Commonwealth History

by

P. Mc G. BULWER

BLANDFORD PRESS
LONDON

167 High Holborn, London W.C.1

Set, Printed and Bound in Great Britain
by Richard Clay (The Chaucer Press) Ltd., Bungay, Suffolk
Blocks made by Half-Tone Engraving Ltd.

COMMONWEALTH HISTORY

Companion Volumes

by P. Mc G. Bulwer and G. K. Tull

BRITAIN AND THE WORLD IN THE NINETEENTH CENTURY

BRITAIN AND THE WORLD IN THE TWENTIETH CENTURY

AN HISTORICAL INTRODUCTION TO THE TWENTIETH CENTURY

by R. W. HARRIS

Contents

Acknowledgements

Acknowledgement is due to the following for their kind permission to reproduce illustrations, to which reference is given by page number:

Australia House 82, 85, 91, 96, 98, 99 (2)
British Museum 12
Canadian Government Travel Bureau 77
Public Archives of Canada 31 (2), 34, 35, 63, 64, 67, 70, 71, 73 74, 75
Camera Press 183, 184, 187, 192, 195, 197, 199, 200, 202, 203, 231, 236, 238, 239, 243 (3), 249
High Commissioner for New Zealand 103, 105, 108
Hull Museum 212
India House 168 (2), 169
Radio Times 8, 9, 10 (4), 14, 15, 23, 24, 26, 27, 28, 40, 59, 60, 73, 78, 128, 129, 130, 138, 143, 144, 148, 151, 152, 157 (3), 158, 159 (2), 160, 161, 164, 167, 177, 179 (2), 180 (2)
South Africa House 110, 112, 114, 117, 118, 121, 123, 130, 132, 133 (2), 135
United States Information Service 43, 44, 54

We also wish to acknowledge the work of Mr Michael Carr and Mr Victor Farmer who drew the maps and diagrams for this book.

SIR HUMPHREY GILBERT'S MAP

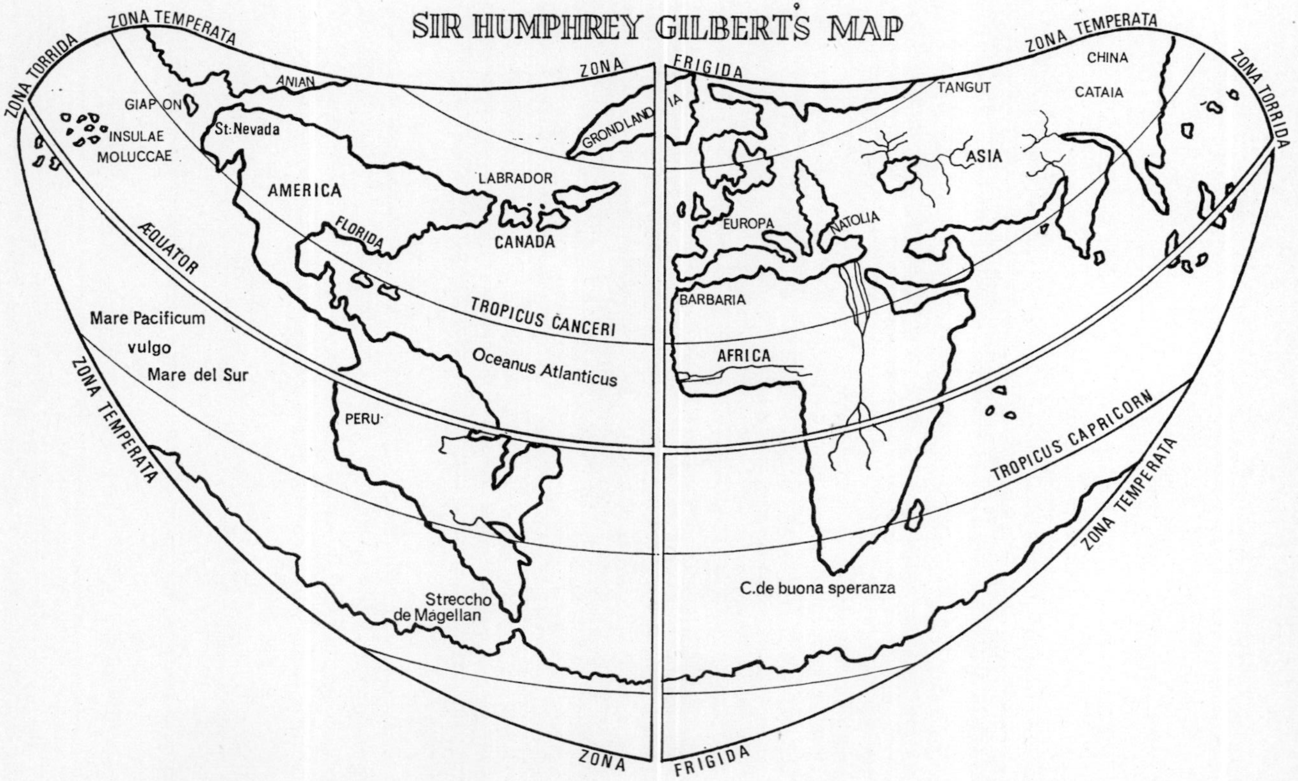

1 : The Age of Discovery

Early Discoveries

THE Renaissance did more than bring back to prominence the ideas and the knowledge of the men of science and letters of the Ancient World; it awakened the craving for knowledge of the men of vision of the later Middle Ages, not the least the desire to know what lay beyond the great seas.

Although the Norsemen had sailed the Atlantic to the New World in very early days, it was the end of the fifteenth century before the interest of Europe was aroused by the thought of voyages across the Atlantic. Even so it was a wish to find a route to the East which resulted in the discovery of the twin continent of the Americas.

Southern Europe had been trading with the fabulous East for years, making contact through the merchants of Egypt, Syria, Asia Minor and the shores of the Black Sea. In the Middle Ages, 'the Indies' meant any region to the East of Europe and the known world. In the thirteenth century Marco Polo made contact with China, or Cathay as it was known.

However, journeys to the East were difficult and dangerous, and the quest for the sea route to the long-sought-after Indies began.

In 1487 Bartholomew Diaz made a perilous journey to the Cape, buffeted by storms, and so discovered the southern tip of Africa. This paved the way for another Portuguese seafarer to make an adventurous voyage round the Cape in 1497, when da Gama reached India.

In the meantime (1492) Christopher Columbus had made his first journey across the Western Ocean. He had studied charts and reports of sea captains and had calculated that since the world was round a voyage due west from Spain would bring him to Xipangu, the old name for Japan, or to the Indies. He did not know of the existence of the American continent, and had miscalculated the size of the globe.

By the beginning of the sixteenth century an exciting new world had been opened and Englishmen, Frenchmen and Dutchmen were sailing to the areas which had been claimed by Spain and Portugal. The Spanish, with conquistadores like Cortes and Pizarro, were founding a new empire in Central and Southern America, while the

PTOLEMY'S MAP OF THE WORLD C. A.D. 150

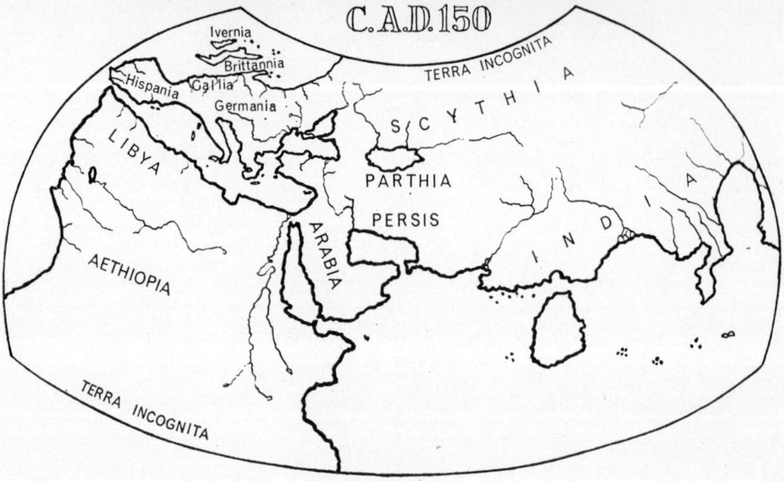

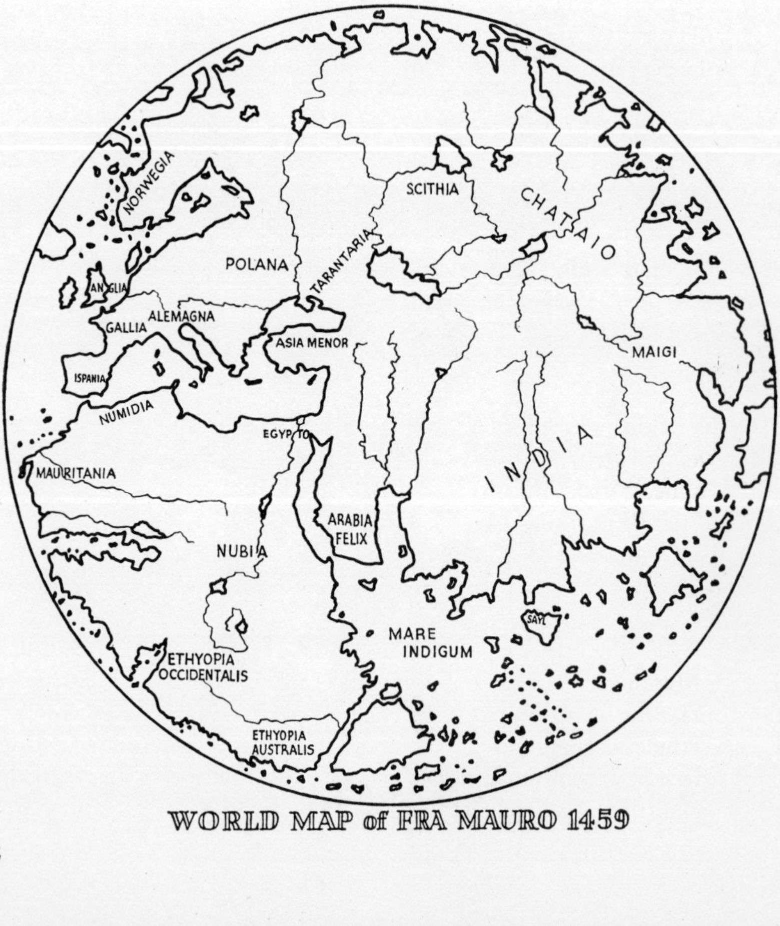

WORLD MAP of FRA MAURO 1459

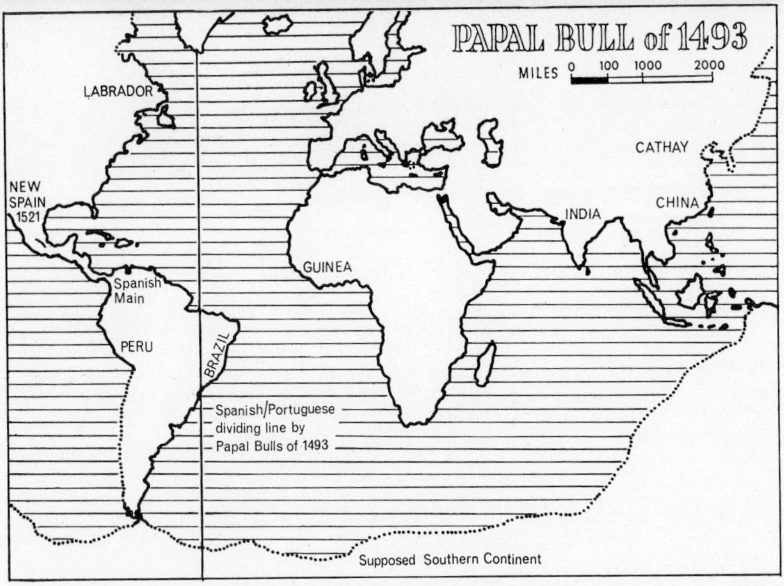

Portuguese had claimed the Indies and the East as their monopoly. The Papal Bull of 1493 which had drawn a dividing line down the 48th line of longitude had given all land in the Americas to the west of the line to Spain and all to the east to Portugal. This was to arouse great resentment in other nations in Europe and particularly in England, and led to the voyages of English sailors which culminated in the Spanish Armada. England was resentful because of John Cabot's voyages to Nova Scotia or Newfoundland in 1497 and 1498 and his son Sebastian's voyage to Labrador. Neither at the time thought that they had found a new continent but as the sixteenth century progressed, the English felt that they had contributed to the discovery of the New World and were entitled to share in it.

England's Commerce in the Middle Ages and After

In the Middle Ages the efforts of English merchants had been overshadowed by great trading groups in Europe. These were the Hanseatic League, consisting of German cities on the shores of the North Sea and the Baltic; the cities of Bruges, Ghent, Antwerp and Ypres in the Low Countries; and Venice, Florence and Genoa in Italy. In the fifteenth century a group of English merchants banded themselves together into a company which they named the Merchant Adventurers, with the purpose of increasing the sales of English textiles. These Merchant Adventurers penetrated to Northern Germany, Denmark and Scandinavia.

Nevertheless, in spite of the vigorous efforts to increase trade, England was not very interested in the newly discovered lands until the second half of the sixteenth century. The old trade with Europe was

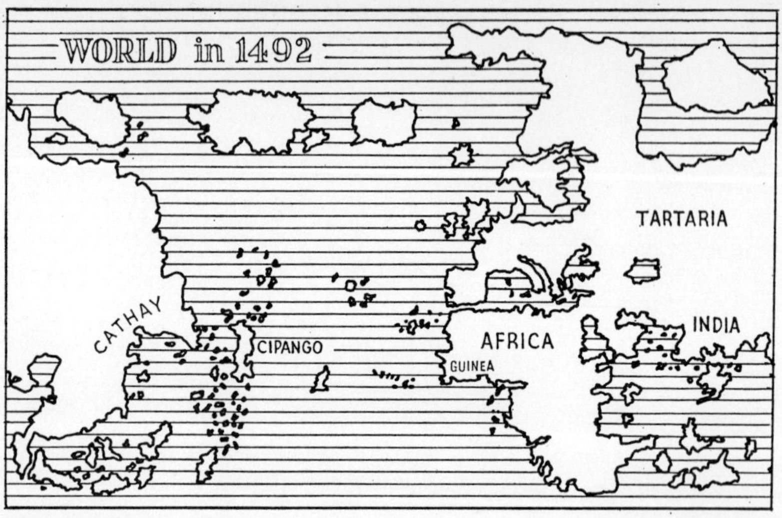

still prosperous, and there was no surplus population making overseas settlement necessary. The spur when it came was far more religious than commercial. Unrest following the Reformation and hardship caused by the dissolution of the monasteries brought a decline in trade and merchants began to look farther afield for their markets. In addition Protestantism and its militant attitude towards Roman Catholics added to the resentment felt at Spain's assumption of ownership of all new land across the Atlantic. English sailors had fallen into the hands of the Inquisition and their reports of their tortures and ill-treatment increased the feelings of hostility towards Spain.

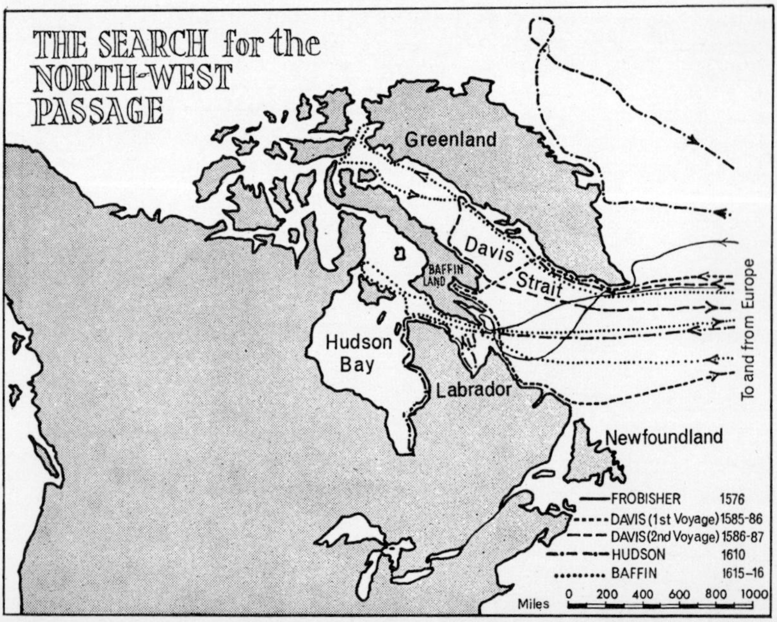

The North-West and North-East Passages

At first attempts were made to find a North-West Passage to the East. As early as 1527 John Rut had sailed for this purpose and pressed on until he was forced to turn back by ice. Before returning home he sailed southwards to the West Indies, the first recorded visit of an English ship. Richard Hore of London made another attempt in 1536 but failed to pass the area of Cape Breton. Sebastian Cabot

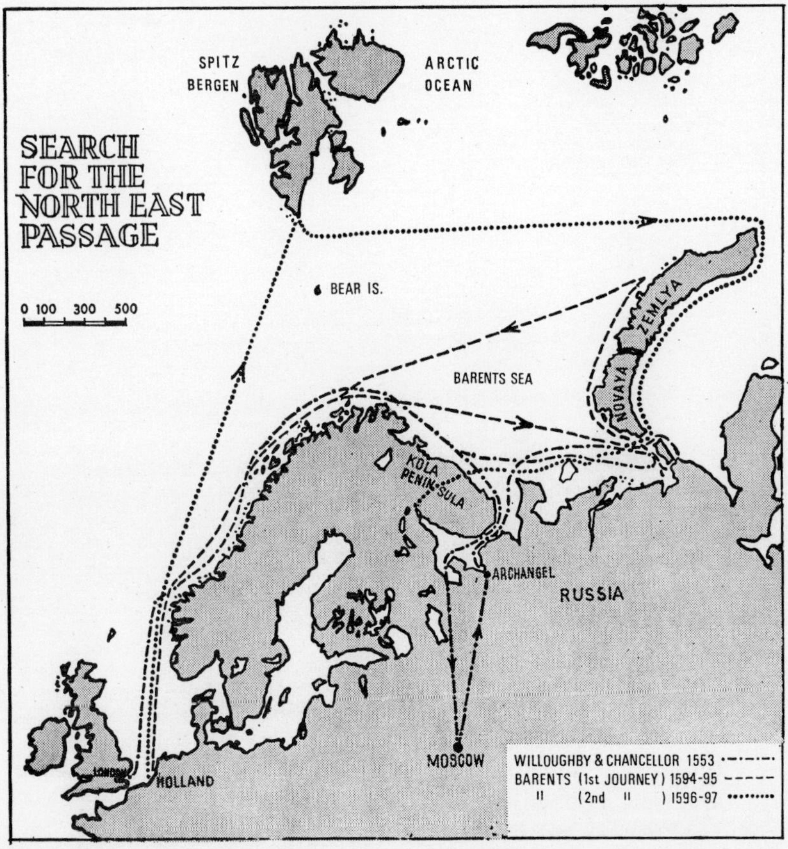

planned a voyage of exploration for the North-East Passage and it set off in 1553 under the command of Sir Hugh Willoughby and Richard Chancellor. Willoughby lost his way and he and all his men died of cold on the northern shores of Russia. Chancellor had pushed on and found the entrance to the White Sea and sailed on to Archangel. He travelled to Moscow to present Edward VI's letter of recommendation to the Czar of Russia, Ivan the Terrible. As the result of this a company of merchants known as the Muscovy Company,

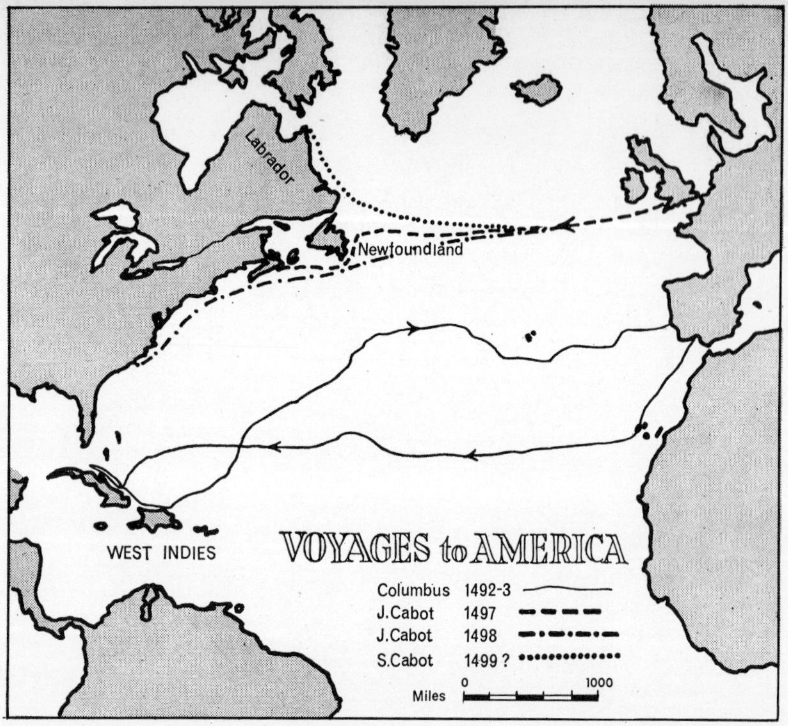

or Russia Company, was founded in 1554 to trade with Russia. A further attempt to find the North-West Passage was made in 1576, when Martin Frobisher sailed to the north of Labrador. The next attempt in 1579, by Sir Humphrey Gilbert, which also failed, nevertheless led to the first effort to found an English colony in the Americas, in Newfoundland. During 1585–87 John Davis set sail on two voyages to find the North-West Passage to the East. He, too, failed, but discovered the strait which bears his name.

Seafaring Trade

The voyages which had been made, together with the other reasons, had stimulated interest in overseas trade. One of the most successful of the seafaring adventurers was John Hawkins, the son of William Hawkins who had sailed to Brazil as early as 1530. John Hawkins sailed to the west coast of Africa in 1562 and began trading in slaves which he found to be most profitable, selling them to Spanish colonists in the West Indies. Although the Spanish Government frowned upon an English ship trading with their possession in the West Indies, the Spanish settlers themselves welcomed the slaves. Hawkins was followed by other captains, notably his nephew Francis Drake, and all had clashes with Spanish warships; and Hawkins and Drake together were treacherously attacked in 1568 by the Spaniards at San Juan d'Ulloa on the Mexican coast. It was fury at this which led to

Drake's voyages of revenge in the 1570s and to the reaction of other English captains. These, in their turn, paved the way for war. Drake's voyage to circumnavigate the world was made from 1577 to 1580.

The war with Spain went on from 1585 until 1604 and is remembered chiefly for the defeat of the Armada in 1588 and Grenville's famous fight in the *Revenge* in 1591. The effect of the war was largely to demonstrate the weakness of Spain, the emergence of England as a seafaring power, and further to stimulate the desire of English merchants and seamen for an expansion of seafaring trade.

Virginia

In 1584 Sir Walter Raleigh, a cousin of Sir Humphrey Gilbert, sent an expedition to explore the coast of America with a view to founding a colony. The reasons for this were the belief that the native Indians would trade with England and a new belief that England was overpopulated. It was still hoped, too, that a passage to the East might yet be found. Sir Richard Grenville took out the colonists in 1585 and the new settlement was named Virginia in honour of Queen Elizabeth. A second party was sent out in 1587, but when the little colony's governor, John White, was forced to return for supplies in 1588, he found on his return, delayed by the war, two years later, that the 150 colonists had completely disappeared. No real trace of them has ever been found. The war with Spain prevented any further attempts at colonisation being made for some years.

The East India Company

Fighting with Spain had made further attempts at colonisation to the West difficult, and the merchants had never given up the idea of increasing trade with the fabulous East. With the opening of the route around the Cape at the end of the sixteenth century and the weakening of Portugal, who jealously guarded it, new interest was aroused.

In 1599 a group of London merchants formed the East India Company with the purpose of promoting trade with India and the East Indies. On 31 December 1600, the company was recognised by the Crown and a long and honourable history began. The first expedition was sent in 1601 under the command of Sir John Lancaster and was a great success. He took four ships, the flagship being the *Red Dragon*, and thirteen months after he left landed at Sumatra. He also visited Java, and returned to England in September 1603, laden with such a rich cargo that the dockers who unloaded his ships were supplied with special suits without pockets!

SUMMARY

Early Discoveries

Effect of Renaissance.—Early voyages of Norsemen.—English and European trade.—Diaz' voyage to the Cape (1487).—Columbus's first voyage (1492).—Vasco da Gama's voyage to India (1497).—Papal Bull of 1493.—John Cabot's voyage to North America (1497).—Sebastian Cabot's voyage to Labrador (1509).

England's Commerce in the Middle Ages and After

Trading groups in Europe.—Hanseatic League.—Merchant Adventurers.—Little interest in new lands.—Religious reasons for quickening interest.—Inquisition.—Hostility towards Spain.

North-West and North-East Passages

Rut (1527).—Hore (1536) to N.W. Passage.—Willoughby and Chancellor to N.-E. Passage (1553).—Chancellor's contact with Ivan the Terrible.—Muscovy Company (1554).—Frobisher to N.-W. Passage (1576).—Gilbert (1579).—First attempt at American colony.—Davis to N.-W. Passage (1585–87).

Seafaring Trade

William Hawkins to Brazil (1530).—John Hawkins begins slave trade from West Africa to West Indies (1562).—Trouble with Spain.—Spanish attack on Hawkins and Drake at d'Ulloa (1568).—Voyages of revenge by Drake and others.—Drake sails round the world (1577–80).—War with Spain (1585–1604).

Virginia

First exploratory expedition sent by Raleigh (1584).—Colonists taken out by Grenville (1585).—New settlement named Virginia.—Second party sent out (1587).—Disappearance of colonists.—No further efforts because of war with Spain.

The East India Company

Group of London merchants form East India Company (1599).—Royal recognition (1600).—First expedition under Lancaster (1601).—Sumatra.—Java.—Returned successfully (1603).

Sebastian Cabot explains his discoveries to Henry VII.

QUESTIONS

Answer the following questions briefly:

1. (a) What did the voyages of Diaz, Vasco da Gama and Columbus do to alter the fifteenth century conception of the world?
   (b) What did the Papal Bull of 1493 say and what was its effect?
   (c) Who were the Merchant Adventurers?
   (d) How did hostility towards Spain develop?
   (e) How was the first settlement in Virginia founded and what happened to it?
2. Describe the many attempts to find a way to the East by means of a North-West or North-East Passage and what resulted.
3. When in 1823, Fowell Buxton introduced a motion into the House of Commons to end slavery, he condemned it as 'repugnant to the principles of the British Constitution and the Christian religion'. This was certainly not the view taken in the sixteenth century.
   (a) Why did John Hawkins begin trading with slaves from West Africa?
   (b) What results did the slave trade with the West Indies have?
   (c) What happened at San Juan d'Ulloa?
   (d) What actions did it provoke?

Columbus discovers America. (*From* Americae Partes *by De Bry.*)

Sir John Hawkins.

Vasco Da Gama.

Sir Francis Drake, with his seal and autograph.

Christopher Columbus.

Oldest authenticated portrait, painted pre-1568. (*In the Uffizi Gallery, Florence*.)

2: Early English Settlements in North America

Virginia

THE death of Elizabeth in 1603 marked the end of an era. The great sea-dogs were already dead and James I, who had succeeded, was determined to end the war with Spain. The end of hostilities meant that peaceful expansion could begin again. However, the first attempt at further colonisation was a second effort to form a settlement in Virginia.

In 1606 James I formed a chartered company, originally known as the London Company but later as the Virginia Company. The first settlers arrived at the coast of Virginia in April 1607 and after sailing into Chesapeake Bay founded Jamestown, fifty miles up the James River. This was the first colony in America.

The new settlement was governed by a council of seven colonists led by Captain John Smith. Smith, although only twenty-seven years old, had considerable experience and proved himself an able and natural leader. Indeed, but for his work, the settlement would have failed within a few months. Attacks from Indians and shortage of food made things very difficult for them. Many of the colonists had hoped for quick wealth by discovering gold and disappointment at their failure to find it, together with disease and lack of food, killed two-thirds of them within a short time.

In 1609 the constitution of the colony was changed. The Company in London controlled the administration but delegated authority to a governor on the spot. The first governor was Lord Delaware. From then on the fortunes of the colony improved and although Lord Delaware was forced to return to England in 1611 by ill-health his good work lived on. He left Sir Thomas Dale, an old soldier, as his deputy, and he ruled the colonists with a rod of iron but his discipline paid dividends.

Gradually, the colonists settled and tobacco plantations grew. Large estates came into being, labourers being provided by paupers, indentured servants, criminals and, after 1619, by Negro slaves. In 1619 the colony was given an assembly based on the English Parliament. However, King James I was displeased with the way the colony

Early adventure in America.
Captain John Smith saved from death by Princess Pocanthas' appeal to her father.

was being administered and he revoked the Virginia Company's charter in 1624 and the governor was afterwards appointed by the King. During the struggle between the King and Parliament and the Civil War which followed, Virginia was loyal to the King. King Charles II repaid this loyalty by granting the freehold of the colony to Lord Arlington and Lord Culpeper in 1672. However, after the revolution of 1688, full rights were restored to Virginia and its assembly. It was by now a thriving settlement.

The New England Colonies

In the early part of the reign of James I a group of Puritans dissatisfied with their treatment after the Hampton Court Conference of 1604 decided to settle in Leyden in Holland, where they hoped that their religion would be regarded more sympathetically. Still not happy in Leyden, they decided to try some of the territory belonging to the Virginia Company which extended far to the north of the actual colony. A group of financiers in London formed the Plymouth Company to support the venture. The party of settlers, who became known as the Pilgrim Fathers, crossed the Atlantic in the *Mayflower* in 1620. Originally, there had been two ships, but the *Speedwell* had to be left at Plymouth and most of the pilgrims, men, women and children, packed into the little *Mayflower*. After a terrible voyage they eventually landed at Cape Cod in Massachusetts in December 1620, considerably farther north than intended. Unprepared for a bitter winter, half the little group perished because of the severe cold, but under the leadership of William Bradford they welcomed the spring with prayer and found the land good. Their little colony was named Plymouth and although not without further hardship it flourished and prospered. At first the governor, William Bradford, ruled through the heads of families but as the colony grew in area and population a representative assembly was founded in 1638.

Plymouth set the pattern for the New England colonies which were to follow. These were not formed for purposes of trade or the desire to win new lands for England. They were founded because groups of people were suffering from religious persecution and desired to find a place where they could worship God in their own way.

In 1621 the new colony was legally recognised and the Plymouth Company became the Council for New England. A further group of Puritans fired by the same reasons as the Pilgrim Fathers, obtained from the Council the right to found a further settlement. They were led by John Endicott and John Winthrop and formed themselves into the Massachusetts Bay Company in 1628, obtaining a royal charter for their colony the next year. The settlers themselves landed in 1628 and 1629 at Salem and Boston. The Company followed and thus the colony became self-governing and almost independent with John Winthrop as Governor. A representative assembly was established in 1634, with the right to vote given only to church members, which not only maintained strict Puritanism but led to some religious intolerance.

Some Dutch settled by the Connecticut River and Puritans from Massachusetts founded a colony there in 1633. For five years it was ruled from Massachusetts, but became separate as Connecticut in 1638.

John Davenport, also from Massachusetts, founded another settlement at New Haven to the west, and this became a part of Connecticut in 1662.

In 1635 Roger Williams, a young Puritan minister, was banished from Massachusetts because he disagreed on certain points of doctrine with the church there. He went with some followers to Rhode Island where he founded the settlement of Providence. As the colony spread it became known as Rhode Island and was noted for its religious tolerance among the strict Puritanism of New England.

To the north further settlements were founded at New Hampshire

Henry Hudson.

and Maine in 1639, both being administered by Massachusetts until New Hampshire became independent in 1679. Maine was not independent until 1783 after the War of Independence.

The New England colonies because of their origin produced people of sturdy independence with little strong loyalty to the Mother country. Agriculture was based upon small farms and this coupled with the temperate climate meant that slavery was virtually unknown. Lumbering, shipbuilding and fishing made up the rest of the economy. An attempt at confederation was made in 1643 between Massachusetts, Plymouth, Connecticut and New Haven, but it lasted only seventeen years. When the Navigation Acts were passed from 1651 onwards they were particularly resented by Massachusetts. The colony reacted so vigorously that its charter was withdrawn in 1683, but it was restored in 1689 when it became a Crown colony.

The Middle Colonies

Henry Hudson, who gave his name to Hudson Bay, made a voyage in 1608 in the service of the Dutch Government. He discovered the river named after him and the Dutch West India Company founded settlements on the banks of the Hudson River, on the coasts nearby and upon Long Island in 1626 and the years which followed. The Dutch settlement was known as New Amsterdam. In 1638 a Swedish colony was planted at the mouth of the Delaware River. The Dutch conquered the Delaware settlement in 1655.

During the Dutch Wars, the rights over the whole territory were given to the brother of King Charles II, the Duke of York, later to become King himself as James II. The Duke of York sent a small expedition under Colonel Richard Nicolls to capture New Amsterdam. The Dutch under their governor, Peter Stuyvesant offered no resistance and the colony fell to the English force on 29 August 1664. It was renamed New York in honour of its royal sponsor. Colonel Nicolls governed the colony wisely, allowing religious freedom and leaving the Dutch settlers in possession of their lands. Stuyvesant and most of the Dutch remained and swore allegiance to the English Crown. The remainder of the Dutch possessions of New Netherlands, including Delaware fell into English hands in 1665. The area between New York and Delaware was settled as New Jersey. The treaty of Breda in 1667 allowed all the old Dutch colonies to be retained by England and they continued to develop with a steady increase in English settlers.

In 1681 William Penn, a Quaker, the son of Admiral Penn the conqueror of Jamaica, accepted a grant of land between New Jersey and Maryland in settlement of a sum of £16,000 owed by Charles II to the Admiral. The next year a party of settlers, mostly Quakers, landed and founded Philadelphia, or the City of Brotherly Love. The colony was named, after its founder, Pennsylvania. Penn used over £6,000 of his own money to help in its development and the colony flourished. Because of his Christian and high principled way of dealing with the Indians they and the settlers lived in complete friendship.

William Penn

Although Maryland really comes in the Middle Colonies group, it far more resembled Virginia because of its climate. It was founded in 1634 by Lord Baltimore, a Roman Catholic, whose father the first Lord Baltimore had obtained a grant of the land from Charles I. It was named Maryland at the King's request in honour of his wife, Henrietta Maria. Lord Baltimore adopted a policy of religious toleration and although the colony attracted many Roman Catholics persecuted at home, it was open to all religions. It was granted a representative assembly in 1647.

The Southern Colonies

The area to the south of Virginia had been granted to Sir Robert Heath by Charles I and had been named Carolina in honour of the King. However, nothing was done about settling it until 1663 when eight prominent men obtained grants of land and established small settlements not of English emigrants but of groups of people from Virginia, Massachusetts and the West Indies. King Charles II granted them a charter and they formed the Carolina Company. There were two settlements, the northern one becoming North Carolina and the southern one, South Carolina. South Carolina developed rather faster and better than the northern colony and Charleston, the capital. became a considerable city. In 1719 the assembly of South Carolina asked to become a crown colony and this request was granted, the rights of the Carolina Company ending in 1729.

Georgia was a much later colony and was founded by General Oglethorpe in 1732 for the purpose of providing a home for insolvent debtors, many of whom were in English prisons. The colony grew slowly to success. The founder had intended both religious toleration and a ban on slavery, but the climate made it necessary for Negro slaves to be imported. Georgia became a Crown colony in 1752.

Nova Scotia and the Hudson Bay Company

Henry Hudson made four voyages in search of a passage to the East between 1607 and 1611, his life ending when he was murdered by mutineers on his fourth voyage, during which he discovered the bay which bears his name.

Nobles and merchants during the reign of Charles II were eager for commercial expansion. A group who wished to exploit the Hudson Bay area obtained the support of Prince Rupert and in 1668 the first voyage to the Bay was undertaken to trade in furs. The Hudson Bay

Company was founded in 1670 with exclusive rights for trade with the shores of the Bay.

The French settled in Acadie in 1604, but a group of Virginians destroyed the settlement in 1613. James I issued a charter to Sir William Alexander and a group of Scotsmen in 1621 who founded a colony which they named Nova Scotia, or New Scotland. Nova Scotia was lost to the French and again became Acadie in 1632. It remained French until the Treaty of Utrecht in 1713 when once again it became Nova Scotia.

The Old Colonial System

Most of the early settlements were inspired by trade and even the New England Puritan settlements were regarded as opportunities for commercial expansion by the Government at home. This emphasis on trade naturally influenced the Government attitude to colonies. The Empire at this time was still small and there was little thought of development of an empire or of the development of individual colonies. This failure on the part of the Government was to come to a head with the American Revolution and to sound the death-knell of the Old Colonial System.

SUMMARY

Virginia

End of war with Spain.—New attempts at colonisation.—Virginia Company (1606).—First settlement on coast of Virginia (1607).—Jamestown.—John Smith.—Control in London with appointed governor (1609).—Tobacco plantations.—Paupers, indentured servants, criminals and Negro slaves (1619) as labourers.—Quarrel with James I (1624).—Civil War.—Rights restored (1688).

The New England Colonies

Pilgrim Fathers.—Plymouth Company.—*Mayflower* sailed (1620).—Hardship.—William Bradford.—Colony of Plymouth.—Assembly (1638).—Massachusetts Bay Company (1628).—Settlements at Salem and Boston (1628–29).—Assembly (1634).—Dutch settlement on Connecticut River.—Colony under Massachusetts (1633).—Became Connecticut (1638).—Settlement at New Haven.—Settlement at Rhode Island (1635).—Settlements at New Hampshire and Maine under Massachusetts (1639).—New Hampshire separate colony (1679).—Maine separate colony (1783).—Attempt at confederation (1643).

The Middle Colonies

Hudson discovered Hudson River (1608).—Dutch settlement as New Amsterdam (1626).—Swedish settlement on Delaware River (1638).—Delaware settlement conquered by Dutch (1655).—English captured New Amsterdam (1664); renamed New York.—Delaware captured (1665).—New Jersey settled.—Treaty of Breda (1667); Dutch colonies retained by England.—Pennsylvania founded (1682).—Maryland founded by Lord Baltimore (1634).—Assembly (1647).

The Southern Colonies

Carolina settled (1663); later became North and South Carolina.—Carolina Company.—Company rights ended (1729).—General Oglethorpe founded Georgia (1732).—Crown colony (1752).

Nova Scotia and Hudson Bay Company

Hudson's voyages (1607–11).—Hudson Bay Company (1670).—French settlement in Acadie (1604).—Colony destroyed by Virginians (1613).—Scots colony (1621) Nova Scotia.—Lost to French (1632).—Regained in Treaty of Utrecht (1713).

The Old Colonial System

Early settlements inspired by trade.—Government attitude to New England settlements.

QUESTIONS

Answer the following questions briefly:

1. (a) What was meant by the Old Colonial System?
   (b) What did the New England colonies have in common?
   (c) Give examples of colonies formed with the motive of helping people.
   (d) Which colonies were originally founded and owned by other countries?
   (e) Give instances of how voyages of exploration led to settlements being founded.
   (f) Did the early settlements always have trouble with the Indians?
2. Give an account of the settlements of the New England colonies.
3. In the sixteenth century it was reported that Virginia was 'a misery, a ruin, a death, a hell'. Sir Thomas Dale was able to describe it in 1612 in this way. 'I have seen the best countries of Europe. I protest unto you, before the living God, put them all together, and this country will be equivalent unto them.'
   (a) How was it that such a change had taken place that the second description was possible?
   (b) Do you think any of the changed conditions were due to the work of any of the governors?
   (c) What effect did Virginia have on later colonies?
   (d) Outline the history of Virginia from 1624 until 1688.

3 : Early Settlement in India

The East India Company

WHEN the first voyage of the East India Company was made in 1601 there was no real thought of establishing settlements in India. The eyes of the merchants behind the Company were far more on the islands of the Indies. Both Portugal and Holland had already begun trade with the East Indies and resented English intervention. The Portuguese by the early seventeenth century were under Spanish rule and the recent war between Britain and Spain had removed Spain as a real rival. With the Dutch it was a different story. They were tough opponents and fought against English trade and influence in the islands which they regarded as their property. They formed their own East India Company and backed it to the full. Pitched battles took place between English and Dutch ships and traders, ending with the Amboyna Massacre in 1623. At Amboyna, in the Moluccas, ten English traders were murdered by the Dutch, after being tortured, on the trumped-up charges that they were plotting to overthrow the Dutch. This was virtually the end of English trade in the Indies and the English East India Company turned their attention to the mainland of India.

Captain Hawkins had obtained permission from the Mogul Emperor in 1607 to set up an English factory at Surat on the north-west coast of India. Portuguese opposition was gradually overcome and by 1622 their influence was in decline, although they retained a settlement at Goa until the twentieth century.

Sir Thomas Roe became ambassador to the Mogul emperor in 1615 and he succeeded in winning respect and further privileges. Factories were established at Masulipatem in 1622, Pipli in 1633, Madras in 1639, Hugli in 1650, Bombay in 1668, Fort St David in 1690 and Fort William or Calcutta in 1696. These factories were purely for the purposes of trade and there was no desire for permanent settlement or to spread the areas of English influence. One of the outstanding governors of Madras at this period was Thomas Pitt, the grandfather of the famous statesman, Pitt the Elder. Trade remained the primary concern until the competition of France, in the shape of the French East India Company, who appeared on the scene in 1622. They

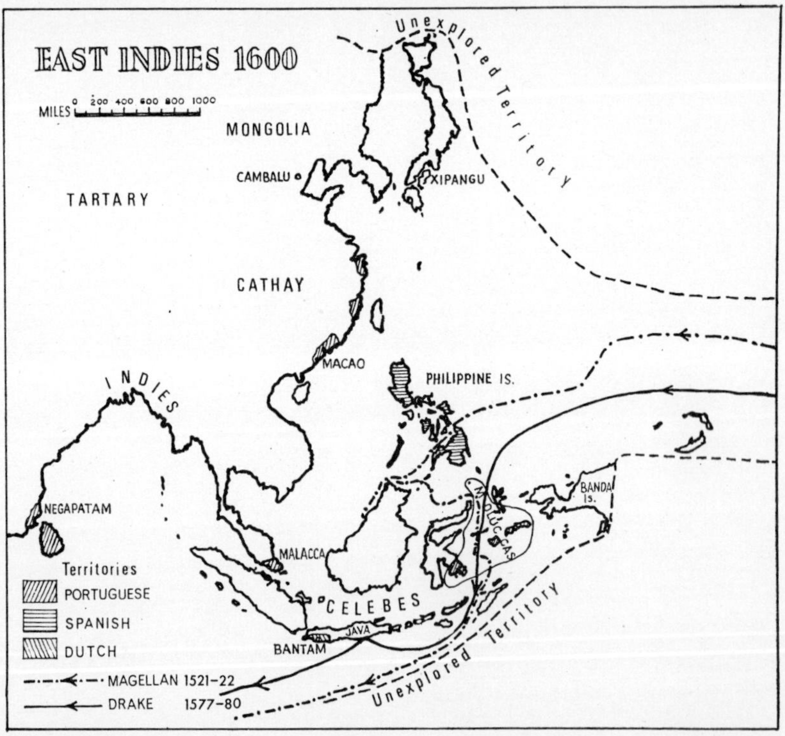

fortified Pondicherry in 1675 and this was followed by settlements at Mahe and Chandernagore. In the next century the French were to interfere in Indian affairs to improve their own position at the expense of the English and this in turn was to lead, not only to conflict, but to English policy switching from trade to obtaining increased status, power and prestige. This change was quickened by the foundation in 1708 of the United East India Company from the fusion of the old original London Company and a rival Company founded in 1698.

The Mogul Empire

In the sixteenth century the Moguls, Mohammedan conquerors, invaded India. Under King Babur of Kabul they founded a dynasty and an empire in 1525. When Babur died in 1556 he left a son of 14 years old, who became known to history as Akbar the Great. The empire lasted for two hundred years. Akbar was succeeded by his son Jahangir in 1605, and after twenty-two years his son Shah Jahan became Emperor. Shah Jahan built the famous Taj Mahal as the mausoleum of his favourite wife and he was buried beside her. He had four sons and one of them, Aurangzeb, overthrew his brothers and became Emperor in 1658 while his father was still alive. Although he was a strong and able ruler, during his reign the authority of the Moguls was challenged by the Marathas, who were a Hindu people. For long the Hindus had resented rule by an alien people with an

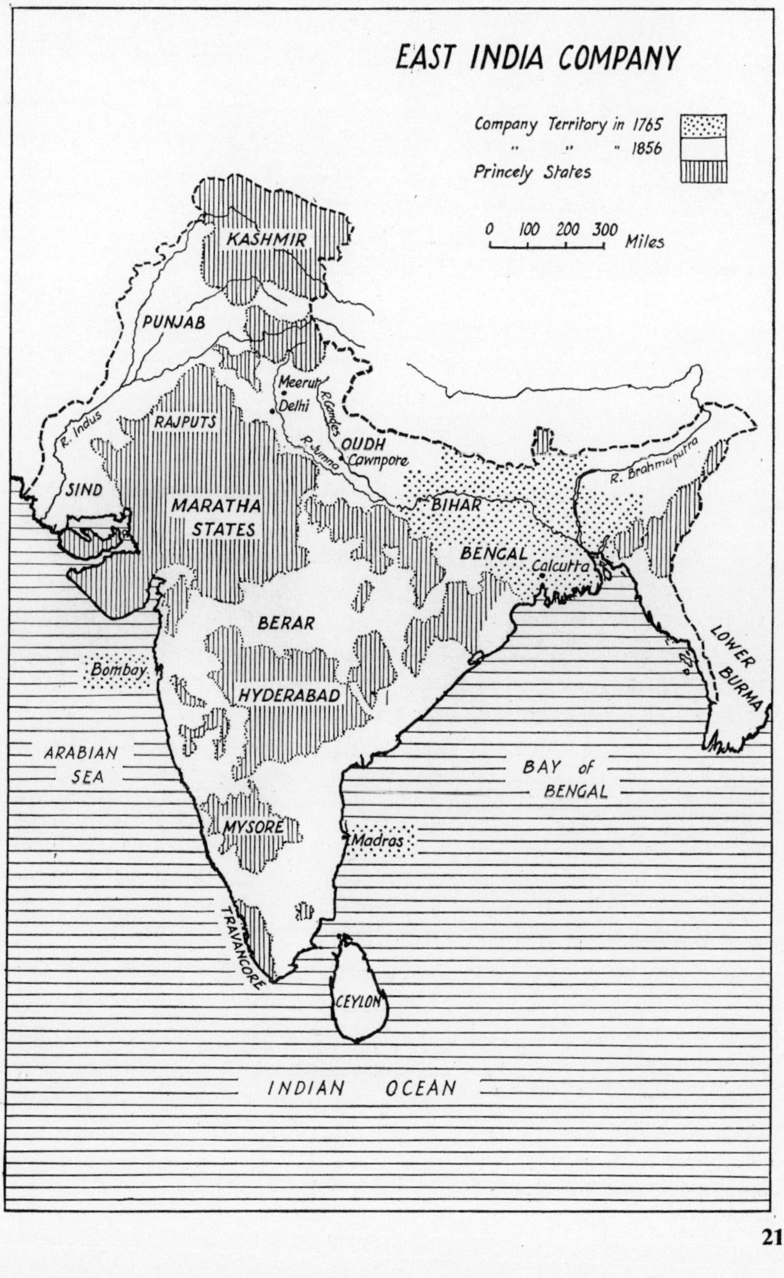

alien religion. After Aurangzeb's death in 1707 his successors were unable to deal with the Marathas or the Afghans and Persians who swept in from the north and within a few years had lost control of the country. India gradually drifted into a state of anarchy at worst, or, at best, separate states or districts who owed only nominal allegiance to the Great Mogul or Emperor, and the central power gradually dissolved and disappeared. It was against this background that the struggle between the British and the French developed.

Dupleix and the Struggle with France

In 1742 Joseph Francois Dupleix was appointed Governor-General of all French settlements in India with his headquarters at Pondicherry. Dupleix had been in the service of the French East India Company since 1720 and was a remarkable man, extremely ambitious and eager to spread French power and influence in India. He had married, in 1741, the widow of a councillor of the Company, who had a wide knowledge of the native dialects and customs and who was to prove of immense help to him in winning the confidence of the Indian princes. Dupleix believed that war was essential to drive the British from India and this opinion was shared by Admiral La Bourdonnais, the French naval commander in Indian waters. Perhaps it was fortunate for the British that Dupleix and La Bourdonnais quarrelled bitterly and intrigued against each other.

The War of the Austrian Succession, which involved both Britain and France in 1744, spread to India in 1746 and a French force besieged and captured Madras in the same year. La Bourdonnais offered reasonable terms, but after his return to France Dupleix refused to carry them out and Madras remained in French hands until 1748.

Clive and Dupleix

In 1743 Robert Clive arrived in India in the service of the Company. A spirited youth who had gone from school to school, neglected his work and been the despair of his father, he had finally been sent to India as the last resort. He hated his job as writer, or clerk, felt homesick, and this and the climate led him even to consider suicide.

He was just 21 years old when the French besieged Madras and he made a thrilling escape, disguised as a native, to Fort St David, twenty miles to the south. He was then commissioned as an ensign in the East India Company army. He found soldiering far more to his liking than writing, but the Peace of Aix-la-Chapelle in 1748 returned Madras to the British and ended the fighting. Clive was forced to return to his duties, as a writer, although his ability as a soldier had been noticed by Major Stringer Lawrence who commanded the British troops at Madras and in the Deccan.

The Nawab of the Carnatic was killed in 1749 by Chunda Sahib. He was supported by Dupleix, who saw a way of obtaining Indian support for his plan to drive out the British. The Nawab had left a son, Mohammed Ali, who, as the legitimate claimant, received British support in opposition to the French nominee. At the same time Dupleix sent his best general, de Bussy, to place a new Nizam on the throne of Hyderabad and further strengthen French influence. This divided Dupleix's forces just at a time when they were needed. Chunda Sahib, supported by the French in 1751, besieged the city of Trichinopoly which was the headquarters of Mohammed Ali, and was held by a few British troops. Major Lawrence was on leave in England and Clive, now a captain, approached Thomas Saunders, the Governor of Madras, with a plan and offered to carry it out. This plan was to capture Arcot, which was the capital of the Carnatic and Chunda Sahib's headquarters. He believed this would force Chunda Sahib to cease attacking Trichinopoly and would immensely increase British prestige. Saunders could only give Clive 8 officers, 200 British and 300 Indian soldiers with 3 cannons. With this small force he marched on Arcot, arriving by coincidence in the middle of a thunderstorm amid flashes of lightning. This so frightened the defenders who, believing Clive and his force to be supernatural, surrendered the city. He treated the inhabitants with such consideration that they rallied to his support and he and his little force were able to hold Arcot in an epic siege lasting for fifty days, during which they were almost without food. Clive's defence of Arcot ranks with the defence of Lucknow as

Robert Clive.

Clive at the Battle of Arcot.

one of the greatest achievements in Indian history. After continuous fighting his force was reduced to 320 men and Chunda Sahib's son Rajah Sahib who had been sent to take Arcot eventually launched a full-scale assault with over 10,000 men led by war-elephants. Clive ordered his men to fire at the heads of the elephants which panicked and fled trampling down many of the enemy soldiers in their flight. Clive completed the rout by sallying forth with his troops and pursuing the beaten force. This so raised the personal prestige of Clive and the prestige of Britain that a force of Marathas now joined him and Dupleix's policy had received a severe set-back.

The next year, in 1752, a strong force under Lawrence with Clive as his second-in-command set out from Madras and relieved Trichinopoly. Chunda Sahib fell into the hands of his Indian enemies and was put to death. The French had been completely defeated in the Carnatic, Mohammed Ali was securely on the throne and in 1754 Dupleix was recalled to France in disgrace.

Clive, too, returned to England on leave and was received as a hero, being promoted to colonel in the Royal army. He was sent back to India in 1756 as Governor of Fort St David, but he never took up the appointment. On his return he found trouble brewing in the province of Bengal.

Clive and Surajah Dowlah

Bengal had been ruled for twenty years by an Afghan adventurer who had made himself Nawab. He had ruled well and British and French merchants had traded with his people. The British had established a headquarters at Calcutta and the French had a fortified post at Chandernagore farther up the river. In 1756, the Nawab died and was succeeded by his nephew, Surajah Dowlah, a weak and vicious youth. He was worried by the presence of both British and French and demanded that they should dismantle their fortifications. The French acceptance of his demand appeared to satisfy him but his anger was aroused by the British attitude. He attacked Calcutta, capturing it in three days. Although some of the British fought well others behaved badly and panicked, fleeing by the river. Surajah Dowlah captured 146 prisoners who had been unable to get away. He had them brought before him and promised them good treatment. It was the hottest part of the year and his officers shut them in a small room with only two small windows. There they remained all night without water. Suffocating, many of them died raving before morning. When the soldiers opened the door in the morning only 22 men and 1 woman were still alive out of the 146. This tragedy is known as the Black Hole of Calcutta. Surajah Dowlah gave no indication of being sorry for the tragedy, nor did he make any attempt to punish the culprits.

The event naturally aroused indignation when the news reached Madras and it was at once decided to send an expedition to recapture Calcutta and obtain revenge for the murders. Clive had just landed on his return from England and he at once was appointed to command the force. He sailed in October 1756, in a fleet under the command of Admiral Watson, with a small force consisting of 900 British troops and 1,500 sepoys. He soon captured Calcutta, defeating a force of 34,000 men, and Surajah Dowlah did little further. In the meantime the Seven Years War had broken out between Britain and France and a French expedition was said to be on its way to India. Clive and Watson attacked and captured the French settlement at Chandernagore.

One of Dowlah's generals, Mir Jaffir, heading a group of conspirators who were dissatisfied with the Nawab's rule, plotted with Clive. Clive was to advance to attack Surajah Dowlah and Mir Jaffir was to ensure that his troops did not fight. After victory Mir Jaffir would replace Surajah Dowlah as Nawab and pay the British the compensation they demanded. Clive had to employ Omichund, a Bengal trader, as a go-between and he demanded payment. A fictitious treaty was signed between him and the British and when Admiral Watson refused to sign, Clive forged his signature, the one act of questionable honesty in his long career which was to be held against him later.

Clive advanced in June 1757 with an army of 1,100 British and

Clive on the eve of Plassey.

2,100 sepoys with 500 sailors and 10 cannon and met Surajah Dowlah's force at the Battle of Plassey. Dowlah's army consisted of 18,000 horse, 50,000 foot and 53 cannon with French gunners. The odds were so great that Clive hesitated and called a council of war. At last he decided to go ahead and attack. A heavy downpour of rain preceded the battle and Clive ordered his gunners to take off their tunics and cover the touchholes of their cannon, something which the French omitted to do. Thus when the battle began the British guns opened up a deadly cannonade and the French were unable to do so. The British then advanced and Dowlah and his men fled in disorder, Mir Jaffir not committing himself until he was sure which way the day was going. This outstanding victory, and that of Calcutta which preceded it, won for Clive the name of Sabur Jung, or 'daring in war', by which he was known to the natives of India.

A few days later Mir Jaffir became Nawab and Surajah Dowlah was put to death by the new Nawab's followers. Clive realised that he could not leave Mir Jaffir unsupported and did not return to Madras. He was appointed Governor of Bengal. Mir Jaffir, not surprisingly, was extremely grateful to Clive for his services and rewarded him generously. Although Clive used much of the money to provide for his troops, this gift was the subject of charges against him on his return to England some years later.

French Activities in the Carnatic

The expected French expedition had landed in the Carnatic under the command of the Comte de Lally in 1758, and immediately captured Fort St David. Although Lally supplied courageous and enthusiastic leadership, his character was more suited to European war than to India. He lacked the support of the French East India Company and was soon short of men and supplies. He failed in his attempt to capture Madras and when a British fleet appeared he marched back to Pondicherry.

In 1759 Clive sent Colonel Forde to recapture Masulipatem, which had fallen to the French, and the whole of that area fell into British hands. The English army in the Carnatic was now under the command of Sir Eyre Coote, who had been at Plassey with Clive. He defeated Lally decisively at Wandewash in 1760, the year Clive returned home. He then advanced on Pondicherry and besieged the town while a British fleet blockaded it from the sea. It surrendered in January 1761. This was really the end of the Seven Years War in India; French power had been broken and the British were supreme. Although Pondicherry and Chandernagore were returned to France under the Treaty of Paris of 1763, they were to be unfortified, solely peaceful trading posts. The British were in control of the Carnatic, the Circars and Bengal, thus the French posts were surrounded by British-controlled territory.

SUMMARY

The East India Company

Trade as original motive.—Focus on trade with Indies rather than India.—Portuguese and Spanish influence.—Decline of Portuguese influence in early seventeenth century.—Dutch power and influence—Dutch East India Company (1602).—Amboyna Massacre (1623).—English East India Company turned to

Central Office of the Dutch East Indies Company in Bengal.

Indiaman, type of ship used by the East India Company.

India.—First trading settlement at Surat (1607).—Factories established at Masulipatem (1622), Pipli (1633), Madras (1639), Hugli (1650), Bombay (1668), Fort St David (1690) and Calcutta (1696).—French East India Company (1662). —Fortified settlements at Pondicherry (1675), Mahe, Chandernagore.—United East India Company formed (1708).

The Mogul Empire

Mohammedan conquerors invaded India in sixteenth century.—Babur (1525–56). —Akbar the Great (1556–1605).—Jahangir (1605–27).—Shah Jahan (1627–58). —Aurangzeb (1658–1707).—Authority of Great Mogul challenged by Marathas. —Afghan and Persian invasion after death of Aurangzeb.—Decline of Mogul Empire.—Anarchy.—Separate princeling states.

Dupleix and the Struggle with France

Dupleix appointed Governor-General of French settlements (1742).—La Bourdonnais.—Madras captured by French (1746).—Dupleix's policy of driving out British.

Clive and Dupleix

Clive arrived in India as clerk (1743).—Commissioned into East India Company army (1746).—Rival claimants to throne of the Carnatic.—Chunda Sahib supported by French.—Mohammed Ali supported by British.—De Bussy placed French nominee on throne of Hyderabad (1750).—Trichinopoly besieged by Chunda Sahib (1751).—Clive captured Arcot (1751).—Held against Rajah Sahib's attacks.—Increase in British and decline in French prestige.—Marathas supported British.—Lawrence and Clive relieved Trichinopoly (1752).—Mohammed Ali as Nawab of Carnatic.

Clive and Surajah Dowlah

Surajah Dowlah became Nawab of Bengal (1756).—Dowlah captured Calcutta (1756).—Black Hole of Calcutta.—Clive and Admiral Watson sailed from Madras with small force.—Battle of Calcutta (1756).—Chandernagore captured (1756).—Mir Jaffir's intrigues against Dowlah.—Omichund as go-between.—Clive forged Watson's signature.—Battle of Plassey (1757); Dowlah defeated and killed.—Mir Jaffir became Nawab of Bengal.—Clive appointed Governor of Bengal (1757).

French Activities in the Carnatic

Lally landed with French force (1758).—Fort St David captured.—Lally's failure—Forde recaptured Masulipatem (1759).—Coote decisively defeated Lally at Wandewash (1760).—Coote captured Pondicherry (1761).—French power broken.—Pondicherry and Chandernagore returned to French by Treaty of Paris (1763).—British in control of much of India.

QUESTIONS

Answer the following questions briefly:

1. (a) Why was the East India Company formed?
   (b) What was the Amboyna Massacre?
   (c) Why were British settlements founded in India?
   (d) Who were the Moguls?
   (e) Why did the Mogul Empire decline?
   (f) Who was Dupleix?
   (g) Who was Surajah Dowlah?
   (h) How was French power finally broken?
2. Describe Clive's capture and defence of Arcot and his victory at Plassey.
3. When Clive finally returned to England he was charged with fraudulent conduct while in Bengal. In his defence of his own conduct before the House of Commons in 1773, he said of the reward he received from Mir Jaffir:

   > Am I not rather deserving of praise for the moderation which marked my proceedings? Consider the situation in which the victory at Plassey placed me. A great prince was dependent upon my pleasure; an opulent city lay at my mercy; its richest bankers bid against each other for my smiles; I walked through vaults which were thrown open to me alone, piled on either hand with gold and jewels. Mr Chairman, at this moment I stand astonished at my own moderation.

   He had previously said, '. . . by my exertions the East India Company had acquired an Empire more extensive than any kingdom in Europe. They had acquired a revenue of four millions sterling and trade in proportion.'
   The House of Commons eventually passed a resolution that, 'Robert, Lord Clive, rendered great and meritorious services to his country.'
   (a) Do you agree with Clive's defence of his act in accepting the reward from Mir Jaffir?
   (b) Do you agree with his comment upon the extent of the gains of the Company by his efforts?
   (c) Do you agree with the House of Commons' motion on Clive's services?
   Give your reasons in all these cases.

4: The American Colonies and the Seven Years War

French Colonies in North America

IN 1534 Jacques Cartier discovered on the West coast of North America one of the great rivers of the world. He named the river and bay St Lawrence, and explored its course as far as Montreal. He reported back to France on the fertile valley he found, but the French Wars of Religion allowed no time for much interest to be taken for years.

Apart from the settlement of Acadie in 1604, later destroyed by Virginians, the first real French colony in North America was founded by Samuel de Champlain in 1608 at Quebec on the St Lawrence River. The settlement developed and in 1627 Cardinal Richelieu formed the Company of New France to develop trade in North America. Its charter actually gave it authority to develop colonies from Florida to the Arctic Circle! In spite of the new company, the progress of Quebec was slow and in 1664 King Louis XIV gave a charter to a new Company of the West, which not only took over the old company's task but also that of developing the French West Indies and Guiana. The new company lasted ten years and from then onwards the colony was administered directly by the French Government.

Exploration helped the colony's expansion. La Salle made many voyages, not the least one down the Mississippi to its mouth in 1682. Here a new colony was founded in 1699, being named Louisiana after Louis XIV. This new settlement was linked with Canada by a line of forts. Jesuit missionaries also explored new territory trying to convert the Indians, and the Great Lakes and other rivers were discovered and mapped, largely by La Salle, Joliet and Marquette.

Anglo-French Rivalry

The British settlements on the east coast had largely been in the fertile area between the Alleghany Mountains and the sea, and there had been little penetration beyond the mountains by the middle of the eighteenth century.

Naturally, many British colonists thought of moving to the west and the Ohio Valley was an obvious place for further settlement. However, the French too sought to move into the same area. They would be able to use the Ohio River as a way to the Mississippi and the

Jacques Cartier. (*By Th. Hamel.*)

Samuel de Champlain.

south. When in 1753 the young Major George Washington led a small party across 500 miles of unexplored country from Virginia to the Ohio valley to contact the French commander there, he was left in no doubt as to French intentions. He was told that the French determined to annex Ohio and drive on to the sea. Quite apart from the war in Europe and elsewhere which was to break out between the British and the French, it was becoming increasingly evident that a clash was coming in North America.

What were the respective strengths which were soon to be opposing each other? The French had rather less than 100,000 people in their colonies against a population of almost a million in the British colonies. Nevertheless, the French strength was greater than it might appear. They had a number of strongly fortified posts, well garrisoned, and they were used to working together. The British had few forts and the thirteen colonies were jealous of each other and had never worked together. In addition, there were few regular troops in the British colonies, while the French had many. What is more, the French were successful in persuading many of the Indians to join them.

Border clashes had been going on for some time but from the time of the War of the Austrian Succession, from 1743 to 1748, fighting went on continuously until it merged with the Seven Years War. Several attempts were made to capture Fort Duquesne, later to become Fort Pitt and the city of Pittsburgh, from the French. Colonel George Washington led an unsuccessful attack in 1754 and General Braddock's attack was repulsed in 1755, Braddock being killed. The following year the Seven Years War broke out and the two nations were officially at war. The same year the Marquis de Montcalm became Governor of Canada and commander-in-chief of the French troops.

The Seven Years War

The Earl of Loudoun, commander-in-chief of the British forces, seemed unable to deal with the French attacks and the colonists appeared to lose heart. In fact, the war was going badly in Europe where Cumberland was defeated at Hanover, and at sea where Byng gave up Minorca. These disasters led to the resignation of the Duke of Newcastle as chief minister and William Pitt took his place at the end of 1756. Pitt proved to be the ideal leader and was the architect of the victory which was to emerge, although it was 1758 before the tide began to turn.

Montcalm had taken Fort Oswego in 1756 and Fort William Henry in 1757 and it appeared that the French advance would continue. When Fort William Henry, gallantly defended by Colonel Monroe, eventually surrendered after a long siege, because of shortage of water and supplies, it was on the undertaking that the women and children should have a safe passage to the nearest fort. This Montcalm gladly gave, but he was unable to control his Indian allies who fell upon the women and children and massacred them, the disarmed British troops being powerless to help. The indignation at this swept through the British colonies and did much to arouse the spirit of the colonists. 'Remember Fort William Henry', became the battle-cry for British regular troops and colonists alike. At the end of 1757, Pitt sent more troops and supplies and in 1758 Forts Oswego and William Henry were recaptured, British troops under Lord Amherst captured Fort Frontenac and Louisburg, while Fort Duquesne was also taken.

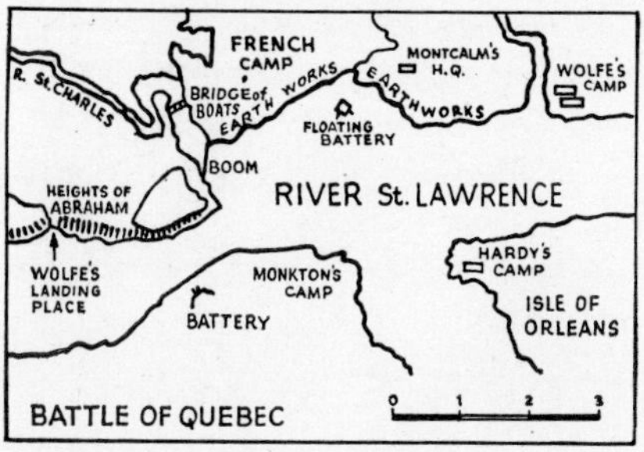

Louisburg had been captured after a siege, and the surrender of the great fortress was a blow to the French.

In 1759, Admirals Boscawen and Hawke defeated French fleets at Lagos and Quiberon Bay and the command of the seas was securely in the hands of the Royal Navy. This meant such a successful blockade of North America that not only were supplies and reinforcements prevented from reaching the French, but in that year for a period of three months Montcalm did not receive a single dispatch from France.

Against this background, Pitt decided to make an attempt to finish the war by capturing the French capital and headquarters at Quebec. To command the expedition he chose a young little-known general who had distinguished himself with Amherst at Louisburg. This was James Wolfe, newly promoted Major-General, and thirty-two years of age. Wolfe's force, carried in a fleet commanded by Vice-Admiral Sir Charles Saunders, was to sail up the River St Lawrence to Quebec, while Amherst was to attack northwards by Lake Champlain.

The task of navigating the St Lawrence was a difficult one and the French believed it impossible to sail large ships up to Quebec. Commanding one of Wolfe's transports was Captain James Cook, later to become famous for his voyage to Australia and New Zealand, and he declared that it was 'as easy as sailing up the River Thames'. The French were amazed to find the fleet off Quebec on the morning of 27 June 1759. Wolfe's problems were only just beginning. Montcalm's defending army was larger than Wolfe's, Quebec lay at the junction of two rivers, heavily fortified and protected to its flanks and rear by steep cliffs of the high ground known as the Heights of Abraham. Wolfe tried an attack on Quebec itself which was repulsed with heavy losses. After a period of some weeks, during which the general himself fell ill and the spirits of the troops dropped lower and lower, he recovered and noticed what appeared to be a small path up the cliffs, the Anse du Foulon now Wolfe's Cove. He sent an officer to reconnoitre and decided to attack there. The French kept a force on the

Heights watching the British and this was deceived by sailing vessels up and down the river until it gave up trying to follow them. The attacking force was moved up the river dropping back quietly at night to climb what turned out to be a very difficult, steep, goat's path. When dawn broke on the morning of 13 September 1759 the small force of some 5,000 men was drawn up on the Heights of Abraham facing Quebec. In the battle which followed the French were decisively defeated, and Wolfe and Montcalm died from wounds received. Both left behind famous last words. Wolfe, on asking how the battle had gone and being told that the French were in full retreat, said, 'Now God be praised, I die happy—I trust that my country will think that I have served her well.' Montcalm, on asking a similar question and receiving the news that the French had lost the day, said, 'I pray that the English will treat my people well.' This prayer was to be answered.

Wolfe's great victory had really made a British victory in Canada certain, but it was some time before it was complete. General Murray, Wolfe's successor, was besieged in Quebec for six months before a relieving fleet reached him and Lord Amherst did not fight his way through to the St Lawrence until the summer of 1760. By September of that year the last of the French troops surrendered to Amherst at Montreal.

The Siege of Quebec. (*By F. Swaine.*)

Major-General James Wolfe.
(*From an engraving.*)

The Treaty of Paris

It was the master touch of Pitt which had brought Britain victory in the Seven Years War, not only in North America but elsewhere. Inspiring leadership, his happy choice of generals and his realisation of the importance of sea-power were the main reasons for success. He was determined to make Britain a great imperial power. However, in 1760 King George II died and his grandson who became King, George III, held very personal views on kingship and had little time for Pitt. He believed that the great minister was preparing for war with Spain and the King wished to end the war. This was indeed true since Pitt thought that Spain was waiting for the right moment to strike. George III refused to accept his advice and Pitt resigned in 1761. His policy was proved right when Spain declared war soon afterwards. However, it made little real difference to the course of the war which ended in 1763.

The peace terms were decided at the Treaty of Paris in 1763. Britain restored to France some of the islands she had taken in the West Indies, Pondicherry and other factories in India and the fishing rights in Newfoundland. Spain was given Havana in Cuba and Manila in the Philippines. However, the whole of the French possessions in North America, or New France as it was known, became British, with the exception of Louisiana which France gave to Spain just after the Treaty. Several West Indian islands taken from France were retained by Britain and Spain was forced to give up Florida to Britain. French rule had disappeared from North America and British control seemed to be secure. Events were soon to prove that this was not so.

SUMMARY

French Colonies in North America

Jacques Cartier discovered St Lawrence (1534).—No settlement for over 70 years.—Champlain founded Quebec (1608).—Company of New France (1627).—Company of the West (1664).—La Salle explored Mississippi (1682).—Louisiana founded (1699).—Great Lakes explored.

Anglo-French Rivalry

British settlements between Alleghany Mountains and the sea.—Common interest in Ohio valley.—Washington's journey to Ohio.—French intentions to annex Ohio.—Relative strengths.—British numerically stronger.—French strongly fortified posts.—Border clashes.—Attacks on Fort Duquesne (1754 and 1755).—Montcalm as Governor of Canada (1756).

Seven Years War (1756–63)

Early British failures everywhere.—Loudoun's failure in North America.—Cumberland's failure in Hanover.—Defeats at sea.—Loss of Minorca.—William Pitt as chief minister (1756).—Pitt's leadership.—Montcalm captured Fort Oswego (1756), Fort William Henry (1757).—Pitt sent troops and supplies.—Forts Oswego and William Henry re-captured (1758).—Amherst captured Fort Frontenac and Louisburg (1758).—Fort Duquesne surrendered to British (1758).—Boscawen and Hawke's naval victories at Lagos and Quiberon Bay (1759).—Royal Navy won command of sea.—French in North America cut off from France.—Wolfe captured Quebec (1759).—Amherst advanced north by Lake Champlain.—Murray besieged at Quebec.—Relieved (1760).—Last French troops surrendered to Amherst at Montreal (1760).

Treaty of Paris (1763)

Pitt's skill as leader.—His choice of generals.—His insistence on importance of sea-power.—Death of George II.—George III's disagreement with Pitt.—Pitt resigned (1761).—Spain declared war (1761).—War ended (1763).

Terms of Treaty of Paris: Britain restored some West Indian islands, Indian factories and fishing rights in Newfoundland to France; Spain given Havana and Manila; all New France except Louisiana became British; some West Indian islands taken from France retained by Britain.—France later gave Louisiana to Spain.—Spain surrendered Florida to Britain.

QUESTIONS

Answer the following questions briefly:

1. (a) How did the French first become interested in Canada?
   (b) Why was there a delay before the first settlements?
   (c) When and how were the first French settlements made?
   (d) What important journeys of discovery were made by French settlers?
   (e) Where were the British settlements?
   (f) Where and when did the British and French first clash?
   (g) Why did Britain's fortunes in the Seven Years War change in 1758?
   (h) What factors finally brought Britain victory?
2. Describe how Wolfe captured Quebec.
3. When William Pitt came to power in 1756 he said, 'I know that I can save this country and that no one else can.'
   Frederick the Great, on hearing of Pitt's appointment, said, 'England has long been in labour, but at last she has brought forth a man.'
   In his despatch containing his orders to Amherst in 1758, Pitt wrote:

   > It were much to be wished that any Operations on the side of Lake Ontario could be pushed as far as Niagara, and that you may find it practicable to set foot on some Enterprise against the Fort there, the Success of which would so greatly contribute to establish the uninterrupted Dominion of that Lake, and at the same time effectually cut off the Communication between Canada and the French Settlements to the South.

   (a) What are your comments on the above quotations?
   (b) In what ways do you think Pitt proved his own words in the first quotation to be right?
   (c) How does the third quotation illustrate Pitt's plans?
   (d) Do you consider that the terms of the Treaty of Paris were a fulfilment of Pitt's ambitions for Britain? Give your reasons.

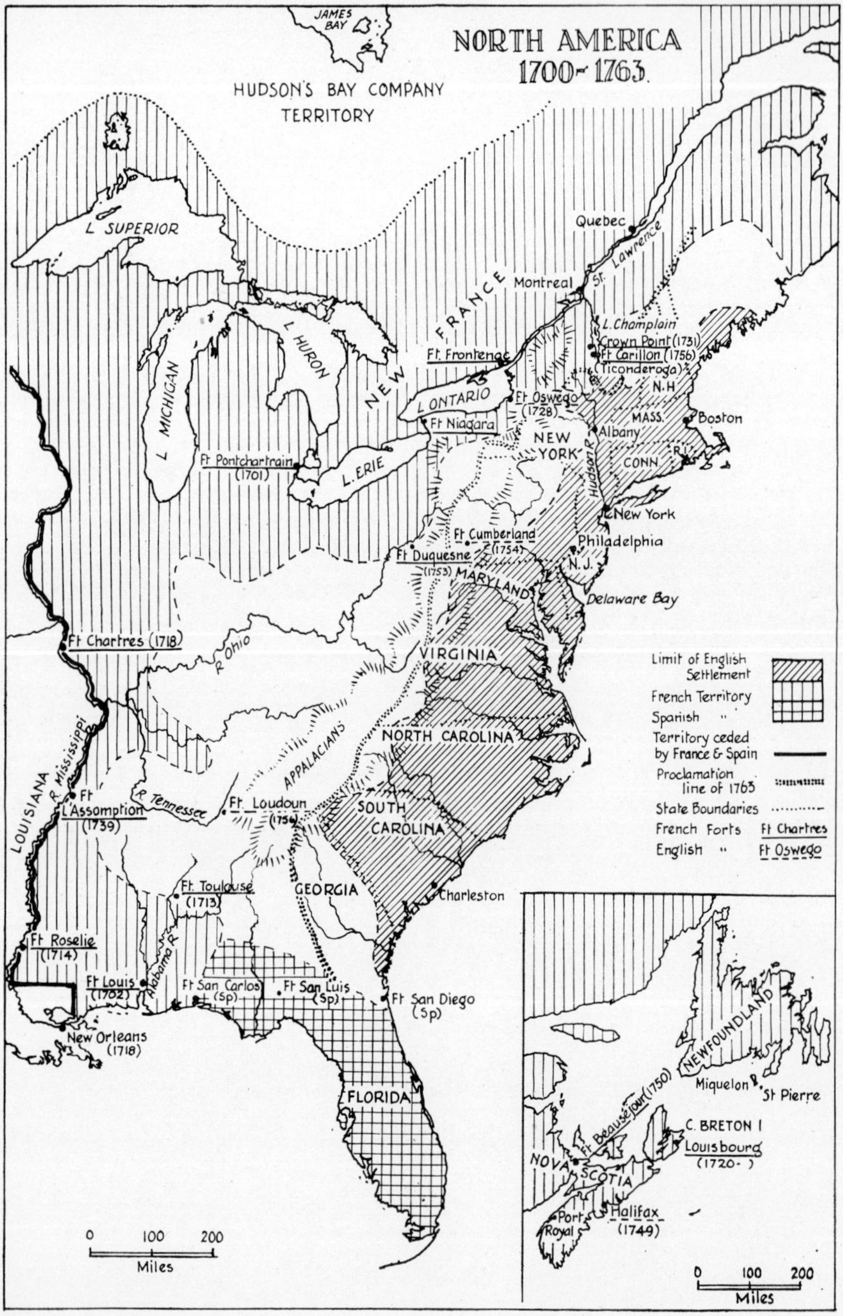
NORTH AMERICA
1700-1763
JAMES BAY
HUDSON'S BAY COMPANY
TERRITORY
L SUPERIOR
L MICHIGAN
L HURON
NEW FRANCE
L ONTARIO
L. ERIE
Quebec
St. Lawrence
Montreal
L. Champlain
Crown Point (1731)
Ft Carillon (1756)
(Ticonderoga)
Ft. Frontenac
Ft Oswego
(1728)
Ft Niagara
Ft Pontchartrain
(1701)
N.H
MASS.
Boston
Albany
NEW
YORK
Hudson R.
CONN.
R.I.
New York
Ft Cumberland
(1754)
Philadelphia
Ft Duquesne
(1753)
N.J.
MARYLAND
Delaware Bay
Ft Chartres (1718)
R. Ohio
VIRGINIA
APPALACIANS
NORTH CAROLINA
R. Mississippi
LOUISIANA
Ft
L'Assomption
(1739)
R. Tennessee
Ft Loudoun
(1756)
SOUTH
CAROLINA
GEORGIA
Charleston
Ft. Toulouse
(1713)
Alabama R.
Ft Roselie
(1714)
Ft Louis
(1702)
Ft San Carlos
(Sp)
Ft San Luis
(Sp)
Ft San Diego
(Sp)
New Orleans
(1718)
FLORIDA
0 100 200
Miles
Limit of English
Settlement
French Territory
Spanish "
Territory ceded
by France & Spain
Proclamation
line of 1763
State Boundaries
French Forts Ft Chartres
English " Ft Oswego
NEWFOUNDLAND
Miquelon
St Pierre
Ft. Beauséjour (1750)
C. BRETON I
Louisbourg
(1720-)
NOVA SCOTIA
Port
Royal
Halifax
(1749)
0 100 200
Miles

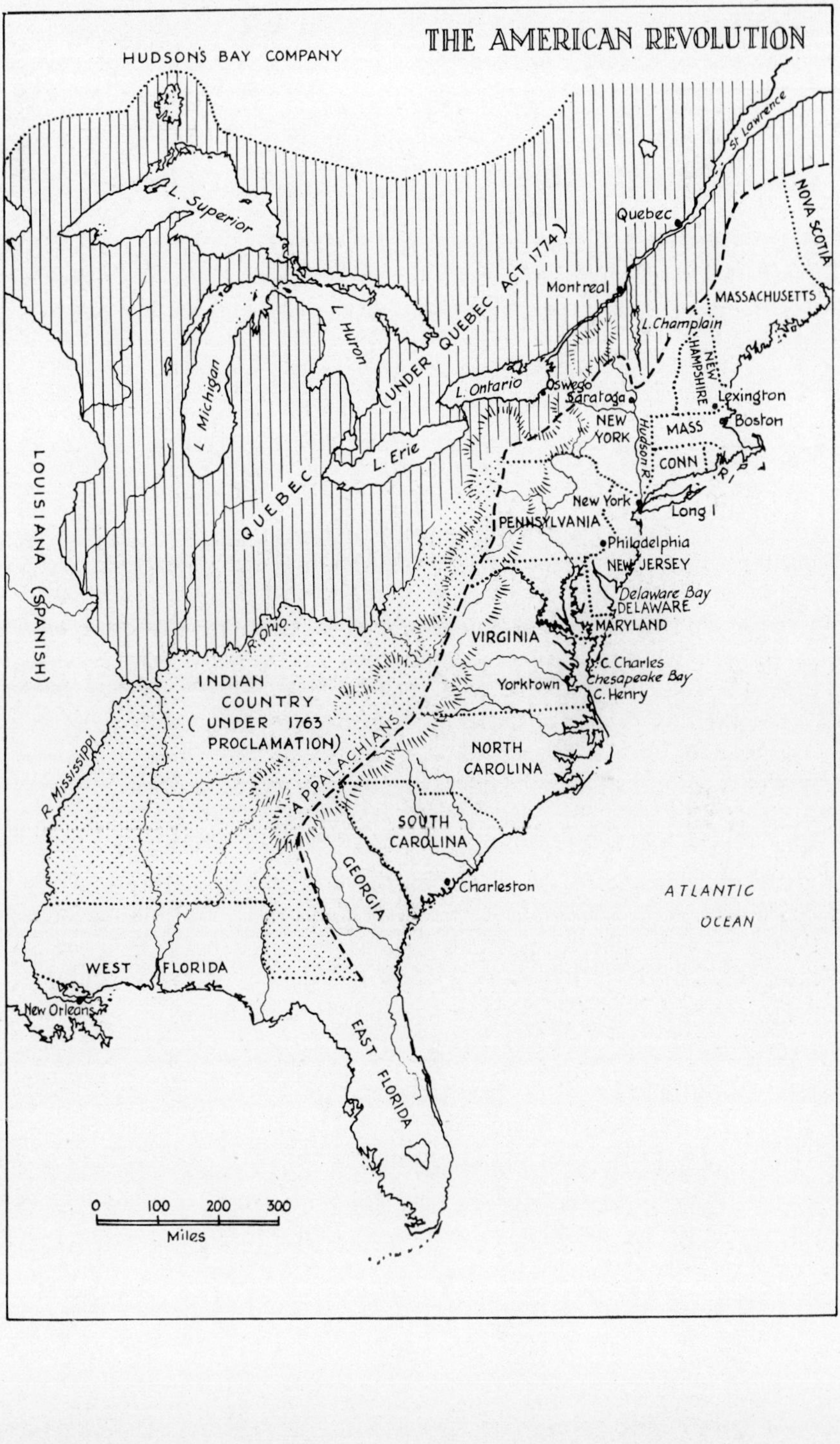
THE AMERICAN REVOLUTION
HUDSON'S BAY COMPANY
L. Superior
St Lawrence
Quebec
NOVA SCOTIA
(UNDER QUEBEC ACT 1774)
Montreal
MASSACHUSETTS
L. Champlain
NEW HAMPSHIRE
L. Michigan
L. Huron
L. Ontario
Oswego
Saratoga
Lexington
Boston
NEW YORK
MASS
Hudson R.
L. Erie
CONN
R.I.
LOUISIANA (SPANISH)
QUEBEC
New York
Long I
PENNSYLVANIA
Philadelphia
NEW JERSEY
Delaware Bay
DELAWARE
MARYLAND
R. Ohio
VIRGINIA
C. Charles
INDIAN COUNTRY (UNDER 1763 PROCLAMATION)
Yorktown
Chesapeake Bay
C. Henry
R. Mississippi
NORTH CAROLINA
APPALACHIANS
SOUTH CAROLINA
GEORGIA
Charleston
ATLANTIC OCEAN
WEST FLORIDA
New Orleans
EAST FLORIDA
0 100 200 300
Miles

5: The Loss of the American Colonies

The Situation After the Seven Years War

THE story of the loss of the British colonies in America is one of complete lack of understanding and consideration on both sides. Nevertheless, it is true to say that the great victory in the Seven Years War and the fruits that it brought in the form of the new British Empire in North America contributed directly to the situation which made the quarrel not only possible but much more likely.

The thirteen colonies had always looked upon themselves as separate independent settlements looking only towards Britain. They had been constantly aware of the menace of French ambitions, particularly so towards the latter years before the war, and were naturally pleased to receive British protection. They were equally happy to have British military assistance against the unfriendly Indians. Indeed the great Indian rising of Pontiac, chief of the Ottawas, in 1763, was finally crushed by British regular troops, the colonial militia taking a very small part. The colonists considered it the duty of the British Government to protect them.

Yet the end of the war had brought a greatly changed situation. The menace of the French had disappeared. The whole of North America was now British and the French Canadians were now British subjects although the British colonists still looked on them with suspicion, while no longer fearing possible attack. The need to join together against the French during the war had brought about the beginnings of co-operation between the colonies. Some colonists felt that they were able to defend themselves against the Indians while most still looked for British protection. These latter, however, did not expect to pay for their protection.

The very removal of the French threat was to contribute directly to the quarrel to come.

The Causes of the Quarrel

The character of the colonies and their people must be remembered and understood. The New England colonies had been founded by Puritans who had been driven from their old country by the policies of James I and Charles I. The feeling of grievance had lived on in their descendants and there was a sturdy independence among them. The Middle and Southern Colonies did not share this feeling of grievance but they had no great feelings of love or gratitude for the Mother Country. Their populations were of mixed descent, they were prosperous and tolerant in matters of religion. What is more, the rule which had been exercised over them through their governors had often been inefficient and corrupt and sometimes tyrannical. Yet they would never have revolted without the leadership of New England. There the spirit of independence was strongest. There the centre of opposition began and remained.

Nevertheless, there were grievances which were shared by all. The Navigation Acts, originally passed by Cromwell in 1650 and 1651, to challenge the seafaring trade of Holland, had always been regarded with suspicion by the colonists. These laid down that the British colonies must not trade with foreigners and that goods imported by the colonies must be carried in ships of the country of origin or in British ships. A later Act in 1660 said that certain goods could only be exported from the colonies to an English port and all goods imported by the colonies must come through England. In fact the Acts had been allowed to lapse and customs officers had over the years allowed trade to develop in contravention of them. George III was determined that the colonists should contribute not only to the cost of the Seven Years War but to the cost of British troops for their protection in as many ways as possible. Measures were taken to enforce the Navigation Acts and further Acts were passed to strengthen the Government's control. The Molasses Act had been passed in 1733 to protect West Indian sugar growers. It created a West Indian monopoly in sugar but had been evaded by the colonists who had sold their goods to the West Indies in exchange for molasses. In 1764, Parliament passed the Sugar Act which re-enforced the old Molasses Act and placed a duty on produce from the West Indies. These measures which made trading extremely difficult angered colonists everywhere in the old settlements. As one merchant put it, 'The restrictions which we are laid under by Parliament put us at a stand how to employ our vessels to any advantage, as we have no prospects of markets at our own islands and cannot send elsewhere to have anything that will answer in return.'

There were by this time nearly two million colonists who regarded themselves, however, as Englishmen rather than as Americans. The grievances, particularly with reference to the restriction on trade, they regarded as violations of 'rights of Englishmen'. What is more, the colonists of pure English descent thought of an England of past centuries and since general emigration to the colonies had virtually ceased, those who came were mostly criminals, either transported or

Washington crossing the Delaware, 1776. (*By Leutze.*)

indentured labourers. These, not very good examples, were taken by the colonists to represent the people at home.

The defeat of the French had brought vast new areas west of the Alleghanies under British rule and the colonists looked upon this territory as theirs to do with as they wished. In 1763, the British Government, very sensibly realising that trouble with the Indian tribes inhabiting the new territory would be disastrous, declared it an Indian reserve and forbade further settlement. This aroused bitter resentment and even George Washington himself said, '. . . I can never look upon that proclamation in any other light than as a temporary expedient to quiet the minds of the Indians,' and ordered his agent to claim valuable land in the Ohio valley. The frontiersmen could not see the point of protecting Indians. They believed in the saying that the only good Indian is a dead Indian.

George III was determined to rule as a King, and he was not prepared to make any concessions to those whom he regarded as 'his subjects in the colonies'. Consequently, his Chancellor of the Exchequer, George Grenville, who had been responsible for the Acts restricting trade, followed with further measures. It was considered that to protect the colonists a regular army of 7,500 men was needed. Grenville believed that the colonies should help to pay for this and invited suggestions from them as to how this could best be done. It is important to note this, as Grenville would have undoubtedly welcomed suggestions, but not one of the colonies replied as they did not wish to contribute anything. So, in 1765, Grenville passed the Stamp Act which imposed duties on documents and newspapers similar to those already in force in England. The colonists, already burning with resentment, reacted at once, declaring that the British Government had no right to tax the colonies other than by customs duties at the ports. Whether this was true or not has been argued ever since, but it is certainly true that it had not been done before. Nine colonies sent protests to Parliament, there were riots in New England, Pennsylvania and New York, and officials found the tax impossible to enforce and collect. It was claimed that Englishmen could only be taxed by their own representatives and since the colonists had no representatives in the English Parliament, the tax was invalid. The cry became, 'No taxation without representation!' It rang round the colonies. The great William Pitt said, 'In my opinion this kingdom has no right to lay a tax on the colonies. . . . I rejoice that America has resisted.' Grenville resigned and his successor, Rockingham, repealed the Stamp Act in 1766. However, the good done by the repeal was somewhat undone by his Declaratory Act of the same year which reaffirmed the Government's right to tax the colonies if it so desired.

Rockingham was dismissed in 1767 and once more Pitt, now Earl of Chatham, took office. Unfortunately, he was in very poor health and during absence through illness government was continued by men of lesser stature. In the same year Townshend tried subtler means of raising the required money. He introduced the American Import Duties Act which placed increased duties on tea, glass, red and white lead, painters' colours and paper. It was hoped to raise £40,000 per year to help in payment of salaries of colonial governors and officials. The colonists had always conceded the right to levy customs duties but the seething resentment and the obvious intention of the Act to supplant the Stamp Act meant that it was opposed vigorously.

It will be seen that feeling was growing increasingly stronger against the Home Government and this together with the deep-rooted grievances were in the main the real causes of the conflict which was soon to follow. This conflict was made more and more inevitable by the chain of events which followed.

The Events Leading to the War

For some years there had been a Radical element bent on independence, but it was a minority movement. However, after the Stamp Act in 1765 the movement grew, led by Samuel Adams and James Otis in Massachusetts, Patrick Henry in Virginia and Christopher Gadsden in South Carolina. Organisations known as 'Sons of Liberty' sprang up everywhere, pledged to oppose the actions of the British Government. The desire for full independence which had been held by a very small minority was now gaining support.

Whipped on by the 'Sons of Liberty', opposition to the new Townshend Acts grew, and tax collectors were roughly handled and often pitched into the harbour at the ports, where customs duties were due to be paid. Many colonists joined together in the 'Association' by which they refused to trade in any way with Britain. By refusing to buy British goods they denied themselves both luxuries and essentials, and the trade boycott also caused distress in England.

Pitt died in 1770, and was succeeded by Lord North, who was essentially a 'King's man' and supported the ideas of George III. However, North removed all the duties except that on tea. This was to maintain the principle of the right of taxation and the colonists regarded it as such and reacted against it, as would be expected. Riots and disorders continued, but George III and North were determined now upon repression and that there must be no compromise. In Boston a rioting crowd surrounded a small force of British troops, who had received strict orders not to open fire without permission. The crowd was in an ugly mood and the troops were nervous. For some reason, never properly known, the troops opened fire and several colonists were killed and others wounded. This was known as the 'Boston Massacre' and increased ill-feeling, particularly between the colonists and the British soldiers. An American eye-witness said that he had never seen troops so goaded and admired their self-control. Samuel Adams made the most of the incident and encouraged still more resistance. 'Committees of Correspondence' were set up in seventy-five towns in Massachusetts, and with Patrick Henry forming a standing committee of the Virginian assembly to keep in touch with other colonies, the means for organising revolution was appearing. Other colonies soon followed Virginia's example and soon the colonies were co-operating with each other. In 1772, rioters captured and burned H.M.S. *Gaspee*, a British revenue cutter off Rhode Island which had been suppressing smuggling.

The East India Company at this time had a surplus of tea and so in 1773 they were permitted by the Tea Act to take it directly to America, thus evading the English tax. This meant that the Americans could buy tea more cheaply than the English could, but the colonists did not see it that way and took it as an attempt to make them pay the hated tea-tax. When a cargo of tea arrived at Boston, a Town Meeting decided that it should not be landed. The governor ordered that it should, so on the night of 16 December 1773, a party of men disguised as Red Indians and organised by Samuel Adams, boarded the East Indiaman in Boston Harbour, overpowered the crew, and tipped the whole cargo of tea, 340 chests valued at £17,000, into the sea.

The Boston Tea Party.

As in the case of the *Gaspee* it was impossible to discover the culprits, as the townspeople protected them. This incident has been known ever since as the Boston Tea Party.

Opinion in Britain was now beginning to harden against the colonists, even among some of those who had sympathised with them, and the feeling was that they had gone too far. When the Government proposed strong action it was generally approved, and General Thomas Gage, commander-in-chief at Boston also felt that firm measures were necessary, and he was known to be friendly towards the colonists.

Four 'Coercion Acts' were passed by the English Parliament in 1774. These became known to the colonists as the 'Intolerable Acts'. The first closed the port of Boston to all trade until compensation had been paid to the East India Company; the second suspended the Massachusetts Assembly, bringing the colony directly under the Crown; the third made it possible for offenders to be taken to England for trial; and the fourth, which applied to all the colonies, was the Quartering Act, providing for the billeting of British troops to maintain order. In the same year the Quebec Act was passed and this made Canada a Crown colony and gave religious toleration to Roman Catholics. It also placed the territory north of the Ohio under the control of Canada, which incensed the Puritan New Englanders. The American colonists mistakenly believed that the Canadians, lately enemies, were being given more freedom than they themselves possessed.

George Washington and Paul Revere.

An open break was now very near. The Assembly of Virginia proposed that there should be a meeting of the representatives of all the colonies and the First Continental Congress was held at Philadelphia in 1774. The Congress agreed to support Massachusetts and demanded the repeal of the Four Coercion Acts and the Quebec Act. It hoped also to win the support of the French Canadians, but this it failed to do. The Massachusetts Assembly, still meeting in spite of the Act forbidding it to do so, formed a group of militiamen to be ready for action at a minute's notice, to be known as 'minute men'. The Second Continental Congress, meeting a little later in the year, made its last appeal to the King in 1775 with the Olive Branch Petition, expressing loyalty to him and asking for a peaceful settlement. At the same time it was preparing for an invasion of Canada. Lord North made an offer to all colonies of exemption from all taxation except customs duties if they would make a voluntary contribution towards the cost of British troops. Both these approaches were too late and each was viewed with suspicion by the other side.

At Boston, General Gage, realising that war was inevitable, was determined to seize all arms and ammunition that he could. On the night of 18 April 1775 he sent a force of 800 infantry to Concord, some twenty miles from Boston, to destroy the military stores, and to arrest Samuel Adams and John Hancock, another leader. The colonists were watching and the warning was flashed by lantern from the steeple of North Church in Boston. Paul Revere then made his famous ride to Lexington, rousing the 'minute men' and warning

Adams and Hancock. The British troops succeeded in destroying the stores, but Adams and Hancock escaped, and the force was ambushed in the woods near Lexington and harried all the way back to Boston, considerable casualties being suffered by both sides. These were the first shots in the war and the engagement is known as the Battle of Lexington.

The Second Continental Congress chose George Washington as its commander-in-chief and set about raising an army. This was a sure sign that even the more moderate elements realised that a peaceful settlement was now out of the question.

In the summer of 1776, the Third Continental Congress met again at Philadelphia and issued the Declaration of Independence. The United States of America had become a new nation.

The Course of the War: The First Phase

General Thomas Gage had in April 1775 about 7,000 troops at Boston, far too few to carry out any offensive operations in the face of the large number of recruits rushing to join the militia, which provided some 20,000 men. General Sir William Howe arrived in May with reinforcements which brought the British strength to 10,000. The Americans decided to attempt to take the town and with this in view moved on to two hills overlooking it, Bunker Hill and Breeds Hill; and proceeded to fortify them. They were bombarded by British ships and then Gage decided to attack them. For some reason he attacked frontally and although he captured both he did so after two attacks were repulsed and at the cost of 1,000 killed and wounded out of 3,000 engaged. Although it was a British victory the American defenders were treated as heroes by the colonists and were greatly encouraged to find that they could stand up with some success to British regular troops.

Gage's plan for the attack is open to much criticism and his inaction afterwards to even more. Britain suffered from not having a Wolfe or a Clive for the whole of the war, but the generals may have appeared worse than they really were by the nature of the struggle. There were many on both sides who had little stomach for the fight. It is often suggested that Gage had much sympathy with the colonists and certainly some other commanders, particularly in the early stages of the war, were half-hearted because they disliked fighting what was almost a civil war against Englishmen. The troops often felt the same. The colonists, too, were divided and the extent of that division is shown by two things. The first was that over 25,000 loyalist colonists fought for the British and that after the war over

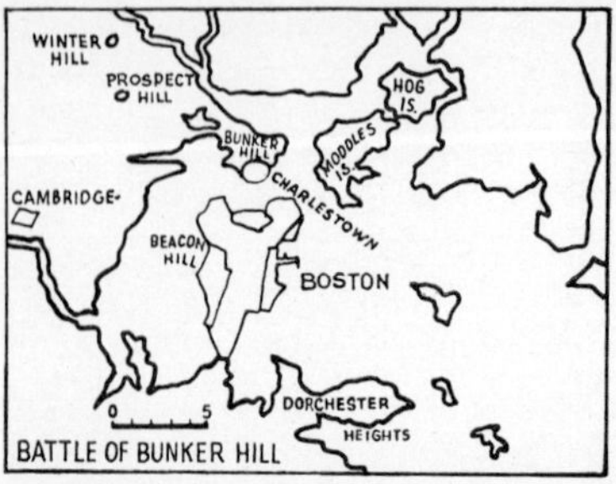

60,000 moved north into Canada rather than leave the rule of the Mother Country. The second was that, although there were some 280,000 colonists fit to fight, Washington could never gather an army of more than 25,000 and usually it was far less.

Gage was recalled in disgrace in October 1775. Sir William Howe, who had led the first troops up the path to the Heights of Abraham in 1759, replaced him and decided to evacuate Boston and move to Halifax early in 1776. Washington had now seized Dorchester Heights overlooking the port of Boston and a withdrawal which should have been made earlier was now forced upon the British.

Meanwhile in 1775 the colonists decided to attempt an invasion of Canada. The main American force was commanded by General Montgomery, a former British officer. Another force was under Benedict Arnold who was later to become infamous. The forts at Ticonderoga and Crown Point had been surprised and captured by Arnold and Ethan Allen just before and were used as a jumping-off point. Montgomery took Montreal and both forces converged on Quebec, defended by General Sir Guy Carleton. The Americans were suffering from sickness and desertion and the attack on Quebec was beaten off, Montgomery being killed and Arnold wounded. This was the last attempt on Canada.

Howe now decided to attack New York. This was the first step in a larger plan; to drive up the Hudson Valley, join with a force driving southwards from Canada and so isolate the New England colonies. These colonies were the hot-bed of independence enthusiasm and had the plan been successful it might have ended the war, since the South was not yet enthusiastic for the rebel cause.

Howe and his army sailed from Halifax to Staten Island, just off New York, in June 1776 and in the following month was joined by his elder brother, Admiral Viscount Howe, with a considerable fleet and reinforcements from England. General Howe now had an army of some 25,000 men and showed considerable skill in his next operations. The fact that he failed to follow them up may be due less to inefficiency than to the fact that both he and his brother were sympathetic to the colonists' cause and hoped for a peaceful settlement right up until 1778. The Americans were driven out of Long Island after heavy fighting and the British crossed to the mainland and captured New York. Washington retreated skilfully, but with more energy in pursuit Howe might have completely destroyed the American army. New York remained the British headquarters for most of the war. Howe then captured Fort Washington on Manhattan Island, while General Lord Cornwallis took Fort Lee in New Jersey. Cornwallis followed this up by overrunning New Jersey and Washington retreated beyond the River Delaware. The morale of the American troops was now at its lowest and they deserted in large numbers. If Howe could have pushed on and captured Philadelphia and then carried out his plan to advance up the Hudson River, the war might well have been over by the end of 1776. However, Howe did little during the winter and thus gave Washington the opportunity to strike back. Twice crossing the Delaware, Washington struck first to surprise a party of Hessian troops at Trenton on Boxing Day, 1776, killing and wounding 106 and capturing 900 of them with only 5 American casualties. The second attack was at Princeton on the rearguard of a British force and this was also successful. Washington had now regained a large part of New Jersey. The employment of German Hessian troops by the British caused anger among the colonists and Washington's success against them was a great boost to morale. Most of them were drunk after Christmas festivities anyway!

It was now time to put the New England plan into operation. At the end of 1776, General Sir Guy Carleton had advanced southwards from Canada and captured Crown Point. He built ships to assist him across Lake Champlain, but by now it was winter and he decided to delay his attack on Ticonderoga until the spring. He was recalled early in 1777 and General Burgoyne, of whom it was said that he was more at home in the world of London politics and fashion than on the battlefield, took his place. Burgoyne continued the advance in the spring. For the success of the plan it was essential that Howe should advance northwards to meet him. Howe was anxious to capture Philadelphia and Pennsylvania and certainly received muddled orders from England. He sailed by sea to Chesapeake Bay in July 1777 with 14,000 men and proceeded to occupy Pennsylvania, defeating Washington at Brandywine and Germantown, and captured Philadelphia with a force under Cornwallis in October. Howe had left General Sir Henry Clinton with an army of 8,000 to meet Burgoyne but sent for 4,000 of these to reinforce his own army soon afterwards.

Clinton moved northwards towards Burgoyne but could only reach West Point. Burgoyne, with many Hessians among his force, continued his progress southwards short of food and supplies, harried by American irregulars and out of touch with everyone. After defeat at Freeman's Farm and Bemis Heights in September and October by General Gates' force, he was surrounded by a vastly superior army of New England militia and forced to surrender with 6,000 men at Saratoga on 16 October 1777. This was a disaster to the British in every way. The plan to isolate New England which might have ended the war was a total failure. A considerable army had been forced to surrender and the morale effect on the Americans was tremendous.

Howe had captured Pennsylvania but, once again, had not followed up his success and had allowed his enemy to escape.

Washington made his headquarters at Valley Forge during the winter of 1777–78 and his work in holding together and training his army was perhaps his supreme achievement. Short of food, clothes and equipment and suffering from bitter cold, the army dwindled to a few thousand at one time. Yet Howe made no attempt to attack and destroy them and Washington employed Baron von Steuben, a German regular, to train his men for the battles to come.

The Second Phase: Intervention of European Powers

There now began a new phase of the war. France had been helping the Americans with arms, supplies and volunteers, notably the Marquis de Lafayette, later to be famous in the French Revolution. Eager to avenge herself for the loss of India and Canada, France seeing the British failure to end the fighting quickly declared open war on Britain in February 1778. This meant that Britain now had a second war to worry about and the Royal Navy lost control of the seas. The navy had been neglected since the Seven Years War but, since the Americans had very little in the way of a fleet, it had not really mattered until now. Although John Paul Jones had achieved a great deal with his small squadron for the Americans, the Royal Navy had been able to maintain control of the seas and support the land operations. Now the French navy was to gain a temporary command of the Atlantic which was to prove an embarrassment to the British armies in America.

General Sir William Howe was recalled early in 1778 and General Sir Henry Clinton replaced him. Clinton left Philadelphia and returned to New York fighting the Battle of Monmouth Court House on the way. Soon after this General Benedict Arnold, who had helped to lead the attack on Canada earlier, left the American cause and joined the British, an event which caused great indignation among the colonists.

In 1780 Clinton decided on a new plan by which he would reconquer the south, where he believed support for independence was lukewarm, and move northwards to join with the army in the Middle Colonies. He sailed for South Carolina with an army and captured Charleston. He then returned to New York, leaving the southern campaign in the hands of General Lord Cornwallis, probably the best British general of the war. Cornwallis drove northwards from Charleston, defeating Gates at the Battle of Camden, and Greene at Cowpens and Guildford Court House.

The French had made an attempt to send an army to America under D'Estaing, but they were driven off by Admiral Howe. Soon after Admiral Rodney defeated a French fleet in the West Indies, but 5,000 French troops under Comte de Rochambeau landed at Newport, Rhode Island, where they were blockaded by Rodney's fleet.

Cornwallis now found himself in need of supplies and reinforcements, although he had been joined by a force sent by Clinton under Benedict Arnold. He then made for Yorktown in Chesapeake Bay. When he got there he found that Admiral de Grasse had landed a French force of 3,000 in Virginia, Washington and Greene's armies, with a second French army under Lafayette, were surrounding him on the landward side and instead of the British fleet he expected in Chesapeake Bay he found de Grasse's fleet blockading Yorktown. So with 8,000 Americans and 9,000 French besieging him and no hope of reinforcement, he was forced to surrender his army of 7,000 on 19 October 1781 after a gallant defence of three weeks. On the very samc day Clinton sailed from New York with a relief force, but on hearing of Cornwallis' surrender turned back. This was the end of the American War of Independence, although the war against France, and against Spain, who had entered the war in 1779, and Holland who had come in in 1780, continued until 1783. During this time Gibraltar withstood a siege by the French and Spanish from 1779 until 1782, Admiral Sir Hyde Parker defeated the Dutch fleet at the Dogger Bank in 1780 and Rodney defeated a French fleet under de Grasse in 1782.

The Treaty of Versailles

Under this treaty, signed in 1783, the independence of the United States of America was recognised, although a treaty had been signed in November 1782 directly with the American Government. The United States was to include all eastward of the Mississippi River. Spain had, however, regained Florida which was not included in the United States and recovered Minorca from Britain. The French gained the West Indian island of St Lucia and Senegal in West Africa and had the trading stations in India, which Britain had taken during the war, returned to her.

Causes of British Defeat and the Results of the War

Why had Britain lost the war? She had first-class regular troops against an army which was mainly irregular and which was never fully supported by the American people. The reasons may be summarised in this way. The British Government were too long realising that they had a major war on their hands and too slow in reinforcing the British troops in America. The distance between Britain and America made supply and reinforcement difficult. Consequently, there were never sufficient British troops available. Those who were there were unfamiliar with the country, while the Americans knew it well. The British were trained for European war, and the Americans used methods more suited to the terrain. It was a mistake to introduce Hessian troops who, apart from being of only average efficiency, incensed the colonists. Although there were at least 25,000 loyalist colonists willing to fight for the British, they were never fully and properly used and were treated badly. Howe's inaction, his failure to pursue and destroy a beaten enemy, and, above all, his failure to carry out the plan to meet Burgoyne and cut off New England, were major reasons for the British defeat. Once France, Spain and Holland had entered the war and the Royal Navy had lost command of the sea, the chances of British victory receded even farther. Above all, the Americans who took an active part believed their cause to be just and were fighting for their own homeland, and they had inspiring and inspired leadership from Washington.

The results of the war were far-reaching. Not only was a new and independent nation created—a nation destined to become a world power—but it marked the end of the Old Colonial System. A new British Empire was to emerge with a Government which looked upon it in an entirely new way. A New Colonial System was evolved by which the colonies in the Empire were eventually to grow to independence themselves. The move of United Empire Loyalists, as they came to be called, to Canada changed the history of that country.

Yet there were other results. For years convicts had been transported to the Carolinas and Virginia. This now had to stop and indirectly this was to lead to the settlement of Australia. The French troops who returned to their own country carried with them the ideas of freedom and rebellion which were to contribute to the French Revolution in 1789.

SUMMARY

The Situation After the Seven Years War

Thirteen colonies as separate settlements.—Fear of French before the war.—British protection.—Fear of Indians.—Pontiac's rising (1763).—French menace removed after the War.—Co-operation between colonies during war continued afterwards.—British troops no longer considered necessary by colonies.

The Causes of the Quarrel

Character of colonies.—New England Puritans.—Middle and Southern Colonies' mixed populations.—Common grievances.—Navigation Acts (1650, 1651, 1660).—Molasses Act (1733).—Sugar Act (1764).—Restrictions on trade resented.—Colonists felt that their 'rights as Englishmen' were threatened.—British Government's action in forbidding settlement west of Alleghanies (1763).—Resented by colonists.—Policy of George III.—Government's decision that colonists should pay part of cost of maintaining British troops.—Stamp Act (1765).—Protests and riots.—'No taxation without representation'.—Stamp Act repealed (1766).—Declaratory Act (1766).—Townshend Act (1767).—Growth of desire for independence.

The Events Leading to the War

Independence movement led by Samuel Adams, James Otis, Patrick Henry, Christopher Gadsden.—'Sons of Liberty'.—Further disorders.—Lord North as chief minister (1770).—Supported ideas of George III.—Boston Massacre (1770).—'Committee of Correspondence'.—Co-operation between colonies.—Burning of *Gaspee* (1772).—Tea Act (1773).—Boston Tea Party (1773).—British opinion hardening against colonists.—Firm action proposed.—Four 'Coercion Acts' (1774): port of Boston closed, Massachusetts Assembly suspended, billeting of British troops, removal of offenders to Britain for trial.—Quebec Act (1774).—Further colonial resentment.—First Continental Congress (1774).—Massachusetts Assembly recruited 'Minute-men' (1774).—Olive Branch Petition (1775).—Lord North's offer.—Both rejected.—Battle of Lexington (1775).—Second Continental Congress (1775).—George Washington as commander-in-chief.—Third Continental Congress. (1776).—Declaration of Independence (1776).

The Course of the War: The First Phase

General Gage and 7,000 troops at Boston.—General Howe and 3,000 troops arrived.—20,000 militiamen around Boston—Battle of Bunker Hill (1775).—Reluctance to fight on both sides.—Loyalists among colonists, 20,000 fought for British and 60,000 moved to Canada after war.—Washington's difficulties in raising and maintaining army.—Gage replaced by Howe.—Boston evacuated (1776).—Howe at Halifax.—Attempted invasion of Canada under Montgomery and Arnold (1775).—Crown Point and Ticonderoga captured.—Failure of invasion.—Carleton evacuated Montreal but held Quebec.

Howe's Plan

Howe's plan to attack New York and isolate New England.—Howe sailed to Staten Island (1776); joined by Admiral Howe and fleet.—Howe brothers' hope for peace.—Long Island and New York captured by British.—Fort Washington captured.—Fort Lee captured by Cornwallis.—Washington retreated beyond the Delaware.—Howe's inertia.—Washington crossed the Delaware.—American victories at Trenton and Princeton (1776–77).—Carleton advanced southwards from Canada (1776); captured Crown Point; delayed further advance until spring; replaced by Burgoyne (1777).—Burgoyne continued advance (spring 1777).

Failure of Plan

Howe's failure to carry out New England plan.—Howe sailed to Chesapeake Bay and advanced into Pennsylvania (1777).—Washington defeated at Brandywine and Germantown.—Cornwallis captured Philadelphia.—Clinton left at New York.—Clinton, with small force, moved northwards towards Burgoyne.—Halted at West Point.—Burgoyne's difficulties.—Defeated at Freeman's Farm and Bemis Heights.—Surrounded and forced to surrender at Saratoga (Oct. 1777).—Washington wintered at Valley Forge (1777–78); hardships; force trained by von Steuben.—Howe's failure to press home his advantage.

The Second Phase: Intervention of European Powers

French help to Americans.—Lafayette.—France entered War (Feb. 1778).—Weakness of Royal Navy.—Achievements of Paul Jones; Britain lost control of seas.—Howe recalled (1778).—Replaced by General Clinton.—Philadelphia evacuated (1779).—Clinton returned to New York.—Battle of Monmouth.—Defection of Arnold.—Clinton's plan to capture South (1780); sailed to South Carolina; captured Charleston.—Clinton returned to New York leaving Cornwallis in Command.

Campaign of Cornwallis

Cornwallis drove northwards.—Victories at Camden, Cowpens, Guildford Court House.—Admiral Howe drove off French fleet under D'Estaing.—Rodney defeated French fleets in West Indies.—5,000 French troops under de Rochambeau landed at Rhode Island.—Blockaded by Rodney.—Cornwallis joined by force under Arnold; marched to Yorktown for supplies and reinforcements.—French force in Virginia.—Washington, Greene and Lafayette with their armies besieged Yorktown.—French fleet under de Grasse blockaded from sea.—Cornwallis and army surrendered (Oct. 1781).—Virtual end of War of Independence.—Fighting against France, Spain and Holland continued until 1783.

Treaty of Versailles (1783)

Independence of U.S.A. recognised.—Spain regained Florida.

Causes of British Defeat and Results of the War

Causes of defeat.—British Government's failure to give early recognition to danger of war.—Distance between Britain and America.—Shortage of British troops; unfamiliar with country; trained for war in Europe.—Hessian troops.—Treatment of loyalists.—Howe's inaction and failure to pursue New England plan.—Entry of European powers.—Loss of command of sea.—Americans' belief in just cause.—Washington's leadership.

Results of war.—New nation of U.S.A.—End of Old Colonial System.—New British Empire and New Colonial System.—Loyalists moved to Canada.—Colonisation of Australia.—Contribution to causes of French Revolution.

QUESTIONS

Answer the following questions briefly:

1. (a) Why did the colonists in America welcome British troops before the Seven Years War?
   (b) Why did their attitude change after the War?
   (c) What were the Navigation Acts?
   (d) What was the effect of the Declaratory Act (1766)?
   (e) What was the Boston Massacre?
   (f) Who were the 'Sons of Liberty'?
   (g) What were the 'Intolerable Acts'?
   (h) What was the Olive Branch Petition?
   (i) Who was Benedict Arnold and why is he well known?
   (j) Why is it suggested that the British commanders were half-hearted?
   (k) Who were the United Empire Loyalists?
   (l) What happened at Valley Forge?
2. What do you consider to be the main causes of the quarrel between the colonists and the British Government? Give the main events leading to the War.
3. Give your reasons for the failure of the British and the success of the American colonists in the War of Independence.
4. King George III's attitude to the grievances of the British colonists in America is shown by his own words:

   > It is with the utmost astonishment that I find any of my subjects capable of encouraging the rebellious disposition which unhappily exists in some of my colonies in America. Having entire confidence in the wisdom of my Parliament, the Great Council of the Nation, I will steadily pursue those measures which they have recommended for the support of the constitutional right of Great Britain and the protection of the commercial interests of my Kingdom.

   Benjamin Franklin, a great American who was representing the colonies in London, in 1773 wrote:

   > . . . There seem to be among us some violent spirits who are for an immediate rupture; but I trust that the general prudence of our country will see that by our growing strength we advance fast to a situation in which our claim must be allowed, that by a premature struggle we may be crippled and kept down . . . that between governed and governing every mistake in government, every encroachment on right, is not worth a rebellion . . . remembering withal that this Protestant country (our mother, though lately an unkind one) is worth preserving, and that her weight in the scales of Europe and her safety in a great degree may depend on our union with her.

   William Pitt, Earl of Chatham, believed that the colonists treated well could become 'a willing, giving people'. Speaking at the outbreak of fighting in 1775 he said:

   > it is not repealing this act of parliament, it is not repealing a piece of parchment, that can restore America to our bosom; you must repeal her fears and resentments; and you may then hope for her love and gratitude.

John Adams, cousin of Samuel Adams, wrote after the Boston Tea Party:

> This is the most magnificent movement of all. There is a dignity, a majesty and sublimity in this best effort of the Patriots that I greatly admire. . . . This however is an attack upon property. Another similar exertion of popular power may produce destruction of lives. Many persons wish that as many dead carcases were floating in the harbour as there are chests of tea.

(a) Comment upon these different points of view from both sides of the Atlantic. How do you think they illustrate the fact that the conflict might have been avoided?

(b) Which do you think contributed most towards the quarrel and the war which followed?

(c) Say what you think might have been done by both sides to keep the peace.

(d) What parts of the Declaration of Independence (Appendix A) indicated the main grievances of the colonists?

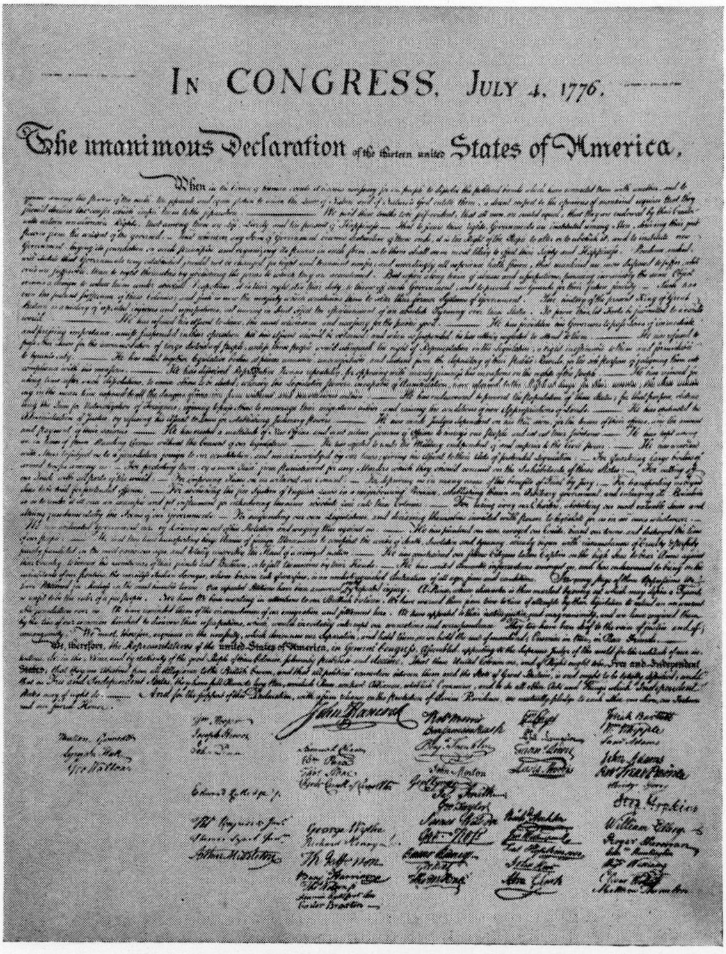

IN CONGRESS, JULY 4, 1776.

The unanimous Declaration of the thirteen united States of America,

Original document—Declaration of Independence.

APPENDIX A

In CONGRESS, July 4, 1776

The unanimous Declaration of the thirteen united STATES OF AMERICA

When in the Course of human events it becomes necessary for one people to dissolve the political bands which have connected them with another, and to assume among the powers of the earth, the separate and equal station to which the Laws of Nature and of Nature's God entitle them, a decent respect to the opinions of mankind requires that they should declare the causes which impel them to the separation.—We hold these truths to be self-evident, that all men are created equal, that they are endowed by their Creator with certain unalienable Rights, that among these are Life, Liberty and the pursuit of Happiness.—That to secure these rights, Governments are instituted among Men, deriving their just powers from the consent of the governed.—That whenever any Form of Government becomes destructive of these ends, it is the Right of the People to alter or to abolish it, and to institute new Government, laying its foundation on such principles and organizing its powers in such form, as to them shall seem most likely to effect their Safety and Happiness. Prudence, indeed, will dictate that Governments long established should not be changed for light and transient causes; and accordingly all experience hath shewn that mankind are more disposed to suffer, while evils are sufferable, than to right themselves by abolishing the forms to which they are accustomed. But when a long train of abuses and usurpations, pursuing invariably the same Object evinces a design to reduce them under absolute Despotism, it is their right, it is their duty, to throw off such Government, and to provide new Guards for their future security.—Such has been the patient sufferance of these Colonies; and such is now the necessity which constrains them to alter their former Systems of Government. The history of the present King of Great Britain is a history of repeated injuries and usurpations, all having in direct object the establishment of an absolute Tyranny over these States. To prove this, let Facts be submitted to a candid world.—He has refused his Assent to Laws, the most wholesome and necessary for the public good.—He has forbidden his Governors to pass Laws of immediate and pressing importance, unless suspended in their operation till his Assent should be obtained; and when so suspended, he has utterly neglected to attend to them.—He has refused to pass other Laws for the accommodation of large districts of people, unless those people would relinquish the right of Representation in the Legislature, a right inestimable to them and formidable to tyrants only.—He has called together legislative bodies at places unusual, uncomfortable and distant from the depository of their public Records, for the sole purpose of fatiguing them into compliance with his measures.—He has dissolved Representative Houses repeatedly, for opposing with manly firmness his invasions on the rights of the people.—He has refused for a long time, after such dissolutions, to cause others to be elected; whereby the Legislative powers, incapable of Annihilation, have returned to the People at large for their exercise; the State remaining in the mean time exposed to all the dangers of invasion from without, and convulsions within.—He has endeavoured to prevent the population of these States; for that purpose obstructing the Laws for Naturalization of Foreigners; refusing to pass others to encourage their migrations hither, and raising the conditions of new Appropriations of Lands.—He has obstructed the Administration of Justice, by refusing his Assent to Laws for establishing Judiciary powers.—He has made Judges dependent on his Will alone, for the tenure of their offices, and the amount and payment of their salaries. He has erected a multitude of New Offices, and sent hither swarms of Officers to harass our people, and eat out their substance. He has kept among us, in times of peace, Standing Armies without the Consent of our legislatures.—He has affected to render the Military independent of and superior to the Civil power.—He has combined with others to subject us to a jurisdiction foreign to our constitution, and unacknowledged by our laws; giving his Assent to their Acts of pretended Legislation:—For quartering large bodies of armed troops among us:—For protecting them, by a mock Trial, from punishment for any Murders which they should commit on the Inhabitants of these States:—For cutting off our Trade with all parts of the world:—For imposing Taxes on us without our Consent:—For depriving us in many cases, of the benefits of Trial by Jury:—For transporting us beyond Seas to be tried for pretended offences:—For abolishing the free System of English Laws in a neighbouring Province, establishing therein an Arbitrary government, and enlarging its Boundaries so as to render it at once an example and fit instrument for introducing the same absolute rule into these Colonies:—For taking away our Charters, abolishing our most valuable Laws and altering fundamentally the Forms of our Governments:—For suspending our own Legislatures, and declaring themselves invested with power to legislate for us in all cases whatsoever.—He has abdicated Government here, by declaring us out of his Protection and waging War against us.—He has plundered our seas, ravaged our Coasts, burnt our towns, and destroyed the lives of our people.—He is at this time transporting large Armies of foreign Mercenaries to compleat the works of death, desolation and tyranny, already begun with circumstances of Cruelty & perfidy scarcely paralleled in the most barbarous ages, and totally unworthy the Head of a civilised nation.—He has constrained our fellow Citizens taken Captive on the high Seas to bear Arms against their Country, to become the executioners of their friends and Brethren, or to fall themselves by their Hands.—He has excited domestic insurrections amongst us, and has endeavoured to bring on the inhabitants of our frontiers, the merciless Indian Savages, whose known rule of warfare, is an undistinguished destruction of all ages, sexes and conditions. In every stage of these Oppressions We have Petitioned for Redress in the most humble terms: Our repeated Petitions have been answered only by repeated injury. A Prince, whose character is thus marked by every act which may define a Tyrant is unfit to be the ruler of a free people. Nor have We been wanting in attentions to our Brittish brethren. We have warned them from time to time of attempts by their legislature to extend an unwarrantable jurisdiction over us. We have reminded them of the circumstances of our emigration and settlement here. We have appealed to their native justice and magnanimity, and we have conjured them by the ties of our common kindred to disavow these usurpations, which would inevitably interrupt our connections and correspondence. They too have been deaf to the voice of justice and of consanguinity. We must, therefore, acquiesce in the necessity, which denounces our Separation, and hold them, as we hold the rest of mankind, Enemies in War, in Peace Friends.—

WE, THEREFORE, the Representatives of the UNITED STATES OF AMERICA, in General Congress, Assembled, appealing to the Supreme Judge of the world for the rectitude of our intentions, do, in the Name, and by Authority of the good People of these Colonies, solemnly publish and declare, That these United Colonies are, and of Right ought to be FREE AND INDEPENDENT STATES; that they are Absolved from all Allegiance to the British Crown, and that all political connection between them and the State of Great Britain, is and ought to be totally dissolved; and that as Free and Independent States, they have full Power to levy War, conclude Peace, contract Alliances, establish Commerce, and to do all other Acts and Things which Independent States may of right do.—And for the support of this Declaration, with a firm reliance on the protection of divine Providence, we mutually pledge to each other our Lives, our Fortunes and our sacred Honor.

6 : The British in Canada

Canada After the Seven Years War

When Montcalm, Governor of French Canada, fell at the Battle of Quebec, he expressed concern for the fate of his people and a hope that the British would treat them well. The military rule which followed the end of the war provided three governors who, indeed, carried out Montcalm's wishes.

In 1763 Canada consisted of a strip of about one hundred miles wide on the northern bank of the St Lawrence and a narrow strip on the southern bank, with a population of over 60,000 people, all of French descent. Nova Scotia, Prince Edward Island and Newfoundland were all completely separate colonies, while the remainder of Canada was not yet settled. It must be remembered that this was before the French Revolution and that the society of the French colony was a reproduction of pre-revolutionary France. There were large landowners of noble birth, known as seigneurs, and a largely peasant population, known as habitants. They were, of course, Roman Catholic and the administration of the Church, the religious orders and parish priests were similar to those in France. As in their mother country, there was no democracy and the people were used to absolute rule.

This was an entirely new situation for British statesmen and the fact that British rule was so successful was largely due to the fact that the Government accepted the idea of military rule and appointed men of high character and considerable ability as governors. These men were soldiers, themselves accustomed to discipline, who governed firmly but with great fairness and understanding.

After a short period when General Lord Amherst, the commander-in-chief in Canada, was military governor and began the firm and fair rule which was to continue, General James Murray, who had defended Quebec, became military governor in 1763. The Canadians themselves reacted favourably to the treatment they received. The laws and customs of the country were respected, they were left to worship as they wished, and indeed the compulsory military service and forced labour which had been a part of French government ended under British rule. The introduction of a representative assembly and English law and at the same time measures to protect the Indians by forbidd-

Lord Amherst.

Earl of Durham.

ing the purchase of land from them by private persons were promised in 1763. The French settlers themselves were not yet ready for democracy and the demand for the assembly was taken up by the few hundred Puritan New Englanders who had come to Canada to settle. Not only were they used to representative government but their Puritanism was violently opposed to the Roman Catholicism of the French. They asked for an assembly from which Roman Catholics would be debarred, something which could not be granted as it would obviously have been unjust to the French. The Puritans accused Murray of partiality towards the French and he was recalled to England in 1768. General Sir Guy Carleton, who was to defend Canada in the American War of Independence and lead the first force southwards to meet Howe until replaced by Burgoyne, then became military governor. Carleton carried on Murray's policy and refused to allow the minority of New Englanders to dominate the French. It was largely due to him that the Quebec Act was passed.

The Quebec Act, 1774

This Act was a wise and statesman-like measure to deal with a situation which was a problem, but it could only be a temporary solution. It made Canada a Crown colony under a governor who was to be assisted by a nominated council of from seventeen to twenty-three members. The Roman Catholic religion was recognised, with tithes collected by the priests, the French seigneurial system of land

Quebec in 1841. (*Engraving by W. H. Barlett, 1841.*)

tenure was accepted, and while English Criminal Law with trial by jury was introduced, French law and custom were allowed to remain in civil matters. It defined the boundaries of Canada and the inclusion of land southwards to the Ohio river was greatly resented by the British colonists in America. In fact this and the toleration shown by the Act to Roman Catholics were one of the causes of the War of Independence. The First Continental Congress at Philadelphia, said, 'we wish to express astonishment (to the British people) that a British Parliament should ever consent to establish in that country (Canada) a religion that has deluged your island in blood, and dispersed impiety, bigotry, persecution, murder and rebellion through every part of the world'. The Puritan New England settlers in Canada also naturally disliked the Act. Nevertheless it ensured the support of Canadians during the War of Independence. The seigneurs and the church were enthusiastic in their support of the British cause, and while the habitants were far less enthusiastic they refused the invitation of the Americans to join them. This, and the skill of Carleton, saved Canada from American invasion in 1775.

The effect of the War of Independence was nevertheless considerable in Canada. The Treaty of Versailles re-drew the boundaries to run through the centre line of the Great Lakes. The greatest single change was brought about by the move to Canada of the United

Empire Loyalists. Each family was granted 200 acres of land and tools, supplies and seeds were given to them. Some of the Loyalists settled in Nova Scotia, some in the area to the west of Nova Scotia which became a separate colony in 1784 as New Brunswick, but the majority settled on the northern shores of Lakes Ontario and Erie in what became known as Upper Canada. These settlements changed the whole political situation in Canada. As well as nearly doubling its population it produced a new people, Protestant, independent, proud of their loyalty to Britain, and used to democratic government. The provisions of the Quebec Act were now no longer effective.

The Canada Act, or Constitutional Act, 1791

Carleton had been succeeded as governor in 1777 by Sir Frederick Haldimand, but in 1786 he returned for a second tour as Lord Dorchester. It was William Pitt, the Younger, who had to deal with the new problems and his method was not approved by Lord Dorchester who believed that Canada should not be divided into two. Pitt's solution appeared to be the best at the time and his Canada Act, or Constitutional Act as it is also known, of 1791 made two provinces: Upper Canada or the British area to the west; and Lower Canada or the French area to the east. Canada was to have a governor with a lieutenant-governor in each province. Each province was to have a nominated Legislative Council with an elected Legislative Assembly. The Act also said that while the Roman Catholic Church was still to receive tithes, the Anglican and Presbyterian Churches were to be given areas of land known as Clergy Reserves. This not only caused complaints from Methodists and other denominations not included but was to provide a future problem.

The Canada Act was not really a success. In Lower Canada or Quebec in particular the officials appointed were mainly English. The effects of the French Revolution were beginning to reach Canada. The seigneurs were beginning to lose influence and the ordinary people, while there was no desire for reunification with France, began to think of independence from Britain. In Upper Canada, the Loyalists were inclined to resent the influx of settlers from America who had not the same traditions of loyalty.

The war with America from 1812–14, however, proved the loyalty of most of the Canadians, French or British. With very little help from British regular troops the Canadian militia defeated the American invasion at nearly every point.

Instead of the solidarity shown by the settlers in the war continuing afterwards, once again the provinces slipped into discontent.

Grievances and Rebellions

Apart from settlers from the United States, immigrants from Britain were now arriving in Canada, ex-soldiers, crofters from Scotland, and peasants from Ireland.

The discontent began to appear as a racial struggle. In Lower Canada there were constant deadlocks between the Government and the Assembly. There was now a real British minority in the province, since apart from a small number of British there in the early days more had gradually settled on the southern bank of the St Lawrence in what became known as the Eastern Townships. The British had no representation in the Assembly and suffered from oppression. They also paid more than their share of taxation. Yet on the Legislative Council the French were barely represented, and consequently bad feelings between the British and French developed and there arose a French movement for independence. In both provinces the real power was in the hands of a small group of Loyalists. In 1831 the Assemblies of each province received the authority to control finance provided that they paid the salaries of the governor and officials. The Assembly in Lower Canada refused to do this and a deadlock resulted. In Upper Canada the control of the Council was also in Loyalist hands, a small clique of Loyalists often related, but so tightly controlled that it became known as the Family Compact. There was a minority among recent immigrants from the United States who wished Upper Canada to join with the new nation of America. A Reform Party was formed to combat the Family Compact and this increased agitation. It has been said that during this time in both provinces, 'the quiet man went back from war to his plough, worked from dawn to dark, conquered the wilderness, bred sons as worthy as himself, and founded a nation'. It is true that the truly discontented were probably a minority as was shown by the two rebellions which broke out, but the grievances were real. Two further grievances were the lands allotted to the clergy as Clergy Reserves which were often left uncultivated, and the duties charged by the Government of Lower Canada on the commerce from Upper Canada which had to pass through it on the way to the coast.

The two rebellions broke out simultaneously in Upper and Lower Canada in 1837. That in Upper Canada was led by William Lyon Mackenzie, the editor of an anti-Government newspaper, and a member of the Reform Party, who aimed at an independent republic. In Lower Canada the rebels were led by Louis Joseph Papineau. Both risings were quickly crushed, the leaders escaping to the United States and, in fact, had received very little popular support. Although

Attack on St Charles, Lower Canada, November 1837. (*By A. Beauclerk.*)

few of the discontented felt strongly enough to join the rebels, the risings were symptomatic of the feelings of grievance and the Home Government took action.

The Durham Report

In 1838, the Earl of Durham was sent to Canada as Governor-General and Lord High Commissioner with almost dictatorial powers. He took with him as an adviser Edward Gibbon Wakefield whose ideas on colonial settlement were just becoming known. Durham saw Canada as a great colony and wished to bring many more people to settle there. He wanted to improve racial relations and recast the political and governmental structure. The constitution of Lower Canada had been suspended since the risings and, in addition to his vast powers, Durham's methods were somewhat high-handed. When there was another small rising he banished the ringleaders to Bermuda. He had power to hang them but not to banish them and he was much criticised at home. Taking offence at this he resigned in 1839 but left behind him a magnificent Report upon which the new Canada was founded.

He analysed the causes of the revolt and made some strong recommendations. These included the re-union of Upper and Lower Canada, the construction of an intercolonial railway to improve communications and to link the Maritime Provinces of Nova Scotia and New Brunswick with the rest of the colony. He advocated

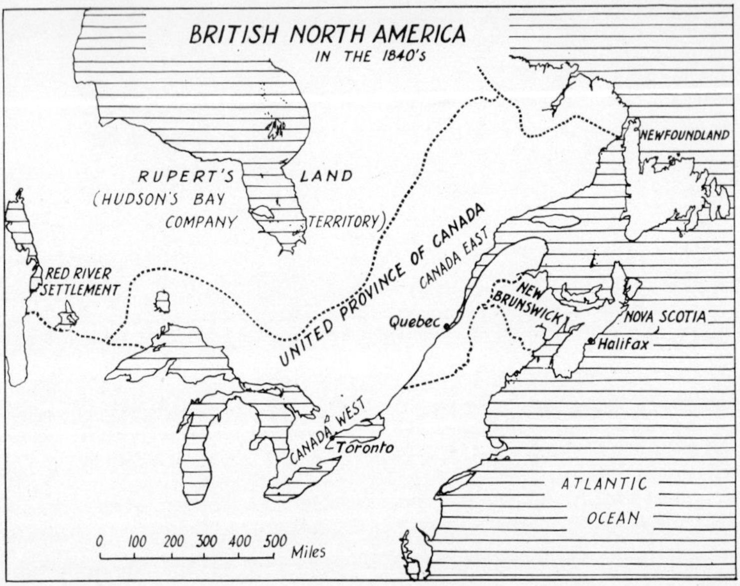

responsible government for Canada in which a Ministry similar to that of Great Britain should govern, responsible to the elected Assembly and holding office provided only that it held a majority in that Assembly. He also suggested improvements in local government. His report recognised that the British Parliament still needed to be supreme in making laws for Canada as a whole, in any alterations of the constitution, in trade, public lands and in foreign affairs.

The Report was in many ways ahead of its time. Few statesmen at home were yet ready to grant responsible government to any colony, but some of the ideas were incorporated in the legislation which followed.

The Re-Union Act, 1840

The Act following the Durham Report was passed in 1840. Under it Upper and Lower Canada were to be united. There was to be a Parliament of two houses; a Legislative Council appointed for life and a Legislative Assembly which was elected. The two provinces, known in future as Ontario and Quebec, were to have equal representation although the French population still outnumbered the British. It is interesting to note that later Ontario was discontented at not receiving greater representation when her population became larger in numbers than that of Quebec. The English language was made official although soon afterwards the French language was recognised too. Nothing was said about responsible government, which evolved during the next ten years as soon as the necessary conditions were present. These were a neutral governor and a reasonable two-party system in Parliament. Lord Elgin, appointed in 1847, was neutral and sympathetic to responsible government, and the party system gradually grew up.

With the adoption of the principle of Free Trade by the Mother Country and the repeal of the Navigation Acts, Canada's trade grew, her population increased and she became more and more prosperous.

This was by no means the end of difficulties, however. The Assembly passed in 1848 the Rebellion Losses Act which compensated people in Quebec for losses in the rising of ten years before. Elgin accepted it, but it provoked an outburst of anti-French feeling. The question of the Clergy Reserves still remained and were a constant source of irritation until 1854 when they were given up, the clergy being provided for in another way. In spite of difficulties slow progress was made towards self-government, British troops being gradually withdrawn except for a small garrison at Halifax, Nova Scotia.

Charlottetown and Quebec Conferences, 1864

The Canada which had existed since the Re-Union Act did not include the Maritime Provinces, nor any land west of Ontario. Other parts of Canada had been developing during this time. Rupert's Land, to the north, had been looked after by the Hudson's Bay Company. Another fur-trading company had been founded in 1783 to develop trade beyond the Hudson's Bay Company area to the west and north-west. In 1789, Alexander Mackenzie sailed down the river which bears his name to the Arctic Ocean, and crossed the Rocky Mountains in 1793. He then founded a new company known as the X.Y. Company which joined with the North-West Company in 1805. In 1821, after bitter rivalry, the Hudson's Bay Company virtually took over the North-West Company. There were a few trading settlements west of the Rockies and although a part of the Hudson's Bay Company territory, were under the Lieutenant-Governor of Upper Canada. Discovery of gold brought many more people into the area and in 1858 the Hudson's Bay Company's monopoly for trade west of the Rockies was ended, and the territory became a Crown colony as British Columbia, a representative assembly being granted in 1864. Vancouver Island, named after the man who explored the coast between 1792 and 1794, had become a British colony in 1849, and the two were united in 1866.

Boundary disputes between Canada and the United States had been going on for some time and the boundary line in the east was decided by the Ashburton Treaty of 1842. The western boundary was disputed by both sides and led to a risk of war in 1844, but the Oregon Treaty in 1846 agreed on the 49th Parallel as the border and that Vancouver Island should be British. However, there were many in America who were pressing for Canada to enter the Union. When the American Civil War ended in 1865, this pressure became greater.

By 1864 Canadian politics were in rather a muddled state and it was realised by wiser men that with the demand for the Maritime Provinces to be associated with the rest of Canada and the fear of American pressure for union of Canada with the United States, it was time for action.

The initiative really came from the Maritime Provinces. A conference of their delegates met in the summer of 1864 at Charlottetown in Prince Edward Island to consider federation among themselves. The Ministers of the Canadian Government invited them to come to Quebec to discuss with Canadian representatives the question of a greater federation. The Quebec Conference met in October 1864. Prince Edward Island withdrew, but Nova Scotia, New Brunswick and Canada sent delegates. A federation was proposed and it was suggested that it should be called the 'Kingdom of Canada'. It was thought that this might cause resentment in the United States, so one delegate quoted from the 72nd Psalm, 'He shall have *dominion* also from sea to sea, and from the river unto the ends of the earth.' His proposal for a name was adopted and the Dominion of Canada came into being in 1867, when the British Parliament embodied the proposals of the conference in the British North America Act. A large part of the credit for this complex act which gave birth to the first great dominion is due to Mr (later Sir) John Macdonald, leader of the Canadian Conservative Party.

SUMMARY

Canada After the Seven Years War

British governors' fair treatment of French settlers.—French Canadian life similar to that of pre-revolutionary France.—Seigneurs and habitants.—Roman Catholic religion.—No representative government.—Military governors of ability: Amherst, Murray, Carleton.—Settlers from New England demanded representative assembly.—Carleton's firm and fair rule as preliminary to Quebec Act.

The Quebec Act, 1774

Canada made a Crown colony under a governor and nominated council.—Roman Catholic religion recognised.—Tithes for clergy.—Seigneurial system of land tenure.—English Criminal Law and trial by jury.—French Civil Law.—

An east view of Montreal at the end of the 18th Century. (*By Thomas Patten.*)

Resentment of American colonists.—Canadians loyal in War of Independence.—Treaty of Versailles: boundaries through Great Lakes.—United Empire Loyalists moved to Canada.—Land grants.—Government help.—Change in political situation.—Quebec Act now out of date.

The Canada Act, or Constitutional Act, 1791

Two provinces: Upper Canada and Lower Canada.—Governor for Canada with lieutenant-governor in each province.—Each province to have nominated council and elected assembly.—Roman Catholic Church still to receive tithes.—Anglican and Presbyterian Churches to receive land grants as Clergy Reserves.—Difficulties; officials in Lower Canada mostly English; independence movement; Loyalist clique in Upper Canada.—War of 1812–14 proved loyalty of colonists.—Further discontent after the war.

Grievances and Rebellions

Immigrants from Britain: ex-soldiers, crofters, paupers and Irish peasants.—Difficulties in Lower Canada.—Deadlocks between council and assembly.—British minority.—Loyalist cliques ruled both provinces.—Difficulties over colonial finance especially in Lower Canada.—Family Compact in Upper Canada.—Reform Party formed to combat Family Compact.—Grievances over Clergy Reserves and commerce from Upper Canada being taxed by Lower Canada—Rebellions (1837) under Mackenzie in Upper Canada and Papineau in Lower Canada easily crushed, little popular support.

The Durham Report

Earl of Durham sent as Governor-General and Lord High Commissioner (1838); dictatorial powers; high-handed methods; resignation.—Durham Report (1839); analysed causes of revolt.—Recommendations: Re-union of Upper and Lower Canada.—Intercolonial railway.—Responsible government.—Improvements in local government.—British Government to retain powers to legislate for Canada, to change constitution, on trade, public lands and foreign affairs.

The Re-Union Act, 1840

Upper and Lower Canada to be re-united.—Parliament of two houses, Legislative Council appointed for life; Legislative Assembly elected; equal representation for provinces; English language official; no mention of responsible government.—Responsible government with the evolution of two-party system and appointment of sympathetic governor in Lord Elgin (1847).—Further difficulties.—Rebellion Losses Act (1848).—Clergy Reserves ended (1854).

Charlottetown and Quebec Conferences, 1864

Remainder of Canada.—Rupert's Land administered by Hudson Bay Company. —Mackenzie's voyage down Mackenzie River (1789); crossed Rocky Mts. (1793).—X. Y. Company and North West Company joined (1805).—Taken over by Hudson Bay Company (1821).—Gold discovered west of Rockies.—British Columbia (1858); representative assembly (1864).—Vancouver Island became colony (1849); joined British Columbia (1866).—Boundary disputes with U.S.A.; Ashburton Treaty (1842).—Oregon Treaty (1846) agreed on 49th Parallel as border.—Maritime Provinces' desire for federation.—Charlottetown Conference (1864).—Government of Canada invited delegates to Quebec for Conference (1864).—Withdrawal of Prince Edward Island.—Dominion of Canada through British North America Act (1867).—John Macdonald.

QUESTIONS

Answer the following questions briefly:

1. (a) What form did the social organisation of French Canada take in 1763?
   (b) Who were the outstanding military governors in the early days of Canada?
   (c) What were the main provisions of the Quebec Act?
   (d) Why was it necessary to pass the Canada Act of 1791?
   (e) What were the main provisions of the Canada Act?
   (f) How did British Columbia become a colony?
   (g) How were the boundary disputes between Canada and the U.S.A. settled?
2. Describe the grievances which led to the rebellions of 1837. What were the main recommendations of the Durham Report and what were its results?
3. In his report in 1839, Lord Durham said:

   > It is not by weakening but by strengthening the influence of people on its government—by confining within much narrower bounds, and not by extending, the interference of the imperial authorities in the details of colonial affairs—that harmony is to be restored where dissension has so long prevailed.

   In 1855, Lord John Russell said in a speech, that the British Commonwealth was to be held together by 'ties which, though light as air, are as strong as links of iron', by the 'participation of freedom, that sole bond, which originally made, and must still preserve, the unity of the Empire'.
   (a) How far did the Re-Union Act of 1840 go in putting Durham's ideas into practice?
   (b) How do you think the ideas in both these quotations came to be put into practice in the British North America Act of 1867?
   (c) Why did the conferences in 1864 in Charlottetown and Quebec take place?

7 : Canada as a Dominion

The British North America Act of 1867

THE Act which was passed by the British Parliament in March 1867 founded the first independent state within the Empire, laid the foundations for what was to become the Commonwealth and gave a new meaning to an old word. Dominion came to mean a colony which had achieved independence within the British Empire.

The Dominion of Canada was born on 1 July, 1867, and within it were united the two provinces of Ontario and Quebec, and the two Maritime Provinces, Nova Scotia and New Brunswick, which were present at the Quebec Conference. Prince Edward Island did not join the federation, but the Act made express provision for other provinces to be admitted later. There was to be a governor-general with lieutenant-governors in each province appointed by the Governor-General on the advice of the Dominion Ministers. The Dominion Parliament itself was modelled upon that of the United Kingdom. The Upper House, to be known as the Senate, consisted of members appointed for life, and the Lower House, to be called the House of Commons after the British Lower House, would have representatives of the provinces proportionate to population. Each province was to have a Parliament of its own. There were two problems which the Quebec Conference had resolved and which were included in the Act of 1867. The first of these was that of representation of the provinces in the House of Commons. It provided that Quebec should have 65 members and the other provinces should have members the same in ratio to 65 as their population was in ratio to that of Quebec. Quebec's representatives could be increased in number but the

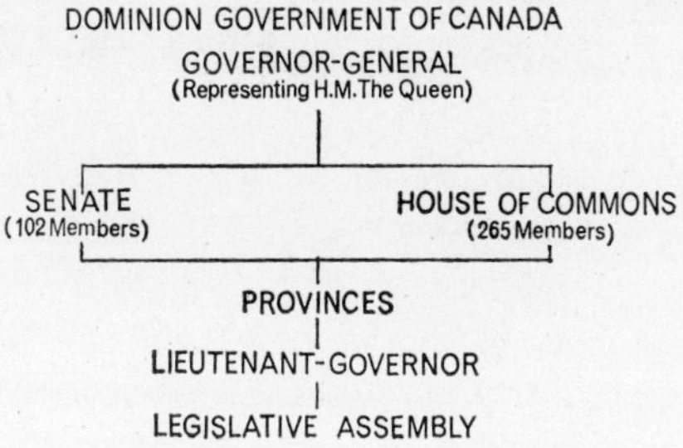

number of members for the other provinces would also be increased in proportion. In fact Quebec's representation remained at 65 until 1952 when it was raised to 75. The second problem dealt with by the Act was that of relative powers of the Dominion and provincial parliaments. The authors of the Act did not wish to see the same independence that the States of the United States of America enjoyed; this they regarded as a weakness in the American constitution. Consequently, the Act provided that certain specific functions such as direct taxation, prisons, hospitals, provincial railways, education and marriage laws should be granted to the provinces, but everything else, or the residuum as it was called, should be left with the Dominion Parliament. This not only meant that the central government controlled defence, foreign affairs, trade, railways, customs duties and company law but also that any new function of government would be assumed by the Dominion Parliament. Consequently the central government's powers have tended to grow while those of the provinces have diminished. The Act also specifically said that the Dominion was to have 'a constitution similar in principle to that of Great Britain,' and this implied fully responsible government, a neutral Governor-General representing the Crown and a Cabinet of Ministers responsible to and dependent upon the support of the House of Commons. The provinces also had responsible government as far as their limited functions allowed. Nevertheless, in spite of the limitations on the powers of the provincial parliaments, they have retained a great deal of authority since 1867. The Act gave the Dominion Parliament the right to disallow laws passed by the provincial governments but in practice it has rarely been used, and, indeed, the Canadian courts have tended to uphold the rights of the provinces.

The first Prime Minister of the new Dominion was Sir John Macdonald, one of the architects of the Act which founded it.

North West Mounted Police, 1875.

Riel on trial: addressing the Jury Court House, Regina, 1885.

The Development of Canada

Prince Edward Island, one of the original colonies represented at the Quebec conference, joined the Dominion as the seventh province in 1873. Yet, if Canada were to develop as a nation, independent economically of the United States, it was essential that all possible use should be made of natural resources. In the middle of the nineteenth century no real attempt had been made to open up the vast prairie lands of the middle-west.

In 1869 the Dominion Government took over from the Hudson's Bay Company the West and the North-West, after negotiations which resulted in an agreement to pay the Company £300,000. This was resented by many of the half-breeds employed by the Company living by the Red River who had enjoyed almost complete freedom from control by the Law. They rose in revolt in 1870 under the leadership of Louis Riel. He set up a provisional government with himself as President but a British force led by Colonel Wolseley soon suppressed the rising after some fighting. Riel had been backed by some American plotters who hoped to seize the area for the United States. The province of Manitoba was then founded, stretching from the shores of Hudson's Bay to the borders of the United States. An old Hudson's Bay post, Fort Garry, was renamed Winnipeg and became its capital.

The colony of British Columbia was separated from the new Dominion by nearly a thousand miles and the Rocky Mountains. Communication was difficult; often it could be maintained only through the United States. British Columbia agreed to join the Dominion in 1871 on condition that a trans-continental railway linking her to the rest of the federation should be built within ten years.

Between Manitoba and the Rocky Mountains was a vast prairie region inhabited by Indians and fur trappers. In theory the Lieutenant-Governor of Manitoba controlled it with the Council of the North-West appointed by the Dominion Government to help him. In order to maintain law and order over this area and other new territories, the North-West Mounted Police was formed in 1874. The famous 'Mounties' later to become the Royal Canadian Mounted Police and cover the whole Dominion, were a small and well-disciplined force, largely recruited in Great Britain at that time, who won a tremendous reputation for daring, energy and resource in enforcing the law.

Two years after this the North-West Territories were formed under a separate lieutenant-governor, consisting after 1882 of Assiniboia, Athabasca, Alberta and Saskatchewan territories. Each of these had a lieutenant-governor and Representative Assemblies. There was discontent in Saskatchewan among half-breeds, many of whom were concerned in the Red River Rebellion of 1870, and when Louis Riel crossed the border from the United States to lead them, they rose again in revolt in 1885. Once again the rebellion was soon crushed after some heavy fighting, and Riel was hanged. Assiniboia and Saskatchewan became the province of Saskatchewan, and Athabasca and Alberta joined to form the province of Alberta in 1905.

Gold was discovered in the Yukon in 1896 and this resulted in a gold rush. Yukon became a separate territory in 1898. The part of Canada to the north which had not been included in the provinces of Manitoba, Saskatchewan and Alberta now became known as the North-West Territories, divided into the districts of Mackenzie, Keewatin and Franklin. They are administered directly by the Dominion Government.

The island of Newfoundland, which today is the tenth province of the Dominion of Canada, was separate until 1949. It was a colony until 1931 when it was granted dominion status. Unfortunately, it ran into financial difficulties and the British Government suspended the constitution in 1934 and took over the administration once more. When its economic position had improved it was given the choice of becoming an independent dominion or joining Canada and it decided upon the latter in 1949.

When Canada became British in 1763 the population was a few hundred thousand, at the time of the foundation of the Dominion it was just over three millions, by 1900 it had passed five millions and today there are well over eighteen million Canadians. Those of French origin number rather less than a quarter of the population. British immigration went on from the early nineteenth century and today the British elements of the population are about half the total. The

Canadian Pacific Railway being constructed across the mountains, 1884: Chinese at work.

remainder, mostly later immigrants, are mainly of Continental European origin.

Railways

The development of the new Canada was dependent upon improvement of communications, indeed it will be remembered that British Columbia had made the building of a trans-continental railway a condition of entry. The railway was to be completed by 1881, but the story of its construction is marked by difficulties. It was begun in 1872 by the Dominion Government. The next year the Canadian Pacific Railway Company was formed to continue with the work. It was said, however, that Sir Hugh Allan, the president of the Company, had bought this concession by contributing to the election funds of Sir John Macdonald, the Conservative Prime Minister. An investigation was carried out which showed the charges to be true and Macdonald was defeated in the election of 1873. Alexander Mackenzie and the Liberals came to power and they had little belief

Canadian Pacific Railway (formerly known as Great Western Railway) 1889.

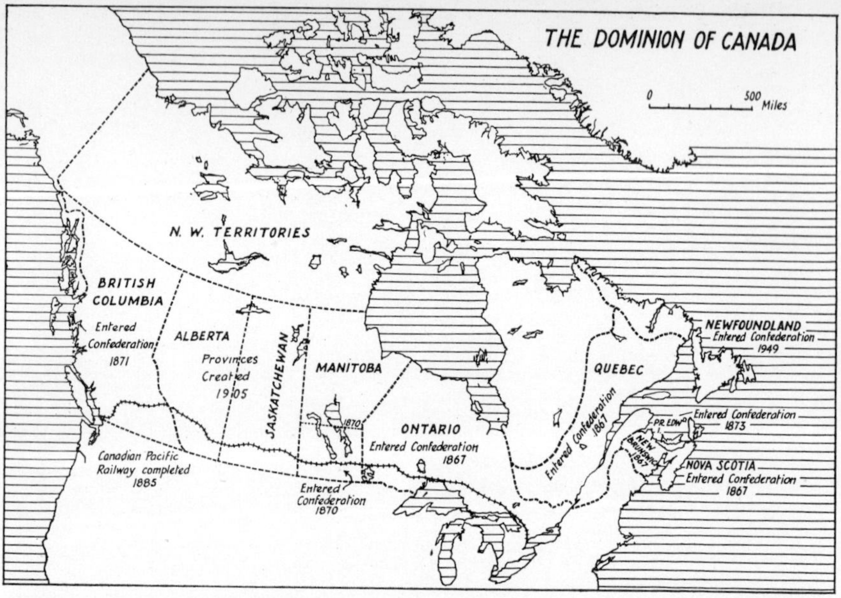

in the need for the railway. Consequently, little further constructive work was carried out. Macdonald and the Conservatives returned to power in 1878 and the task of building the railway continued with increased speed. It was a tremendous task. Between Ottawa and British Columbia were some 500 miles of swamps, rivers and wilderness, 1,000 miles of prairie and 500 miles of rugged mountains. A new Canadian Pacific Railway Company was formed in 1880 and it was granted with the line so far constructed, all the land needed for its completion and a belt of land each side of the line which it could sell to settlers. These generous terms were criticised, but were necessary in order that the line could be completed. It was finally finished in November 1885, four years late, but not before British Columbia had accused the Dominion Government of bad faith by not keeping its promise to complete by 1881. The Canadian Pacific Railway not only joined British Columbia to the rest of the Dominion but enabled large-scale settlement and development of the prairie lands and their great wheat fields and natural resources.

Further railway building followed. The Grand Trunk Pacific Railway was begun in 1903 and completed in 1914. This line, now part of the Canadian National Railways, ran from New Brunswick through northern Quebec and Ontario to Winnipeg and then across the prairies well to the north of the Canadian Pacific line to the Pacific coast. The Inter-colonial Railway linking the Maritime Provinces was completed in 1876. The third line across Canada was completed in 1915. This was the Canadian Northern Railway. With local railways these added up to a total mileage of over 42,000.

Sir Wilfred Laurier.

W. L. Mackenzie King.

Political Events

The party system, which was so necessary if responsible government was to work, had been developing since federation. The first Prime Minister of Canada was Sir John Macdonald who was the leader of the Conservative Party. He had to deal with a crisis concerning Nova Scotia soon after coming to power. Because the people of that province had not been asked for their opinion on the federation a strong movement, led by Joseph Howe, grew up which demanded secession. Howe was sent to England to press for this. Gradually feeling died down and the building of the railway from the Maritime Provinces to Quebec ended all agitation. Macdonald lost the election in 1873, and the Liberals under Mackenzie came to power for five years. When the Conservatives under Macdonald became the Government again in 1878, they began a period of eighteen years in continuous office. Perhaps the most controversial question of policy at that time was trade. There had never been any real protection for Canadian industries, but it was increasingly being realised that if Canada was to withstand economic pressure and competition from the United States, some sort of protection was necessary. This was the view of the Conservatives, and one which the Liberals opposed. This helped Macdonald to win the election and he established a protective tariff in 1879. He remained Prime Minister until he died in 1891. Five years later the Liberals, now led by Sir Wilfred Laurier, came back to power. Although they had pursued a Free Trade policy in opposition, they realised that as a Government they could not end the protectionist policy of the previous Government. They, therefore, worked for far greater trade collaboration with Great Britain, a policy different from that of the Conservatives who had been looking for a trade agreement with the United States. The new Government introduced a system of trade preferences with Great Britain, but it was still inevitable that much of Canada's trade should be carried on with her near neighbour, America. It is worth noting that in 1963 Canada's imports from the United Kingdom were worth some 564,000,000 dollars per year and from the United States, some 4,300,000,000 dollars. This increasing economic co-operation with the United States was inevitable, bearing in mind a common unguarded frontier and that the bulk of the Canadian population was close to it. Their monetary systems were similar and the Canadian people read American newspapers and magazines.

The question of a trade treaty with the United States was the main issue of the election of 1911. The farmers of the prairies desired it but the idea was rejected and the Liberals lost the election. The Conservatives took office under Sir Robert Borden. During the fifteen years the Liberals were in power under Sir Wilfred Laurier, immigration had been encouraged and there was one of the spectacular rises in population, from 5,000,000 to 7,250,000.

Since that time the Conservative and Liberal parties have shared

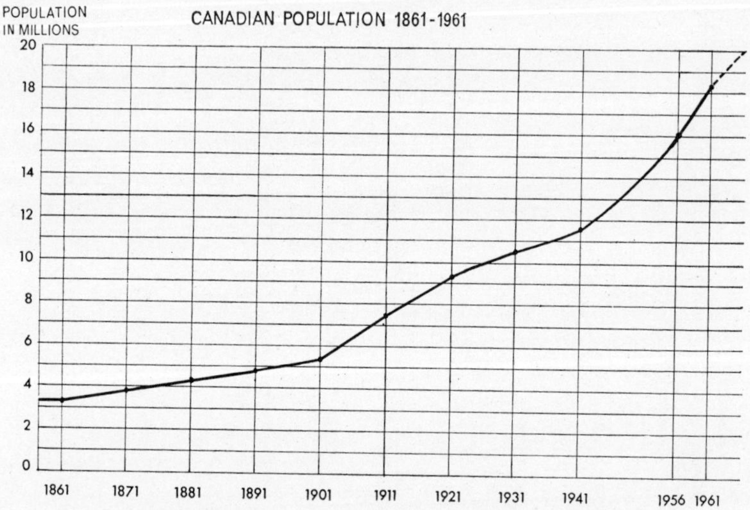

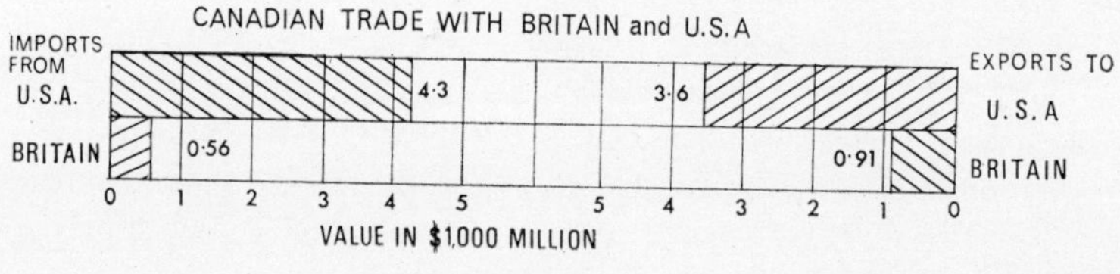

'Mountie' on ceremonial duty outside Canadian Parliament Building in Ottawa.

in ruling Canada. The Commonwealth Co-operative Federation, the nearest Canadian party to the British Labour Party, was founded after the First World War but it has never gained power although it has often been well represented in the Dominion Parliament. Another party which attracted support between the two world wars, and gained power in the provincial parliament of Alberta in 1935, was the Social Credit Party.

Canada entered the First World War under a Conservative Government, and Canadian troops fought in large numbers in Europe and the Dominion played a great part in the war. After the war, in the election of 1921, although no party won a working majority, the Liberals under W. L. Mackenzie King formed a government with some support from the National Progressive Party, formed from farmers and Labour and inclined towards national ownership and freer trade. The new party lasted only a few years, virtually merging with the Liberals. In 1930, dissatisfaction with the Liberals meant a Conservative victory with R. B. Bennett as Prime Minister. The Liberals returned to office in 1935 and under the leadership, first of Mackenzie King and afterwards Louis St Laurent, remained in power until 1957 including the period of the Second World War. Canada's contribution then was even greater than in the First World War. A large Canadian Army fought overseas. Canadians fought in the Royal Air Force, and the Royal Canadian Air Force provided

Royal Canadian Air Force: No. 1 fighter wing.

one-third of Bomber Command. The Royal Canadian Navy played a considerable part, too. After six years of Conservative Government under G. Diefenbaker from 1957, the Liberals were once more the Government with Lester Pearson as Prime Minister.

After the Statute of Westminster, in 1931, Canada became completely independent and since the Second World War has recognised the changed nature of the Commonwealth by recognising Queen Elizabeth II as Queen of Canada. Canada is a member of the United Nations and is represented independently in foreign capitals.

It is a prosperous country and has made splendid use of its great natural resources of agriculture, timber, gold, oil and uranium under both Conservative and Liberal Governments. Canadian engineers shared with Americans in constructing the great Alaskan Highway in 1942. The Trans-Canada Highway 4,860 miles long running east to west through every province, was completed in 1962. Perhaps the greatest achievement of all has been the construction of the St Lawrence Seaway allowing ocean-going ships to sail from the Atlantic to Lake Superior. This, too, was a joint Canadian–American project.

The ties which join Canada to the Mother Country are very strong, for the largest part of the population is of British origin. Nevertheless, there has been considerable nationalistic feeling among the French-Canadians in Quebec, and recently a movement aiming at independence for Quebec has appeared, although its supporters are but a minority of the French-speaking population.

SUMMARY

The British North America Act of 1867

Passed in March 1867, founded first Dominion 1 July 1867.—Four provinces, Ontario, Quebec, Nova Scotia, New Brunswick; provision for other provinces to join later.—Governor-General.—Lieutenant-Governors in provinces.—Dominion Parliament, Senate and House of Commons.—Provincial parliaments.—Representation in Commons on ratio of population with Quebec as base.—Main power with Dominion Parliament.—Provincial parliaments to have specific functions; residuum with Dominion Parliament.—Dominion Parliament's right to disallow provincial legislation; rarely used.

The Development of Canada

New provinces.—First Riel Rebellion (1870).—Manitoba founded and joined Dominion (1870).—British Columbia joined Dominion (1871) on condition of trans-continental railway within ten years.—Prince Edward Island (1873).—Formation of North-West Canadian Mounted Police (1874).—North-West Territories formed (1876).—Second Riel Rebellion (1885).—Saskatchewan and Alberta as provinces (1905).—Gold discovered in the Yukon (1896).—Yukon as separate territory (1898).—Newfoundland, colony until 1931; independent dominion until 1934; became tenth province of Canada (1949).—Population of Canada rose from 3,000,000 in 1867 to over 18,000,000.

Railways

Promise to British Columbia to build trans-continental railway; commenced 1872.—Canadian Pacific Railway (1873).—Conservatives defeated in election (1873).—Railway construction slowed.—Conservatives won next election (1878).—Speed of building increased; completed November 1885.—Inter-colonial railway to Maritime Provinces (1876).—Grand Trunk Railway (1903–14).—Canadian Northern Railway (1915).—Railway mileage 42,000.

Political Events

Conservative and Liberal parties developed.—Macdonald as first Prime Minister.—Problem of Nova Scotia.—Liberals under Mackenzie in power (1873).—Conservatives (1878).—Problem of tariffs or free trade.—Liberals under Laurier (1896).—Policy of trade preferences for Britain.—Conservatives under Borden (1911).—Canada's part in First World War.—Commonwealth Co-operative Federation and Social Credit Parties after the War.—Liberals and Mackenzie King (1921).—Conservatives under Bennett (1930).—Liberals and Mackenzie King and St Laurent (1935).—Canada's part in Second World War.—Conservatives under Diefenbaker (1957); Liberals under Pearson (1963).—Effect of Statute of Westminster (1931); Canada fully independent within Commonwealth.

QUESTIONS

Answer the following questions briefly:

1. (a) Which colonies were represented at the Quebec Conference in 1864?
   (b) Which became provinces of the new Dominion?
   (c) How did British Columbia become a province?

(d) What were the main differences between the Liberals and the Conservatives in the Dominion Parliament between 1873 and 1911?
(e) In what way did Canada contribute to the Allied effort in the First and Second World Wars?
(f) What was the effect of the Statute of Westminster on Canada?

2. Describe the development of the Middle-West and the North of Canada. What part did railways play in this?
3. Lord Blachford, who was Permanent Under-Secretary of the Colonial Office from 1860 to 1871, wrote, 'I had always believed that the destiny of our colonies is independence; and that in this point of view the function of the Colonial Office is to secure that our connexion, while it lasts, shall be as profitable to both parties, and our separation, when it comes, as amicable as possible.'
In 1872, W. E. Forster said . . . 'self-government ought to have been conceded as part of a great policy of imperial consolidation.'
These are surprisingly progressive views on Empire for so long ago.
(a) How do you consider that the British North America Act of 1867 put these views into action?
(b) What particular part of the Act particularly did this?
(c) In what way do you think the Dominion of Canada served as a model for future development of the Empire?

8 : Early Settlements in Australia

Early Exploration

THE maps of some early geographers, particularly that of Humphrey Gilbert, showed a great land to the south which was known as Terra Australis. Luis de Torres, a Spaniard, sailed past the northern tip of Australia, giving his name to that strait, in 1606. In the early seventeenth century Dutch captains sighted a barren coast which is today Western Australia. Nevertheless, it was still believed to be a great continent and it was not until Abel Tasman sailed right round the new land in 1643 that it was proved to be an island. He did not, unfortunately, look at the eastern coast of Australia, as it came to be known, and his report on the dry unattractive north-western coast did not tempt others to make the long voyage. Tasman's view of Australia was supported by William Dampier, an Englishman who visited the west coast in 1688 and 1699 and reported it to be desolate and unable to support human settlement.

Cook's Voyage

In 1768 the Royal Society wished to send an expedition to the South Seas in order to obtain a better view of the transit of Venus. A passage of the planet across the sun was due that year and it was believed that the clearer skies of the Pacific would enable the observations to be carried out with more success. The Admiralty supplied a ship, the *Endeavour*, with Captain James Cook in command, to carry the party of astronomers, scientists and botanists who were led by Sir Joseph Banks. Cook was also asked to make sure that there was no Terra Australis. After a successful scientific observation, Cook turned westward and spent six months sailing around New Zealand in a figure eight. He then sailed for the east coast of Australia which had not been visited by any European. The *Endeavour* reached Cape Howe in 1770 and Cook sailed northwards as far as Cape York. The party landed at Botany Bay and Cook claimed the new land for Britain, naming it New South Wales.

Early Penal Settlements

Nothing was done to settle the new territory in spite of the glowing reports of Cook and Banks. The immense distance from the

Captain Cook proclaims New South Wales a British possession outside Botany Bay, 1770.

Home Country, combined with the fact that the American War of Independence started soon after their return, prevented the interest which might otherwise have been shown in this discovery. It was not until the American colonists' victory presented the British Government with the problem of what to do with the convicts who had previously been sent to penal settlements in America that any interest was taken. For a time they were kept in hulks in rivers and harbours and later an attempt was made to found a convict settlement in West Africa. Sir Joseph Banks had constantly advocated a British settlement in New South Wales and at last his advice was heeded.

In May 1787 a fleet of ships carrying seven hundred and seventeen convicts, of whom one hundred and ninety-eight were women, with two hundred Royal Marine guards under the command of Captain Arthur Phillip, sailed for Australia. They reached Botany Bay in January 1788 and after moving a little northwards founded the first penal settlement at Port Jackson, later to be known as Sydney. A French expedition under La Perouse arrived soon afterwards, but sailed away without attempting a landing.

This first settlement met with great difficulties. There had been no attempt to choose convicts suitable for colonisation with the skills and knowledge which were needed. Many were lazy and unwilling to accept authority and, in addition, inadequate planning had resulted in a shortage of tools, seeds and equipment. The colonists suffered great hardship and the fact that the settlement succeeded was largely due to the leadership of Captain Phillip. He kept a tight control over the convicts, placed them for a time on half rations and insisted on this applying to the guards, officers and himself, and finally won through. He founded a second settlement on Norfolk Island, a thousand miles off the coast, and at both Norfolk Island and Port Jackson agriculture was gradually developed. Until these could supply sufficient food to keep the colonies going, supplies were sent occasionally from the East Indies.

The Government at home thought of New South Wales purely as a penal colony. Phillip believed that it would develop, until it became 'the most valuable acquisition Great Britain ever made'.

In 1803 a penal settlement was established in Van Diemen's Land, or Tasmania as it later became, and this was followed by a free settlement the following year.

There had been no thought of free settlement at first in New South Wales, but convicts whose sentences had finished were given no passage home and stayed as free settlers, and discharged marines were granted up to one hundred and fifty acres of land if they stayed in Australia. Consequently most of the early inhabitants were convicts, but it must be remembered that many of them were not really criminals, having been deported for poaching, stealing to save their families from starving or for illegally combining in trade unions. Many were children.

When Captain Phillip left the colony in 1792, Major Grose acted as governor for three years and during this time allowed rum to be supplied to convicts. This began a racket in which many officers of the colony were involved and made considerable sums of money. Hunter, who succeeded Grose, was unable to deal with this, but his successor in 1799, King, acted vigorously and began to deal with the evil. In 1806, Captain William Bligh, of *Mutiny on the 'Bounty'* fame, became governor, and his methods of dealing with the illegal trafficking were so severe that he was deposed and imprisoned by the military commander. Colonel Lachlan Macquarie became Governor of New South Wales in 1810 and this marked the beginning of a period of great development for the colony.

From then onwards, and particularly after the French Wars ended in 1815, free emigrants from home began to arrive in increasing numbers. Captain John MacArthur realised that the hinter-lands were likely to provide excellent grazing for sheep and obtained a licence to select five thousand acres for his sheep and to employ thirty convicts as shepherds. He introduced a breed of Merino sheep which were extremely successful and founded the woollen industry for which Australia was to become famous.

Development of New South Wales: Exploration

Macquarie was governor for eleven years and during this time he began to develop the colony. He did not see it as a place for free settlers, but he began a programme of roads and public works and encouraged exploration. During his term of office New South Wales changed from a mere penal settlement into a colony. Schools and churches were built, a newspaper was published and even a theatre was opened. Encouraged by Macquarie, several important voyages of exploration were carried out. There had been no attempt up until then to move inland west of the Blue Mountains. In 1813 Gregory Blaxland led a party across the mountains and found the pasture lands of the interior. Captain Charles Sturt carried out systematic exploration of the river system of south-eastern Australia, completing it by 1830. The fine new lands naturally attracted settlers, but the Government was not enthusiastic about the discovery since it made the problem of administration and the maintenance of law and order far more difficult. Consequently, in 1829 an imaginary line was drawn in a semi-circle one hundred and fifty miles from Sydney, beyond which settlement was prohibited. This was known as the 'Limit of Settlement'. Within the limit were nineteen counties which became known as the 'Old Settled Districts'. Licences were granted within this area to settlers keeping sheep. As the settlement grew, more land was required for purposes of cultivation and the sheep-farmers were worried lest their pasture lands should be taken from them. As the result of their demands they were allowed to purchase their land, firstly in 1831 at five shillings an acre, rising eventually to a reserve price at auctions of one pound per acre in 1842. The increasing shortage of land was naturally driving settlers westward across the 'Limit of Settlement' line. This was illegal, but it would have required a vast army of police and troops to have prevented it, so the Government was forced to accept it. The 'squatters' who had crossed the line were not allowed to buy their holdings, but they were granted licences. The woollen industry of New South Wales was now growing, particularly as the Industrial Revolution in Great Britain was creating a great demand for wool.

There developed a contest between the squatters and the New South Wales Government. The Waste Lands Act of 1842, passed by the British Parliament, had fixed the minimum price of land at one pound per acre. In New South Wales the Act was applied to the 'squatters' by an ordinance which declared that each holder of a licence for pastoral land must purchase 320 acres of his land at this price. If he did this he would have an undisturbed lease over the whole of his land for eight years. Each time he purchased a fresh 320 acres he would have a further eight years lease on the remainder of his land and thus by continued purchases could obtain the whole holding. The squatters did not like this policy and formed a Pastoral Association demanding the maintenance of their rights on the payment of a licence fee as before. As a result of this a second Act, known as Earl Grey's Waste Lands Act, was passed in 1846 by which leases of fourteen years were granted to the pastoralists. This, like the first Act, applied to all Australian colonies and not just New South Wales. Land in New South Wales was divided into Settled, Intermediate and Unsettled, and squatters leases and rents varied with the type of land.

Meanwhile, constitutional progress was being made. New South Wales became a Crown colony in 1823, with a governor and Council of Officials. In 1842, it received representative government with a Council of thirty-six members, twenty-four of whom were elected. By 1855 it received responsible government, with a Parliament of two chambers, the Upper House having nominated members and the Lower House elected members.

This same Parliament passed in 1861 the Crown Lands Occupation Act which was designed to encourage the tillage of land. The rights of the squatters disappeared and their land might be purchased by

Aborigines with hunting spears, Central Australia.

'selectors' at any time and their leases wiped out. This began a bitter conflict between squatters and selectors which went on for some twenty-five years until an Act of 1884 enabled squatters to obtain a lease over half their land. However, the squatters themselves found a way of hitting back and selected parts of their own land for purchase, often containing the only source of water supply, thus making the rest of the land useless without it. This was known as 'picking the eyes out of a run'. Because the squatters held large runs and because their wool was essential for the progress of the colony their ultimate victory was inevitable. Yet in the intervening period there was a great deal of bitterness and violence and the officials concerned with the administration of the laws were often corrupt.

As the free settlement increased so the demand for the end of transportation had grown stronger, and this was supported by humanitarians in England. The transportation of convicts to New South Wales was formally abolished in 1853, but it ended in practice in 1840. Population had increased rapidly, from 60,000 in 1833 of whom 24,000 were convicts, to 265,000 in 1865 of whom less than 2,500 were convicts.

Tasmania

After the establishment in 1803 of the convict settlement which was to become Hobart, a free settlement was founded at Port Dalrymple on the north coast the following year. The new colony of Tasmania soon developed and in 1812 was separated from New South Wales. Although whaling and sealing were carried on, most of the production of the island depended upon convicts who continued to be sent until 1853. Escaped convicts who became bushrangers gave even more trouble here than in New South Wales and, together with the aborigines who resented the white man because of ill-treatment, were a constant problem. The aborigines were so ruthlessly suppressed that they were virtually wiped out, some being sent to Flinders Island in Bass Strait. Tasmania received responsible government in 1856.

Western Australia

In 1827, Captain Robert Stirling explored the Swan River, and two years later with Thomas Peel, a relative of Sir Robert Peel, and other wealthy men founded the Swan River Colony, later to become Western Australia. Land was sold far too cheaply, virtually at 1*s*. 6*d*. per acre, and the wealthier men obtained huge grants of land, as much as 250,000 acres. This resulted in an extremely scattered population and a great shortage of labour, and the land was not properly culti-

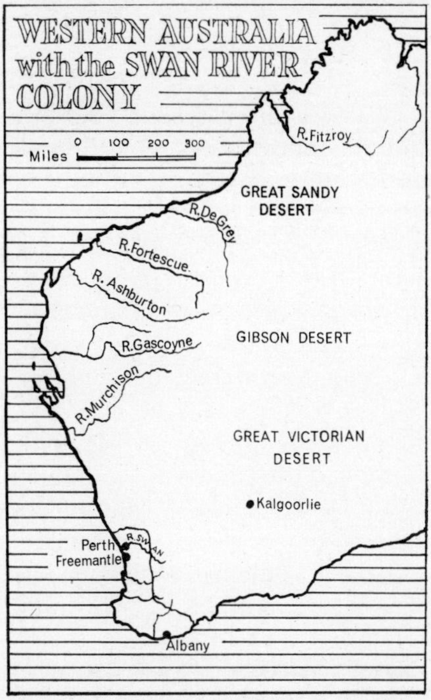

vated. There were no roads and food was scarce, making conditions of great hardship.

Conditions were so bad that immigration had to be checked. The price of land was raised to five shillings an acre in 1832, twelve shillings an acre in 1839 and to a pound per acre in 1842. Gradually the colony recovered from its unplanned beginning and progress was made. Coal, copper and lead were discovered and mined, and vines were cultivated for wine.

Nevertheless, it still needed assistance, and at the request of the colony, because of the shortage of labour, transportation of convicts began in 1849, just when other colonies were ending it. Transportation continued until 1868. In addition, Earl Grey's Waste Lands Act of 1846 was applied to the colony. This divided the land into two classes, A for cultivation and B for pasture. The former was leased at 320 acres at a time for eight years at a fee of one shilling per acre per year. The pasture land was leased at five pounds per year for the first thousand acres and ten shillings for each additional thousand acres. These two measures helped the colony to get on to its feet.

The bad start made by Western Australia made its constitutional development slower than elsewhere. It was ruled directly by a governor until 1840. He was then assisted by a nominated Council until 1870 when a representative Council was formed. Responsible government was granted in 1890.

Gold was discovered at Coolgardie in 1892 and Kalgoorlie in 1893 and was followed by a gold rush. This made the success of the colony certain.

Gibbon Wakefield's Systematic Colonisation

In 1829 Edward Gibbon Wakefield published *A Letter from Sydney* in which he advocated a system of colonisation. He said with some truth that if land was too cheap too many settlers would buy it, resulting in scattered communities, shortage of labour and bad cultivation. Wages would be high and labourers would soon be able to purchase land themselves. He pointed to the Swan River Colony as an example of this and was scathing in his criticism. At the same time he said that if the price of land remained too high, little would be sold; there would be no chance for labourers to save and buy their own and they would be condemned to be labourers all their lives and would lose enthusiasm. This would slow down the progress of a colony. Wakefield believed that a wise policy of dealing with the waste lands of a colony was essential and that land must be of a 'sufficient price'. Unfortunately, he was unable to suggest how this should be found other than by experiment. He believed that money obtained from sale of land should be used for developing roads and communications and for assisting suitable immigrants. He believed strongly that immigrants should be selected. They should be of good character, preferably with some knowledge of agriculture, and young married couples would be the most suitable since they would be interested in the future development of the colony for the sake of their children. Young unmarried people of both sexes would be the next most suitable, as they would probably get married and have the same stake in the future of the colony. He did not turn down the idea of older immigrants if they were of good character and suitable in other respects. Wakefield believed, too, that it was of prime importance for the colony to receive responsible government just as soon as it had developed sufficiently.

These ideas received a great deal of support and the National Colonisation Society was formed in Britain in 1830 to put them into practice. This was followed by the South Australian Association with the specific purpose of colonising South Australia along Wakefield's lines.

South Australia

In 1834 the British Government was persuaded to pass an Act which authorised the establishment of a colony of the type advocated by Wakefield. Land to the value of £35,000 was to be sold at a minimum price of twelve shillings per acre and a guaranteed £20,000 had to be raised before the colony was to be formed. The Commissioners which the Act appointed were to raise a loan of £200,000. There were to be no penal settlements for convicts and provision was made for a constitution when the population reached a figure of 50,000.

Gibbon Wakefield withdrew from the scheme before the settlement began because he believed that the minimum price of land was too low. He believed that it should be two pounds per acre in order to keep the holdings small and ensure a compact settlement of small farms. In spite of Wakefield's withdrawal, the settlement went ahead. It was 1835 before the sales of land reached £35,000 and the colony was founded in 1836, being named Adelaide after the Queen of William IV. Because of lack of previous survey, the colonists arrived without their lands being apportioned. Thus the colony started badly, the settlers often preferring speculation to agriculture. However, once agriculture began the colony appeared to prosper. The expenses of the colony were being paid for out of the loans the Commissioners had raised and not out of revenue, and in 1840 the British Government had to step in and take over the colony because the debts could not be paid. Too much had been spent on public works, and labour had been wasted on them instead of agriculture. Captain George Grey, later to become Sir George Grey and famous for achievements in Africa and New Zealand, became governor of the colony in 1841. He ruled firmly, cut expenditure and diverted labour from public works to agriculture. By 1843 he had brought about the recovery of the colony. Copper was discovered at Kapunda and Burra Burra in 1842 and 1844 and from then onwards the colony prospered.

The Waste Lands Act of 1842 was applied to South Australia and thus sales of land by auction began at the minimum price of one pound per acre. This was virtually the end of Wakefield's principle of a uniform price. Nevertheless, his ideas of systematic colonisation had established a successful colony although the system was now discontinued. It was not his system which had failed but the mishandling of the colony's financial affairs which had caused the difficulties.

By 1856 the colony received responsible government.

Victoria

The area to the south-west of New South Wales was first settled as early as 1834 when a family named Henty settled at Portland Bay. The area was nominally under the New South Wales governor at the time but he and his officials knew nothing of their activities. They raised sheep and cattle and hunted whales. In 1827 a man from Tasmania called John Batman asked for permission to settle the area. This was refused, and in the same year as the Henty family settled he went without permission and established himself at Port Phillip. Both these settlements attracted other people and in 1837 the city of Melbourne was founded, getting its name from Lord Melbourne, the British Prime Minister. The area around was, for a time, known as Australia Felix, and was recognised as a part of New South Wales. This was entirely unsatisfactory to the colonists who pressed for separation and their recognition as a separate colony. In 1851 they won their battle and Victoria was recognised as such with a representative constitution. Fully responsible government was granted in 1855.

A few weeks after separation from New South Wales gold was discovered at Ballarat and Bendigo. This began a gold rush and a large number of people from other parts of Australia and from Europe and America came to Victoria. Although most of the diggers were honest and the diggings were generally peaceful, there were some bad elements and there was some serious trouble at Ballarat. There was an outbreak of fighting at the Eureka Stockade in 1854. In 1861 a discovery of gold in New Zealand attracted many of the diggers from Victoria. Nevertheless, during the gold rush the population of the colony rose from 70,000 to 300,000 and many of them remained.

As in other colonies, the Waste Lands Act of 1842 was applied to Victoria and as a result of this emphasis was placed upon small farms with resident owners. Although the policy was not entirely successful, it helped it to become a rich agricultural colony.

Queensland

The settlement which eventually became Brisbane was founded as a penal colony in 1826. Free settlement was not allowed, but squatters made their way northwards from New South Wales and settled in the Darling Downs area. When the convict settlement closed down in 1839 the inmates made their way over the mountains and established themselves at Moreton Bay. The settlement prospered on the breeding and grazing of cattle and sheep. It was at this time a part of New South Wales and its inhabitants wished to become a separate colony. This came about in 1859 when the colony of Queensland was founded with responsible government. At that time the population was 20,000 and in six years it had passed 100,000.

Gold was discovered in 1867 and this attracted more people.

Further Exploration

In 1840 E. J. Eyre pushed northwards from Adelaide and found two areas of mud and stagnant water known as Lakes Torrens and Eyre. Mitchell and Leichhardt explored northern Queensland in 1844. The latter was lost in attempting to cross Australia from east to west. In 1861 Burke and Wills crossed from north to south but were lost attempting the return journey. McDowall Stuart succeeded in crossing in 1862 and in 1874 Sir John Forrest crossed the middle of the continent from west to east.

By the end of the century most of Australia had been explored, in varying degrees.

SUMMARY

Early Exploration

Search for Terra Australis.—Torres (1606).—Tasman (1643).—Dampier (1688 and 1699).—Reports of unattractive north-west coast.

Cook's Voyage

Royal Society's expedition (1768).—Cook as Captain.—Sir Joseph Banks as leader of scientists.—Voyage around New Zealand (1769).—Sighted east coast of Australia (1770).—Landed at Botany Bay; New South Wales.

Captain Cook.

Early Penal Settlements

Failure to settle new land.—American War of Independence.—Need for new penal settlements.—Banks's advocacy of N.S.W.—Capt. Phillip's expedition, with convicts (1787); Botany Bay and Port Jackson (Sydney) (1788).—Early difficulties.—Norfolk Island.—Penal settlement in Van Diemen's Land or Tasmania (1803).—Free settlement (1804).—Increase in free settlement in N.S.W. —Released convicts.—Difficulties over Rum trade.—Difficulties over Governors. —Macquarie (1810–21).—His considerable achievements.—MacArthur's introduction of sheep.

Development of New South Wales: Exploration

Programme of roads and public works under Macquarie.—Blaxland crossed Blue Mountains (1813).—Sturt explored river system (1830).—'Limit of Settlement' line (1829).—'Old Settled Districts'.—Difficulties over 'squatters'.— Waste Lands Acts (1842 and 1846); Pastoral Association formed to protect squatters; N.S.W. as Crown colony (1823).—Representative government (1842). —Responsible government (1855).—Crown Lands Occupation Act (1861).— Act of 1884.—Struggle between squatters and selectors.—Practical end of transportation (1840); formally abolished (1853).

Tasmania

Convict settlement at Hobart (1803).—Tasmania separated from N.S.W. (1812). —Transportation ended (1853).—Trouble with bushrangers and aborigines.— Aborigines suppressed and sent to Flinders Island.—Responsible government (1856).

Western Australia

Captain Stirling explored Swan River (1827).—Swan River Colony founded (1829); difficulties at start; shortage of labour; transportation of convicts began (1849); ended in 1868.—Waste Lands Act (1846) applied; new lands policy; improvements.—Representative government (1870).—Responsible government (1890).—Gold discovered at Coolgardie (1892) and Kalgoorlie (1893).

Gibbon Wakefield's Systematic Colonisation

A Letter from Sydney (1829).—Advocated systematic colonisation.—Land at 'sufficient price'; selected immigrants; responsible government.—National Colonisation Society (1830).—South Australian Association.

South Australia

Act authorised settlement (1834).—Wakefield withdrew because of low price of land.—Colony founded at Adelaide (1836); bad start; financial difficulties; British Government took over (1840).—Grey as Governor; wise rule; recovery of colony.—Copper discovered at Kapunda (1842) and Burra Burra (1844).— Waste Lands Act (1842) applied.—End of Wakefield's principle of uniform prices. —Responsible government (1856).

Victoria

Henty family settled at Portland Bay (1834).—Batman settled at Port Phillip (1834).—Settlement of Melbourne founded (1837).—Area around part of N.S.W. —Separated from N.S.W. and representative government (1851).—Responsible government (1855).—Gold discovered at Ballarat and Bendigo (1851).—Gold rush.—Eureka Stockade (1854).—Agricultural development.

Queensland

Penal colony founded (1826).—Squatters in Darling Downs area.—Convict settlement closed (1839).—Free settlement at Moreton Bay.—Cattle and sheep.—Part of N.S.W.—Separated from N.S.W. and responsible government (1859) as Queensland.—Gold discovered (1867).

Further Exploration

Eyre discovered Lakes Torrens and Eyre (1840).—Mitchell and Leichhardt explored Northern Queensland (1844).—Burke and Wills crossed continent from north to south (1861).—McDowall Stuart crossed continent (1862).—Forrest crossed continent (1874).

QUESTIONS

Answer the following questions briefly:

1. (a) What was the main task of the Royal Society's expedition which left for the South Seas under Captain James Cook in 1768? What other task was it given?
   (b) How was it that convicts were sent to New South Wales?
   (c) Describe the early difficulties of Western Australia.
   (d) What effect did gold have on the development of Australia?
   (e) How did Queensland become a free settlement?
   (f) When did transportation end in the Australian colonies?
2. Describe the early settlement of New South Wales and its development up until the time it received responsible government.
3. Edward Gibbon Wakefield writing on his plan for 'Systematic Colonisation' said that by using such a method the mother countries and the colonies would:

   > become partners in a new industry, the creation of happy human beings; one country furnishing the raw materials, that is the land—the dust of which man is made; the other furnishing the machinery, that is, men and women to convert the unpeopled soil into living images of God . . . in this honourable and glorious co-partnership, the interests of the mother-country would be greater than that of the colony, and a rupture of their relations would be most injurious to the former.

   (a) What two principles of Wakefield's Systematic Colonisation are brought out in the above passage?
   (b) What were the other main points in his system?
   (c) When were his ideas put into practice and what happened?

9: Australia as a Dominion

Australia Before Federation

IN the latter part of the nineteenth century the new Australian colonies prospered. By 1890, all had received responsible government. Unfortunately much of the prosperity was based upon loans and in 1893 twelve banks in Australia suspended payment because they were unable to raise the money required when the loans were recalled. It was some years before the colonies recovered.

The six colonies were separate democratic states with no thought of joining together. It was no accident that practical democracy came early to the Australian colonies, particularly those which had been penal settlements. Manhood suffrage, vote by ballot and payment of Members of Parliament were achieved long before Great Britain. Many Chartists who had demanded these reforms in the Mother Country were among the convicts who had been transported to Australia and they carried their ideas with them. Others were voluntary emigrants and so progressive ideas were powerful from the first. Women received the vote as early as 1894 in South Australia.

The idea of federation had been suggested as early as 1847 by Earl Grey and Bills were introduced into the House of Commons in 1849 and 1850 to make it possible. They were so unpopular in Australia that they were dropped. In 1871 the British Parliament authorised a uniform customs system but advantage was not taken of this.

The reasons that federation received little or no support in Australia were as follows. Although the borders of the colonies were adjoining, the centres of population were far apart, and communications were difficult. Many railways had been built during the second half of the century, but being planned in separate colonies their gauges were completely different. For example, the gauges in Queensland, South Australia, Central Australia and of some lines in Western Australia were 3 ft 6 in. In New South Wales and the remainder of Western Australia they were 4 ft $8\frac{1}{2}$ in. and in Victoria 5 ft 3 in. Some have been standardised since but not all. Customs barriers between the colonies had prevented the expansion of inter-colonial trade and there was even a certain amount of antagonism between them. What is more, there was no fear of any threat from another power.

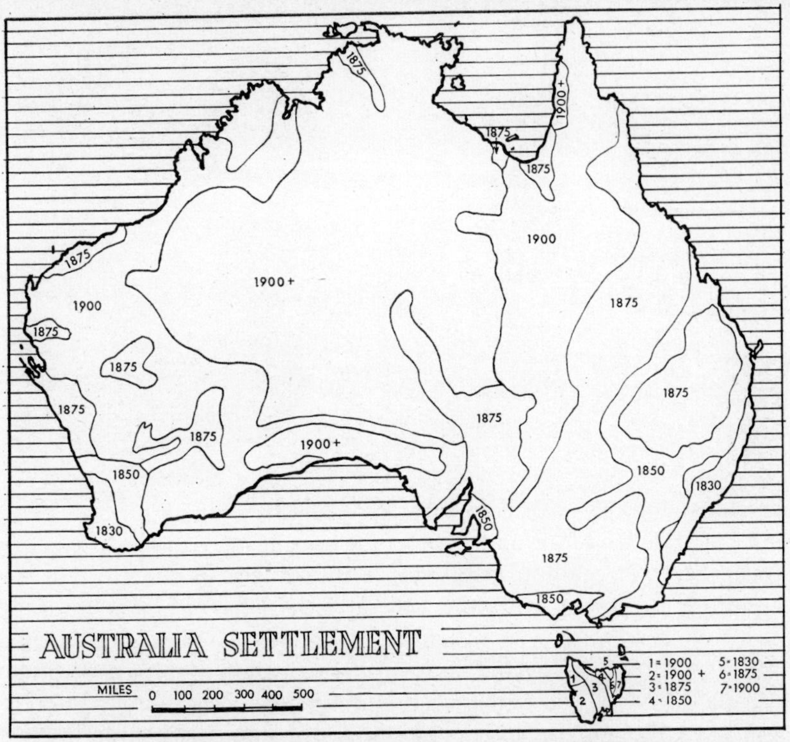

In 1884 Germany annexed a part of New Guinea and at last interest was focused on defence. An unsuccessful conference of Prime Ministers had been held in 1880 and a second one was called in 1884. Lord Derby, who was British Secretary of State, presented a plan for naval defence in the next year. Although this was not put into operation feeling in the colonies was aroused and in 1886 New South Wales, Victoria and Queensland offered subsidies for the Royal Navy. An Act of the British Parliament in 1885 set up a Federal Council for Australia. It had two appointed delegates from each colony. It met every two years but had little power or effect. Neither New South Wales nor New Zealand, which at that time was included in plans for Australia, were represented on it and it was no advertisement for the advantages of federation.

A federation movement was growing in Australia. Its main leaders were Sir Henry Parkes, the Prime Minister of New South Wales, and Mr (later Sir) Edmund Barton. The idea of the establishment of a Dominion of Australia was put forward by Sir Henry Parkes in a speech in 1889. It met with quite a good reception and in 1890 the first of a series of conventions met at Melbourne to discuss the idea. The second meeting was at Sydney in 1891 to draw up plans. By this time New Zealand had withdrawn from the scheme. Considerable discussion as to the form federation was to take took place at Sydney.

Sir Henry Parkes.

Sir Henry Parkes wanted to copy the Canadian model but the traditions of independence and democracy among the colonists led to a strong body of opinion in favour of the American model, with the minimum of power with the central federal government and the maximum remaining with the states. Agreement could not be reached and no further meeting was held until 1897 when it met at Adelaide. There a draft bill was drawn up and it was decided to hold a referendum in each colony in 1898. There was still some opposition in New South Wales and that colony insisted on a vote in favour in its referendum of at least 80,000. No vote was held in Western Australia which was not yet ready for it. In Victoria and Tasmania votes were four to one in favour of federation but in New South Wales the vote in favour only reached 71,000. After slight alterations to the draft bill a second referendum was held in 1899 which included Western Australia, and on this occasion there were large majorities in favour of federation in all six colonies. The climate of public opinion had gradually moved to the support of the idea of federation since it was first suggested in 1889. Apart from the threat of Germany in New Guinea, and also France in the New Hebrides which drove the colonies towards co-operation for mutual defence, there were other reasons. With the growth of industry and commerce there was a desire for increased inter-colonial trade. The people of Australia looked forward to greater social advances under a federal government. At last there could be detected the beginning of pride in Australian nationality and for some time there had been strong feelings in favour of a 'White Australia'. In the 1850s Chinese coolies had been imported to work in the goldfields and Queensland sugar planters had made use of Kanaka labour from the Pacific Islands. This was a threat to the standard of living of the Australian working man and many people believed that Australia was close enough to China to attract workers from that over-populated country. Thus the idea of a 'White Australia' policy grew and it was believed that this was easier to put into operation as a common policy of a federal government.

The Commonwealth of Australia

The federation was brought into being on 1 January 1901 by the Australian Commonwealth Act which was passed by the British Parliament the previous year. The new federation was to be known as the Commonwealth of Australia. It was to have a Governor-General representing the Crown and a Federal Parliament of two houses; a Senate consisting of six members from each state, with a House of Representatives having a minimum of five members from each state but with representation proportionate to the population. There was to be Cabinet Government responsible to the Federal Parliament and State Parliaments were to continue. It was there that the constitution differed from that of the Dominion of Canada. Some powers such as customs, postal services and defence were given to the Federal Government while some were under joint control of the Federal Government and the states. Some powers were to be transferred to the Federal Government by agreement with the states while the residuum was to be with the states. The states were to retain governors and not lieutenant-governors in order to emphasise their independent rights further. However, where there was a clash be-

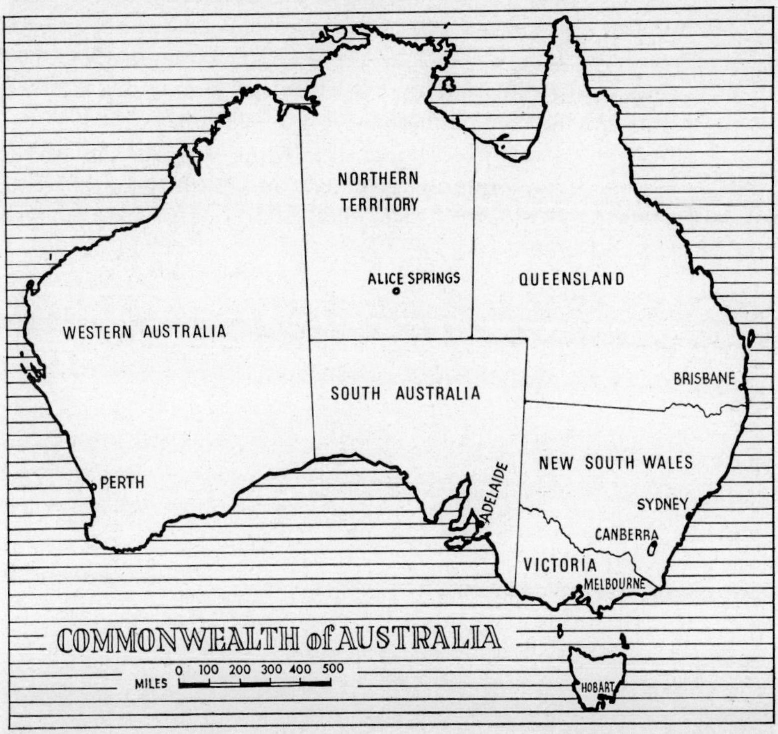

tween a state and the Commonwealth the final decision lay with the latter. In order not to cause inter-state jealousy it was decided to build a Commonwealth capital within New South Wales and not less than one hundred miles from Sydney. Canberra was selected and the capital came into being in 1927 and was surrounded by a thousand square miles of territory which was directly administered by the Commonwealth Government.

The intention of the authors of the Commonwealth Act from the first was to limit the power of the Federal Government and safeguard the powers of the states. In fact, over the years, it has been increasingly recognised that the concentration of greater power in the Federal Government was necessary for progress and this has happened, more and more powers passing from the states to the Commonwealth.

New Zealand did not join the Commonwealth of Australia, preferring to continue as a separate colony as will be seen. This is not surprising considering that it is over 1,500 miles from Australia.

Thus Australia became the second Dominion to take her place as a leader of the British Commonwealth.

Political History

In New South Wales the Labour Party first came to prominence in the election of 1891. As has been stated, progressive ideas came early to Australia and the Labour Party was a strong force in Commonwealth politics long before its sister party was in Britain. At the end of 1925 it was the only official opposition and had held office in every state except Victoria.

In the early part of the twentieth century the main issues were the question of tariffs and the maintenance of a 'White Australia' policy. New South Wales was a Free Trade state while Victoria was Protectionist, and in 1902 a common agreement was reached over a moderate tariff, but it was not until the Labour Party supported the prin-

Royal Australian Navy aircraft carrier H.M.A.S. *Sydney*.

Viscount S. B. Bruce.

Sir Robert Menzies.

ciple of protection that the issue was decided. The Labour Party agreed to this on condition that the workers should have a fair share in the prosperity and a Commonwealth Court of Conciliation and Arbitration was set up in 1904.

By 1907 the question of tariffs had largely ceased to be of interest to the electorate and the Labour Party won power in the election of 1908 and again in 1910 under Andrew Fisher.

Australia played a significant part in the First World War, sending 330,000 troops overseas and sustaining 226,000 casualties of whom 60,000 were killed or missing. William Hughes was Prime Minister for the latter part of the war.

Labour was badly beaten after the war and did not win power again until 1929. It remained the Government until 1932 when a coalition took over under J. A. Lyons.

The other main Australian political parties between the wars were the Nationalist Party and the Country Party. Leaders who came to prominence include S. B. Bruce, Dr Page, Arthur Fadden, John Curtin and Robert Menzies. The latter was to become the dominant figure in Australian politics after the Second World War.

Again Australia loyally supported the Mother Country when war came in 1939. Australian troops served in the Middle East and took a large part in the fighting in the Pacific against the Japanese. The Royal Australian Navy fought alongside the Royal and United States Navies, while Australian airmen served in both the Royal Air Force and the Royal Australian Air Force. When the Japanese had reached New Guinea Australia herself was threatened with invasion. After the war Australia gave generously to assist Britain to recover economically, contributing £25,000,000 in 1947.

This period of Australian history was not without its difficulties. Western Australia was not happy within the Commonwealth, particularly with reference to tariffs, and after a referendum in favour of secession in 1933 it petitioned the British Parliament in 1934. Since the Statute of Westminster in 1931, Australia was fully independent and a Joint Committee of both Houses of Parliament in 1935 ruled that Britain had no right to interfere. After this the Federal Government agreed to consider Western Australia's difficulties and the demand for secession was dropped.

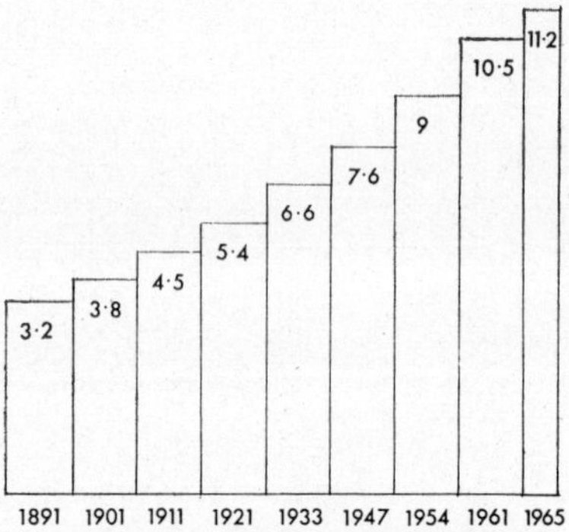

POPULATION OF AUSTRALIA (in MILLIONS)

When the Commonwealth Act of 1900 came into force it did not specifically make provision for the Northern Territory, rather barren and sparsely populated. It was originally under New South Wales and was later taken over by South Australia. This state was unhappy about its responsibility and the Commonwealth Government took over the territory in 1911. It was divided into North Australia and Central Australia in 1927, but this was ended in 1931 and it once more became Northern Territory.

Australia also controls a part of New Guinea and some Pacific Islands.

Today Australia is a flourishing vigorous country, still developing, with a population of over ten millions and still growing. More people is her greatest need, but she feels they must be the right people.

SUMMARY

Australia Before Federation

All colonies had received responsible government by 1890.—Financial crisis (1893).—Early progressive and democratic movements.—Influence of Chartists.—First suggestion of federation by Earl Grey (1847).—Uniform customs system authorised (1871) but not operated.—Little support for federation.—Germany annexed part of New Guinea (1884).—Lord Derby's Naval Defence Plan (1885).—Federal Council for Australia set up (1885); ineffective.—Federation movement launched by Sir Henry Parkes and Edmund Barton (1889).—Growth of support for federation.—Conventions at Melbourne (1890), Sydney (1891), Adelaide (1897.—Referendums (1898 and 1899); vote in favour.

The Commonwealth of Australia

Australian Commonwealth Act (1900).—Federation came into being as Commonwealth of Australia (1901) with a Governor-General, Federal Parliament of Senate and House of Representatives and a Cabinet Government.—Powers divided between Federal Government and states.—Canberra as capital (1927).—New Zealand did not become a member.

Political History

Labour Party's early prominence.—Issues of tariffs and 'White Australia' policy.—First Labour Government (1908).—Labour Government (1929); Nationalist and Country parties; Western Australia's petition for secession (1934).—British Parliament powerless to interfere since Statute of Westminster (1931).—Northern Territory; New Guinea and Pacific Islands.

QUESTIONS

Answer the follow questions briefly:

1. (a) What were the very first steps towards federation in Australia?
   (b) Why was popular feeling generally against federation at this time?
   (c) What changed this feeling?
   (d) How did federation eventually come about?
   (e) Why did the Labour Party become a force in Australian politics so early?
   (f) What democratic progress was made in Australia at the end of the nineteenth century?
   (g) What was meant by the 'White Australia' policy?
2. Outline the main points of the Australian Commonwealth Act and say how Australian federation differed from that of Canada.
3. John Ruskin, when Slade Professor of Art at Oxford University, said at the end of the century:

> Will you youths of England make your country again a royal throne of kings, a sceptred isle, for all the world a source of light, a centre of peace . . . ? This is what England must either do or perish. She must find colonies as fast and as far as she is able, formed of her most energetic and worthiest men; seizing any piece of fruitful waste ground she can set her foot on, and there teaching her colonists that their chief virtue is to be fidelity to their country. . . . If we can get men, for little pay, to cast themselves against cannon mouths for love of England, we may find men also who will plough and sow for her, and who will bring up their children to love her. . . .'

   (a) How do you think this quotation has applied to Australia?
   (b) How have Australians shown their 'fidelity to their country' both before and after federation.
   (c) How do you think the last sentence of the quotation may be applied to Australia and its people?
   (d) What other comment have you on Ruskin's words?

10 : New Zealand

Discovery and the First Settlements

JAMES COOK, with Sir Joseph Banks and his party, sailed around both islands of New Zealand in 1769 and 1770, and mapped them. Cook landed in two places, taking possession of the islands in the name of King George III, but he found the native Maoris fierce, warlike and unfriendly, and did not stay. Between 1770 and 1779, Cook made four other visits. The French also sent expeditions to New Zealand in 1769 and 1772. During the second expedition their leader du Fresne and many of his men were killed by the Maoris.

Ships from Sydney made visits to New Zealand soon after the foundation of New South Wales. The first settlers were escaped convicts and bushrangers who had made the dangerous journey from New South Wales at about the turn of the century, often in small boats which they had stolen. Some were carried in ships by sympathetic sailors. These men were sometimes disreputable characters and they taught the Maoris to use rum and firearms. Some intermarried with the Maoris and tried to build up small private kingdoms. One French adventurer actually called himself King of New Zealand in 1822. By 1839 there were some 2,000 white men of mixed race in New Zealand.

The first British missionaries arrived in 1814 under Samuel Marsden and many others followed. They had a tremendous influence on the Maoris who were a very intelligent race, many becoming Christian. Later, from 1842 to 1869, Bishop Selwyn did a great deal to civilise the natives.

However, it needed strong control from the British Government to clean up what was still a bad situation. In spite of colonisation movements at home, the Government had steadfastly refused to encourage, or even allow, colonisation of New Zealand.

Gibbon Wakefield and the First Official Settlement

A New Zealand Company had been formed in 1825, and a piece of land was bought from the Maoris to the north of North Island. However, the British Government, influenced by Sir James Stephen of the Colonial Office, would not agree to a settlement. In spite of this, the

The arrival of the Maoris in New Zealand. (*By C. F. Goldie and L. Steele.*)

Government did appoint a British Resident in New Zealand, subordinate to the Governor of New South Wales in 1832. This was largely because of the bad state of affairs in the islands but the Resident had little real influence.

Edward Gibbon Wakefield was still determined to press forward with his ideas for colonisation and after his withdrawal from the plans for South Australia, he planned a settlement in New Zealand.

In 1837 a New Zealand Association was formed without effect but two years later a second New Zealand Company was founded by Gibbon Wakefield and his friends. Without waiting for official Government support, because of fear that the French would move in first, an expedition sailed for New Zealand in May of 1839, under the command of Captain Arthur Wakefield, Gibbon Wakefield's brother. They reached Port Nicholson on the south coast of North Island in January of 1840. The settlement began at the spot which is now Wellington. The British Government was forced to act, and Captain William Hobson, a naval officer, was sent from Sydney to act as lieutenant-governor under the Governor of New South Wales. In November of 1840 New Zealand became a separate colony and Hobson became governor. Auckland was the first capital although it was replaced by Wellington in 1865. Once again, as in New South Wales, a naval officer quite arbitrarily selected, proved an outstanding governor.

The feared French expedition arrived off Akaroa in 1840, but Captain Hobson sent Captain Stanley to forestall them. The French

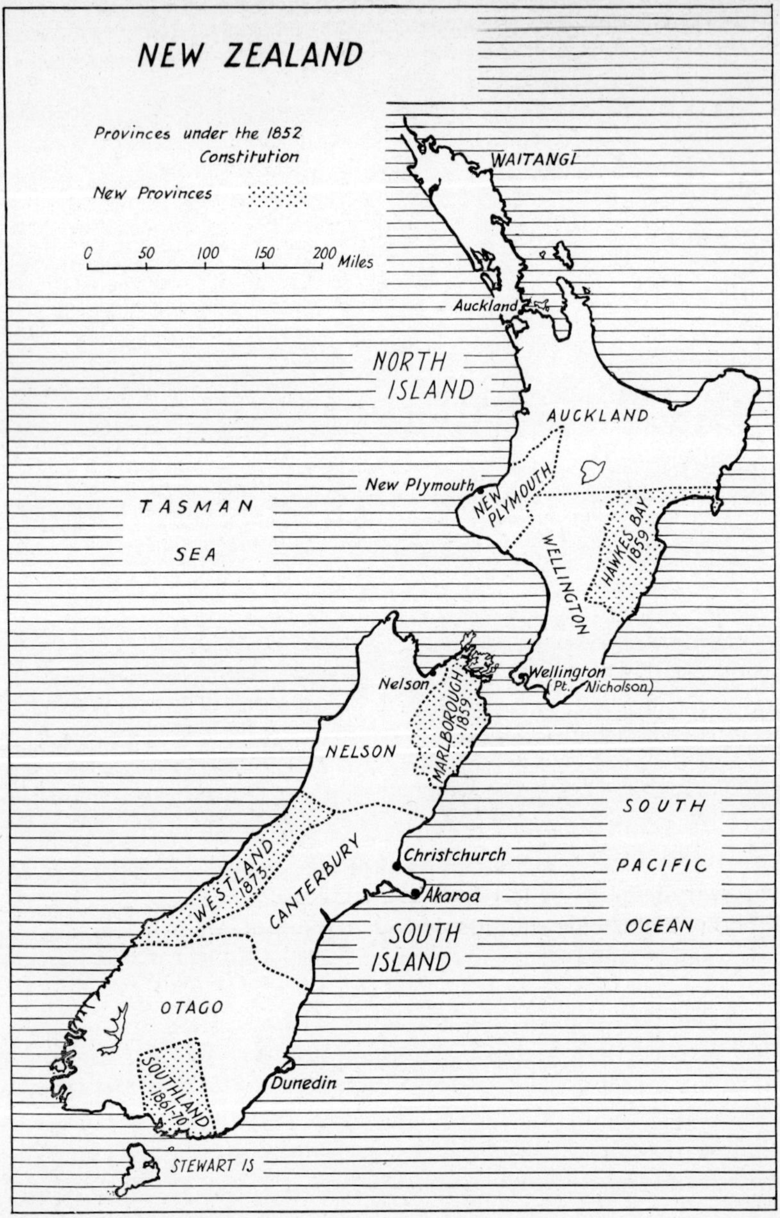

expedition sailed away but a few French remained as colonists under British rule.

The Treaty of Waitangi

At Waitangi the same year, Hobson called a great gathering of Maori chiefs. In the Treaty of Waitangi which followed the chiefs recognised the Great White Queen across the seas; Hobson guaranteed them British protection; the Maori land rights were recognised; it was agreed that they should sell land only to the Government and not to individual settlers or to the New Zealand Company; all land was to be paid for and to be sold only by the tribe as a whole. Hobson had a great understanding of the Maori and certainly won their confidence. The Treaty was very much in their favour and was resented by the New Zealand Company who wished to purchase land cheaply and were guilty of violation of the Treaty in the years which followed. The Maoris, who were of high intelligence, fully understood the Treaty and its failure to work entirely as intended was because of a misunderstanding of the Maori system of holding land. Their land did not belong to the chiefs but to the whole tribe and this made for great difficulty. With both the Company and individual settlers buying land from the Maoris in defiance of the Treaty and some land being sold several times by the same tribe, chaos ensued. In spite of a special Commissioner being sent from Britain to settle the land question, disputes went on for some years. This made the Wakefield system more difficult to put into operation because of the difficulty of fixing a price for land and the fact that no emigration fund could be set up. Nevertheless, it was a successful colony in spite of the early troubles.

Hobson died in 1842 and was succeeded for a short time by Lieutenant Shortland as acting-governor. Captain Fitzroy became

Treaty of Waitangi, 1840:
Plaque in Wellington.

governor in 1843. All were guilty of failure to enforce the Treaty of Waitangi and weakness in dealing with Maori indiscipline. In 1842 the Maoris believing, with some justification, that the Treaty had been violated, murdered twenty-two white men, including Captain Wakefield. Fitzroy failed to take strong action and disorder grew.

The First Maori War, 1845–47

The disorder developed into a war and Fitzroy was replaced in 1846 by Captain George Grey, fresh from his success in South Australia. He took strong action at once. He broke off all negotiations with the Maoris and forbade and ended the sale of arms to them. He then took vigorous military action and crushed the rising. For his successful handling of the situation Grey was knighted.

Perhaps it was after the war that he achieved most. He went out of his way to win the confidence and friendship of the Maoris by a conciliatory policy and scrupulously fair treatment. He learned the Maori language and introduced many reforms to improve their conditions. The Maoris respected a strong governor and a peaceful period followed.

Further Settlement

The Government enabled the New Zealand Company to purchase land in the South Island where there were far fewer Maoris and here the Wakefield system had a far better chance of success. The Company did an excellent job of selecting colonists, assisting them to make the long voyage to New Zealand and to settle them along Wakefield's lines at the end of it. Some of the best settlements were by groups: by Scottish emigrants at Nelson in 1847; by a group of Tories and High Churchmen at Canterbury in 1848 as the Canterbury Association. These were immensely successful and proved the true value of Wakefield's ideas.

The Company continued until 1851. In 1846, Earl Grey's Act had been passed by the British Parliament and set up two provinces New Ulster, or North Island, and New Munster, or South Island. The colony of New Zealand had a governor and each province was given a lieutenant-governor. Each province was given an Executive Council, a Legislative Council, and an elected Assembly. In actual fact the elected Assemblies were not put into operation, because Sir George Grey considered them to be premature.

New Zealand was given responsible government in 1852, when the two provinces of New Ulster and New Munster were abolished, with a nominated Legislative Council and an elected House of Representatives, although full parliamentary government was not in operation until 1856. An Executive Council of Ministers, or Cabinet, was responsible to the elected House. Six provinces, with Provincial Councils, were set up. They were Wellington, Auckland, Nelson, New Plymouth, Canterbury and Otago. All questions concerning the Maori remained directly under the governor. After this, Sir George Grey gave up the governorship. He had been a magnificent governor. Many stories are told of the way he gained the friendship of the Maoris. He once challenged a Maori champion runner to a cross-country race and beat him.

The next twenty years saw two different kinds of struggles; one between the Provincial Councils and central government and the other the Second Maori War.

The Second Maori War, 1860–71

As New Zealand developed settlement spread and this further demand for land in the North Island caused resentment among the Maoris. A clash occurred over some disputed land in 1860 and some of the tribes tried to join together under one of the chiefs who took the title of King. The Maoris were brave and good soldiers and since the departure of Sir George Grey they had been able to obtain firearms. They fought extremely well and the white troops found their task very difficult. Grey became governor again in 1861 and carried on the war with the same vigour as he had shown in the first war. A large number of British troops were engaged but the Maoris built up fortified positions called 'pahs', and they were very difficult to dislodge. Grey soon disagreed with General Cameron in command of the British troops and in 1866 when the revolt had been partially crushed the withdrawal of British troops began. After that much of the fighting against the rebels was carried on by colonial militia and the war did not finish finally until 1871. Grey had been recalled in 1867 and when the war dragged to a conclusion in 1871 the people of New Zealand were unhappy and discontented. They resented the interference of the British Government and some of the more extreme elements even thought of leaving the Empire. After a few years of peace and prosperity things improved.

During the Second Maori War, the control of matters affecting the Maoris was transferred from the governor to the Government.

Political and Constitutional Development

Sir George Grey returned to New Zealand in 1872 and became Prime Minister in 1877 as leader of the Conservatives who were in power from 1872 until 1891. They were replaced by the Liberal Party who were in office until 1912.

New Zealand soldiers at convalescent hospital in England, being greeted by General Gedley on Anzac Day 1917.

Maori representatives took their place in the House of Representatives in 1867.

In 1876 the Provincial Councils were abolished and County Councils were set up in their place. This had the effect of strengthening central government and ended the struggle for supremacy between the two.

Women received the vote in 1893 although they were not eligible to sit in the House of Representatives until 1919.

New Zealand was granted full Dominion status in 1907, its governor becoming governor-general in 1917, while like other Dominions it became fully independent under the Statute of Westminster in 1931.

As in Australia, Labour became an effective force early, forming a separate party in 1910. It did not succeed in winning power until 1928 when a combined Liberal and Labour Government took office under Sir Joseph Ward. The first independent Labour Government was in 1935, led by Michael Savage. Under this Government New Zealand was a pioneer of social legislation. In 1938 a Social Security Act was passed which provided for pensions and health and medical benefits.

There have been changes in the names of other parties, the Conservatives tending to be known first as the Reform Party and then as the National Party and the Liberals as the Progressives.

New Zealand proved loyalty to the Mother Country by the way it entered into the First World War. Large numbers of enthusiastic volunteers came forward for service overseas.

In the Second World War the Dominion's effort was even greater.

Her troops served with great distinction in the Middle East and Italy, as well as in the Pacific area. New Zealand airmen flew with the Royal Air Force and the Royal New Zealand Air Force and the New Zealand Navy served with the Royal and United States Navies. In 1945, New Zealand made a gift of £10,000,000 to help Britain recover from the War.

In 1950 the Legislative Council was abolished and New Zealand adopted a single-chamber Parliament.

This most British of Dominions has continued to develop, but her population is still small, less than two and a half million. There is no doubt that a greater population could be supported, but New Zealand is very anxious to maintain the British basis of her people.

SUMMARY

Discovery and First Settlements

Cook's voyage (1769–70); took possession in name of George III.—French unsuccessful expeditions.—Early settlement by escaped convicts and bushrangers. —British missionaries.

Gibbon Wakefield and First Official Settlement

New Zealand Company formed (1825).—British Resident appointed (1832).—New Zealand Association formed (1837).—Second New Zealand Company formed (1839) on Wakefield's principles of systematic colonisation.—Expedition under Captain Arthur Wakefield arrived (1840).—Settlement founded at Wellington; Captain Hobson appointed lieutenant-governor under Governor of New South Wales (1840).—New Zealand as separate colony and Hobson as governor later the same year.

Treaty of Waitangi—1840

Recognition of Maori land rights.—Private sale and purchase of land forbidden. —All land to be paid for.—Maoris as British subjects.—Difficulties caused by Maori system of land tenure.—Death of Hobson (1842).—Shortland and Fitzroy failed to enforce Treaty.—Maori discontent.—Murder of 22 white men including Captain Wakefield.—Fitzroy's weakness and growth of disorder.

First Maori War, 1845–47

Captain Grey as governor (1846) took strong action.—Won friendship of Maoris.

Further Settlement

Encouragement of settlement on South Island.—Settlements on Wakefield's lines at Nelson and Canterbury (1847 and 1848).—Earl Grey's Act (1846).—Two provinces of New Ulster and New Munster.—Governor for colony; lieutenant-governors for provinces.—Executive Council and Legislative Council for each province.—Responsible government granted (1852).—Two provinces abolished; Legislative Council appointed for New Zealand.—Elected House of Representatives.—Full parliamentary government (1856).—Six provinces set up; Maoris affairs remained under governor.

Second Maori War, 1860–71

New demands for land in North Island.—Resentment among Maoris; clashes; rising under Maori King; bitter fighting.—Grey as governor once more (1861).—Disagreement with General Cameron.—Withdrawal of British troops (1866).—Revolt partially crushed.—Carried on with colonial militia.—Grey recalled (1867).—War dragged to end (1871).—Maori affairs now under Government.

Political and Constitutional Development

Sir George Grey returned to New Zealand (1872); Prime Minister (1877).—Maoris in House of Representatives (1867).—Provincial Councils abolished and replaced by County Councils (1876).—Women received vote (1893).—Rise of Labour Party.—Legislative Council abolished and single-chamber Parliament adopted (1950).

QUESTIONS

Answer the following questions briefly:

1. (a) When and how was New Zealand first mapped?
   (b) When it was claimed for King George III, why was no settlement made?
   (c) How was it first settled?
   (d) What were the causes of the First Maori War?
   (e) What were the causes of the Second Maori War?
   (f) Why did the second war last so long?
2. Describe the constitutional development of New Zealand from the settlement in 1840 until 1950.
3. At the signing of the Treaty of Waitangi a Maori chief, Tamati Waka Nene, who delivered an oration in favour of the Treaty, turned to Captain Hobson and said, 'I say to you, sir, remain, be to us a father, a judge, a peacemaker.'
   (a) How far did Captain Hobson act as 'a father, a judge, a peacemaker'?
   (b) Do you consider that Tamati Waka Nene's remarks could apply to Sir George Grey.
   (c) Why was Sir George Grey so successful with the Maoris?

Jan Van Riebeek, early Dutch settler in South Africa.

11 : South Africa as a Colony

Early Settlement

IN the fifteenth and sixteenth centuries Table Bay was used by British, Portuguese and Dutch seafarers as a stopping place on their way to and from the East Indies. It served as a haven in the storms for which the Cape is famous and a place from which fresh water, fruit and supplies could be obtained. They used it as a kind of unmanned Post Office, leaving letters in canvas bags under large stones to be picked up by the next ship.

No attempt at settlement was made until 1652, when a party of Dutch under Van Riebeek founded a depot at which Dutch ships could call. Even then the intention was not to form a colony but purely to aid the Dutch East India Company's trade. In 1685, after Louis XIV had revoked the Edict of Nantes and persecution of the Huguenots had recommenced, some Huguenot refugees settled at the Cape. Together with more Dutch settlers they helped to form a colony and they were absorbed by the Dutch. These French settlers brought the vine to South Africa.

While some settlers stayed near Table Bay and founded Cape Town, many moved into the interior on isolated farms and became the true Boers, different from the old Dutch. Like the Huguenots, they were of the Calvinistic faith, but of the Dutch Reformed Church, and they lived in the wilderness like the people of the Old Testament.

British Annexation

When the French Revolutionary War broke out in 1792, the French armies invaded the Netherlands and the Stadtholder asked the British to seize Cape Colony. A British expedition under Admiral Elphinstone and General Craig occupied the colony in 1795, only too anxious to prevent it falling into French hands when it could be used as a base from which they could attack British lines of communication with India and the East. It was returned to Holland by the Peace of Amiens in 1802, but when the Napoleonic War broke out and Holland once again was under French domination, British forces under Admiral Popham and General Baird re-occupied Cape Colony in 1806. At the Peace of Vienna in 1814 Britain was given the colony

Landing of Jan Van Riebeek.

as a part of her reward for fighting the French, and it was annexed, compensation of six million pounds being paid to the Dutch. Britain did not really want the colony but was anxious to have the naval base of Table Bay.

British Settlement

At first no attempt was made to persuade British settlers to go to the Cape. The Boers had been fighting constantly with the Kaffirs along the line of the Great Fish River and with other Bantu people who were part of a great migration south to the east coast. They had often asked for help from Cape Town, but the Dutch authorities had not given it. They now asked their new rulers who decided to colonise the area north of the Great Fish River with British settlers. The first settlers arrived and settled in Cape Town about 1815, but by 1820 nearly five thousand settled on the border.

Until this time the British authorities had not interfered with the Boers in any way and had, indeed, been welcomed because of their help against the Kaffirs. For years the Boers had lived in their isolated farms, using quantities of Negro slaves, clinging tenaciously to the strict beliefs of the Dutch Reformed Church which taught them that God had created white men as superior to black men, and adhering to all their old traditions and way of life. Slavery to them was a natural state for the coloured peoples and they could see nothing wrong in it.

Now that British settlers were beginning to arrive, the British

Government began to look upon South Africa as a colony and began to introduce changes. The English language became official in 1822 and was to be universal by 1828. A new system of local government was introduced and English magistrates were appointed and the judicial system was remodelled on the English pattern in 1828. English coinage replaced the Dutch and the British began to dominate the churches and schools. Unfortunately Lord Charles Somerset, the governor, was tactless and overbearing in his treatment of the Boers.

British missionaries had been working in South Africa since the beginning of the century and not only had they set about the task of converting the natives but they insisted upon treating them as brothers in the sight of God. This brought them into conflict with the Boers. The slave trade had been abolished through the efforts of William Wilberforce, Clarkson, Buxton and others in 1807 and feeling at home was mounting against slavery. Dr John Philip and the London Missionary Society were persuading the Government and the Colonial Office not to heed the protests of the Dutch. It was largely Dr Philip's influence which secured the passing of an ordinance in 1828 which made white men and natives equal before the law; this the Boers regarded as unjust.

While there was nothing unreasonable about these measures, they were applied without sufficient thought, particularly bearing in mind the way of life of the Boer farmers. They lived in isolated farm houses surrounded by natives and fear made them believe in the need for keeping the Bantu in subjection. Had more tact been used, it is possible that much of the conflict would have been avoided. Yet the Boers themselves were obstinate, stubborn and difficult; certainly not without blame for the problems to come.

The Quarrel between British and Dutch: the Great Trek

The quarrel was brought to a head by the final success of Wilberforce's life's work in 1833. In that year the Act for the abolition of slavery in all parts of the British Empire was passed by the British Parliament. This was bitterly resented by the Boers, just and humane though it was. Nevertheless, the Dutch farmers did have a genuine grievance. They estimated the value of the forty thousand slaves they were to lose as three million pounds. They were awarded only one and a quarter million pounds. What made it even worse was the method by which their compensation had to be claimed. All claims had to be made in London! This meant the employment of agents at great expense. It is not surprising that the Boers were bitter.

The climax came in 1834. A great body of Kaffirs crossed the Great

Sir Benjamin D'Urban.

Fish River and invaded Cape Colony, killing many people and destroying farms. The governor, Sir Benjamin D'Urban, used troops to drive them back and he decided to protect the farmsteads by annexing the land between the Keiskana and Great Kei rivers to form a new province which would act as a buffer. This was to be known as Queen Adelaide, and later became British Kaffraria. This won the support of the Boers but roused the missionaries and other humanitarians at once who persuaded Lord Glenelg, the Colonial Secretary, to repudiate D'Urban's plan. D'Urban resigned, just at a time when a popular governor might have brought a peaceful solution. The Boers were furious because they believed that the British Government had let them down and surrendered them and their families to be murdered by the Kaffirs. Their indignation was increased by the campaign carried on in London by the missionaries and their supporters accusing the Boers of cruelty to the natives. They could not understand why it was considered wrong to flog natives for misdeeds, when flogging was a regular punishment for British soldiers and sailors for disciplinary offences.

It was the last straw as far as the Boers were concerned. In 1836 there began the Great Trek, although a few had moved northwards the previous year. In quite small groups, with their women and children, in covered wagons similar to those used by the pioneers in the West of America hauled by oxen, and driving their cattle in front of them, some five thousand Boers set out into the unknown lands to the north. They crossed the Orange River to form the Orange Free State; they moved north-eastwards into Natal, only to leave it when British settlers followed them and they trekked even farther northwards to cross the Vaal river and founded Transvaal. The 'Voortrekkers' under the leadership of men like Piet Retief and Pretorius made long and dangerous journeys, short of food and water and menaced all the time by the Zulus and the Matabeles. It was a tremendous achievement and moulded the history of South Africa. Over the course of several years more than ten thousand Boers left Cape Colony.

Retief led his party over the Drakensburg mountains into Natal where they hoped for peaceful settlement. He opened negotiations with Dingaan, the King of the Zulus, and Retief and sixty men met Dingaan at a conference in February 1838. At a signal from Dingaan thousands of Zulu warriors fell upon the Boers and killed them all. The Zulu armies fell upon Boer camps everywhere and there was bitter fighting. The Boers formed their wagons into 'laagers' and beat off the attacks, finally joining together to crush Dingaan's forces at the Battle of Blood River in December of 1838. They then established the Republic of Natal around Pietermaritzburg, with Andries Pretorius as the first President. The British Government refused to recognise the Republic and made it a province of Cape Colony in 1843. Led by Pretorius, most of the Boers then left Natal for the Orange Free State. Even now the British Government did not feel that they could wash their hands of the Boers. They were still British subjects and in need of protection and their continued march northwards made wars with the natives inevitable. In 1848 Sir Harry Smith, Governor of Cape Colony and an able soldier who had fought with Wellington, annexed the Orange Free State, and when the Boers resisted, defeated a force under Pretorius at Boomplatz. Pretorius then led many of the Boers northwards into Transvaal and the city of Pretoria was named after him.

In 1852, Pretorius met Sir Harry Smith at the Sand River Convention where the freedom of the Boers in the Transvaal was recognised and in 1854 the Convention of Bloemfontein recognised the independence of the Orange Free State. A great many of the Boers were dismayed by this, being only too ready to accept British protection against the natives, the Basutos. However, the British remained the paramount power and were recognised as such, with power of intervention if necessary. That power would later have to be used.

Thus there were now two Boer republics; Transvaal and the Orange Free State, although there was a danger at one time that they would break up into several. An attempt was made to form a union of both and for a time a second Pretorius, son of Andries, was President of both.

In the meantime, Natal had become a separate Crown colony in 1845 and had been given representative government, with no African representation, in 1856. Cape Colony had been under military rule until 1833, although it was given a nominated Council in 1825. From 1833 to 1853 it was a Crown colony with a governor, and nominated Executive and Legislative Councils. In 1853 it was given representative government, including representation of coloured people.

Criticism is often made of the feebleness of British policy in South Africa at this time, but to maintain control over such a vast area against the wishes of many of its people would have been impossible without vast numbers of troops which could not have been spared.

From 1854 to 1861, Sir George Grey, famous for his work in South Australia and New Zealand, was Governor of the Cape. He suggested, in 1858, a plan for federation of the two colonies of the Cape and Natal; British Kaffraria; and the Boer Republic of the Orange Free State. He hoped that if the plan were put into operation, Transvaal would later join. Unfortunately, this statesmanlike proposal received no support from the British Government. Had it done so the history of South Africa might well have been far happier.

Trouble with the Basutos began in the Orange Free State and in 1868 Sir Philip Wodehouse, Governor of Cape Colony, annexed Basutoland. This was resented by the Boers who considered that it should have become a part of the Free State.

The Discovery of Diamonds

The Suez Canal opened in 1869 and this diverted traffic to and from the Far East from Cape Town. Naturally, this meant a serious loss of trade and interest was aroused in possible natural resources which could be developed.

In 1869 a Boer child playing on the bank of the Orange River discovered a 'pretty pebble'. This was identified as a diamond and in 1870 the Kimberley diamond field was discovered. The area was north of the Orange River on the border of Cape Colony and the Orange Free State and belonged to the Griqua tribe. The Cape Government annexed the area at the wish of the Griquas and to maintain law and order among the diamond diggers in 1871, it became known as Griqualand West.

The Boers claimed that this was seizure of land rightfully theirs, sincet he Cape Government had agreed not to take overl and north of the Orange River. It must be pointed out, though, that the Boers would almost certainly have been unable to control the diggers. Nevertheless, they had lost a valuable area and this was recognised soon afterwards when Lord Carnarvon, the Colonial Secretary, authorised the payment of £90,000 in compensation to the Orange Free State.

Morning market, Kimberley, 1888.

As the diamond field developed, the individual miners could not continue and mining companies took over. Cecil Rhodes formed the De Beers Mining Company in 1873 and Barnett Barnato formed the Barnato Diamond Mining Company the same year. After years of rivalry the two came together as the De Beers Consolidated Mines in 1891. These diamond interests made Cecil Rhodes' fortune and helped him to the political career which was to have such an effect on Africa.

At this time, in 1874, a second proposal for federation of the two colonies and the Boer Republic was made by Lord Carnarvon. The Orange Free State was still smarting from the annexation of Basutoland and Griqualand West, and Cape Colony was happy with the newly won responsible government, so there was little enthusiasm for the idea. In spite of the passing by the British Government in 1877 of an Act authorising such a federation, the lack of enthusiasm and rather clumsy handling of the plan by Lord Carnarvon meant that nothing further was done.

The Zulu War, 1879

The Transvaal had not been having a happy time during this period. With a more scattered population than the Orange Free State, government was difficult and the Zulus were threatening. Since their defeat at Blood River in 1838 they had been comparatively peaceful, but now they were under a new King, a warlike leader called Cetewayo. Cetewayo, after succeeding in 1872, had pursued an aggressive policy and Sir Bartle Frere, the Governor of the Cape, called upon him to keep the promises he had made to live in peace, and to disband his armes. This Cetawayo refused to do, allowing and even encouraging raids into Natal and the Transvaal. Frere also asked for

A young Zulu looks at his kraal down in the valley.

compensation for the raids and for the end of the traditional custom by which young Zulu men could not marry until blooded in battle.

Frere, realising the danger of the situation, warned the British Government, asking for more troops. His warning was not heeded and he was sent only a few of the troops for which he had asked. Transvaal had been annexed for its own protection in 1877 and with the threat of Zulu invasion few Boers really objected.

In the early part of 1879 a British force under Lord Chelmsford invaded Zululand. It was totally inadequate for its task and had to be split over the large area. At Isandhlwana a battalion of South Wales Borderers, some 800 men, was surprised by an overwhelming force of 10,000 Zulus and fought almost to the last man, only some 40 escaping. The Zulu impis then turned towards Natal. Their way was barred at Rorke's Drift by a small garrison, also of South Wales Borderers, of 80 men with some 30 in hospital, under Lieutenants Chard and Bromhead. The Zulu force of over 4,000 men attacked for several hours, six times getting within the wall only to be driven out at bayonet point. The next morning the Zulus withdrew, leaving their dead behind them. This epic defence of Rorke's Drift had saved Natal from invasion and the massacre of many men, women and children had been averted.

Reinforcements arrived from England and with an army of some 5,000 men, Chelmsford advanced towards Ulundi, the royal kraal. The Zulus attacked with over 12,000 men but the British formed a hollow square and the Zulus were completely defeated. This was virtually the end of the war. Cetewayo was captured and sent to Cape Town. In the operations in Zululand, Louis Napoleon, son of

Napoleon III and Prince Imperial of France, who had accompanied the British troops, was killed.

Zululand was divided into thirteen districts under Zulu chiefs with a British Resident in each. This was not a success and Cetawayo was restored as King. He had lost support of his people, and soon afterwards died, being succeeded by his son Dinizulu, who was not a good ruler. In 1887 Zululand was ruled directly by the British Government and in 1897 it was annexed by Natal.

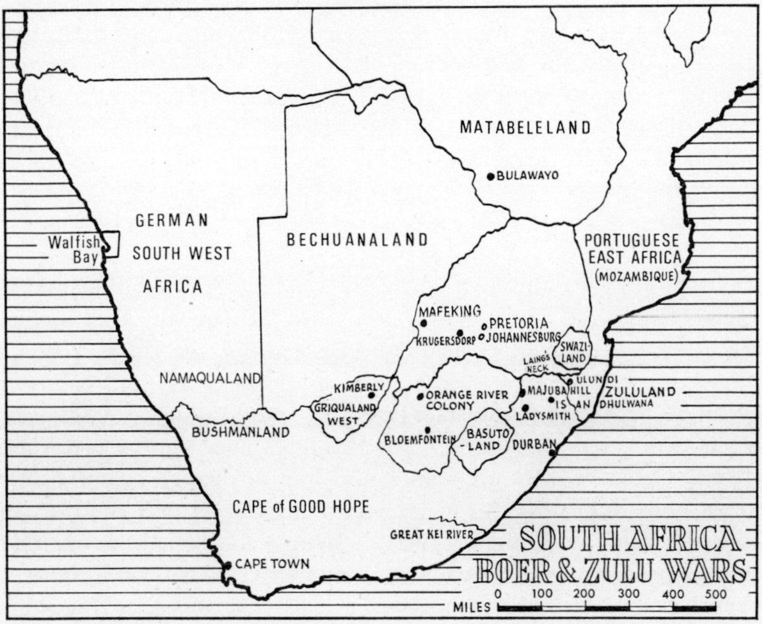

The First Boer War, 1880–81

As soon as the Zulu War was over and the menace of Zulu invasion removed, the Boers in the Transvaal demanded their independence once more. This they hoped to get from the newly-elected British Liberal Government under Gladstone, but many British Liberals were distrustful of the Boers and their attitude towards the natives. Consequently, the Boers grew angry at the Government's inaction. After the Zulus had been defeated most of the British troops had been withdrawn and only a few scattered detachments remained. The President of Transvaal was now Paul Kruger, a man of iron will who hated the British with a hatred born of a boyhood during the Great Trek. He was determined to take advantage of British military weakness and to wait no longer. In December of 1880 the Boers rose and overcame the British troops in the Transvaal. Sir George Colley led a small force from Natal, but he was defeated at Laing's Nek and again defeated and killed by the Boers at Majuba Hill in February 1881. Gladstone then made peace and at the Convention of Pretoria, Transvaal was given independence, although with a British Resident and theoretically subject to the Queen. In 1884 full independence was given, the Resident was withdrawn, and Transvaal was recognised as the South African Republic. Bechuanaland was annexed by Britain in 1885.

This had been a humiliating defeat for the British and a triumph for the Boers. Gladstone had been in error in allowing a war to develop and then surrendering afterwards. The British in South Africa were bitter and humiliated and the Boers were now certain that the British would give way to force. This was to contribute to the causes of the Second Boer War.

Discovery of Gold

In 1886 gold was discovered in the Witwatersrand, south of Pretoria in Transvaal. There was a gold rush, but because the nuggets were in rock it needed scientific mining and this the Boers were not qualified to carry out. Consequently, mining experts and engineers had to be brought in, most of them British, and large companies floated to develop the mines. Cecil Rhodes was a leading proprietor in these. The city which grew up in the area was called Johannesburg and the non-Boer population grew until in 1899 it was equal to the Boers. The Boers still did not like the British and called the intruders 'Uitlanders'. They were treated very harshly, denied any rights of citizenship and forced to shoulder a crushing burden of taxation. When the 'Uitlanders' complained they were told that they had not been asked to come and were welcome to leave if they wished. This was scarcely true since the gold mines could not have been developed without them. Relations worsened and eventually became very strained.

The Events Leading to the Second Boer War

In 1889 Cecil Rhodes had formed the British South Africa Company in order to develop the area to the north of Transvaal in Matabeleland and Mashonaland to achieve his ambition of a Cape to Cairo railway and a British Africa from north to south. When he acquired the territories the Boers felt almost surrounded by British territory

Rhodes became Prime Minister of Cape Colony in 1890 and for

Cecil Rhodes.

several years, with the support of Jan Hofmeyr, the leader of the Boer party in the Cape Parliament, attempted to bring about a peaceful solution to the problem of Transvaal. Kruger would have none of it and was determined to achieve Boer supremacy, although very many Boers in the Orange Free State and even some in Transvaal were in favour of Rhodes' policy.

The situation in which the 'Uitlanders' found themselves in 1895 was so bad that they began to plot an armed rising. The plan was that risings should take place in Transvaal and simultaneously a force of officials, settlers and police led by Dr Jameson of the British South Africa Company should cross the border and invade Transvaal. Jameson's force attacked but the 'Uitlanders' were unready and failed to rise in support. He penetrated far into Transvaal but he and his force were surrounded and captured at Krugersdorp in January 1896. This had been a flagrant invasion of an independent state, Rhodes was implicated in the plot and forced to resign as Prime Minister of the Cape, and it was said that the Colonial Secretary, Joseph Chamberlain, knew of the scheme. It was a foolish adventure as it united the Transvaal Boers under Kruger just when his popularity was beginning to decline and brought the Orange Free State into support of Transvaal, as well as turning world opinion against Britain. The British Government requested that Jameson and his men should be handed over for punishment, but they were dealt with leniently,

Jameson receiving only fifteen months' imprisonment. Boer anger grew and Kruger's mood hardened, as the situation became steadily worse.

In June 1899 Sir Alfred Milner who was now Governor of the Cape and High Commissioner of South Africa had an interview with Kruger at Bloemfontein and tried to obtain minimum rights of citizenship for the 'Uitlanders'. The negotiations came to nothing and the last chance of peace had gone. The bitterness brought about by the treatment of the 'Uitlanders', by the Jameson Raid and the British Government's leniency to the offenders, together with the long-standing hatred of the British by the Boers, made war now inevitable. The failure of the raid had confirmed the impression that the Boers had gained at Majuba Hill; that the British were militarily weak, and would give way to force. Kruger's hand was strengthened by the famous telegram from Kaiser William II of Germany virtually promising support for action against Britain.

The Second Boer War, 1899–1902

Much of the money which Kruger had raised by taxing the 'Uitlanders' had been spent on arms and munitions and the Boers were well prepared for war. There has been great argument about the blame for the war, some blaming the mine-owners whom, it was said, wished to see the Boers crushed, while others said that Kruger and his followers were determined to drive the British out of South Africa. Wherever the blame should be, the war was a long and bitter one, and was a tragic chapter in South Africa's history.

The British Government had not heeded the warnings of the military authorities in Cape Colony and there were far too few British troops. Kruger declared war on 11 October 1899. Boer commandos, under Cronje, besieged Mafeking, and under Wessels, besieged Kimberley. The main Boer force under Joubert invaded Natal. The British forces were outnumbered and taken by surprise both by the skill of the Boer generals and by their numbers and equipment. After bitter fighting the British forces were surrounded in Ladysmith. General Sir Redvers Buller who had been placed in command of the British forces, arrived in Cape Town at the beginning of November with three divisions of troops.

Buller met a critical situation. Natal was virtually in Boer hands, British forces were besieged in Mafeking, Kimberley and Ladysmith, and the Boers were on the point of invading Cape Colony. Quick action was necessary but with the need to relieve Kimberley and recover Natal at the same time as defending Cape Colony, Buller had

Paul Kruger.

to divide his forces into three. General Sir Charles Clery with rather more than a division was sent to Natal; General Sir William Gatacre with about a brigade was left to defend the Cape, while General Lord Methuen with a division was sent to relieve Kimberley. This division of forces was fatal. Methuen was defeated at the Modder River at the end of November, Gatacre was defeated at Stormberg and Methuen again defeated at Magersfontein, both the latter in December in what was known as 'black week'. At Magersfontein the Highland Brigade was caught in the open and lost its general, Wauchope, and 750 men killed. The 'black week' was completed by the defeat of Buller and the Natal force at Colenso. Buller was relieved of his command, and replaced by Field-Marshal Lord Roberts with Major-General Lord Kitchener as his Chief-of-Staff. Extra troops were sent and because of the shortage of regular troops, volunteer regiments and yeomanry served overseas for the first time. In addition, Canada, Australia and New Zealand sent volunteer contingents.

Roberts created a second field army out of units in Cape Colony and leaving Buller in command in Natal, planned to move northwards to relieve Kimberley, invade the Orange Free State and move into Transvaal. After some heavy fighting the advance proceeded successfully and in February 1900, 4,000 Boers surrendered at Paardeburg, the anniversary of Majuba, Kimberley having been relieved a few days before. Ladysmith was relieved by Buller on the day after. Roberts captured Bloemfontein, the Orange Free State capital in

March. The Boer forces were now beginning to break up and with the death of Joubert and the end of March, Boer morale began to decline. In spite of brilliant operations by Boer commandos under de Wet, Roberts' advance continued and a flying column relieved Mafeking on 17th May. This news was received everywhere with great rejoicing since it had been defended with great gallantry by Colonel Baden-Powell. Johannesburg fell in May and on 5 June 1900 Roberts entered Pretoria.

Although this was the end of the major fighting, the war dragged on for a further two years of guerilla warfare before the Boers surrendered. Roberts left Kitchener in command at the end of 1900 and returned to Britain. Kruger fled to Portuguese East Africa and then to Holland.

Kitchener, faced with brilliantly led mounted forces, rounded up the remaining Boers during 1901 and 1902 by building lines of block-houses manned by infantry and driving the Boers into the confines thus formed by cavalry sweeps. Although de Wet led a daring raid into Cape Colony, Kitchener's plan was a success. By early 1902 the complete system of block-houses was finished and the last of the Boers were rounded up by March 1902. He also rounded up the non-combatants, mainly women and children into concentration camps. The Boers sued for peace and this was signed, after a conference at Vereeniging, at Pretoria on 31 May 1902. The main Boer representatives were Botha, de Wet, Hertzog and Smuts.

The war had cost the British nearly six thousand killed and the Boers almost as many.

SUMMARY

Early Settlement

Early use of Table Bay as stopping place on route to East.—Van Riebeek's depot (1652).—Huguenot refugees.—Dutch settlers.

British Annexation

British expedition occupied Cape colony at request of Dutch (1795).—Colony returned to Holland at Treaty of Amiens (1802).—Re-occupied (1806).—Annexed under Treaty of Vienna (1815).

British Settlement

Boers' welcome for British as aid against the Kaffirs.—British colonists arrived in strength (1820).—Introduction of changes by the British.—English language official (1822–28).—New system of local government (1828).—English magistrates and judicial system (1828).—English coinage.—Work of missionaries; differences between British and Boers on attitude to natives.—Slave trade abolished (1807).—White and coloured men made equal in law (1828).

Quarrel between British and Dutch: the Great Trek

Slavery abolished (1833).—Boer resentment.—Unfair system of compensation.—Kaffir War (1834).—D'Urban's plan; repudiated by British Government; further Boer resentment.—The Great Trek (1836).—Difficulties with Zulus.—Republic of Natal (1838).—Natal annexed by British (1843).—Further trek; Orange Free State annexed (1848).—Further trek to Transvaal; Sand River Convention (1852).—Transvaal's independence recognised.—Convention of Bloemfontein (1854); Orange Free State's independence recognised.—Natal became Crown colony (1845); granted representative government (1856).—Cape Colony granted representative government (1853).—Sir George Grey advocated federation of two British colonies and Orange Free State (1858); rejected by British Government.

Discovery of Diamonds

Diamonds discovered near Orange River (1869).—Kimberley diamond field discovered (1870); annexed by Cape Government as Griqualand West (1871).—Boer resentment.—De Beers and Barnato Companies.—Rhodes as mine-owner.—Lord Carnarvon's proposal for federation (1874) met with little enthusiasm.

Zulu War 1879

Zulus' aggressive policy under Cetewayo.—Transvaal annexed (1877) with general Boer agreement because of fear of Zulus.—Massacre at Isandhlwana.—Defence of Rorke's Drift (1879).—Natal saved.—Zulus defeated at Ulundi.—Zululand divided into thirteen districts each under British Resident.—Cetewayo died, succeeded by son, Dinizulu.—Zululand ruled directly by British Government (1887); annexed by Natal (1897).

First Boer War, 1880–81

Boers' demand for independence for Transvaal.—Liberal Government's failure to grant it.—British troops withdrawn after Zulu War.—Paul Kruger, President of Transvaal.—His hatred of British.—Boers attacked British troops in Transvaal (Dec. 1880).—Boers defeated British at Majuba Hill (Feb. 1881).—Independence granted to Transvaal with British Resident (1881).—Full independence (1884).

Discovery of Gold

Gold discovered in Witwatersrand (1886); British miners; Cecil Rhodes as a leading mine-owner.—Johannesburg.—'Uitlanders'.—Increasing trouble.

Events Leading to Second Boer War

British South Africa Company founded by Cecil Rhodes (1889).—Rhodes as Prime Minister of Cape (1890).—Worked with Hofmeyr for peaceful settlement of problems with the Boers.—Kruger's anti-British attitude.—'Uitlanders' intolerable position; Jameson Raid (1896).—Worsening of relations.—Boer belief in British military weakness.—Milner's peace efforts (1899).—War.

The Second Boer War, 1899–1902

Boers prepared.—British unprepared.—Boers invaded Natal; besieged Kimberley, Mafeking and Ladysmith.—Buller's forces split; British defeats at Modder River, Stormberg, Magersfontein and Colenso (Dec. 1899).—Buller replaced by Roberts.—Roberts relieved Kimberley, captured Bloemfontein (Feb. and March

1900).—Mafeking relieved (May 1900).—Roberts entered Pretoria (June 1900).—Roberts returned to Britain.—Kitchener in command.—Mopping up operations —Block-house plan (1901).—Last Boers surrendered (March 1902).—Peace of Vereeniging (May 1902).

QUESTIONS

Answer the following questions briefly:

1. (a) How did European countries first interest themselves in South Africa?
   (b) How did the first Dutch settlement begin and develop?
   (c) In what way did the Cape become British?
   (d) What was the effect of the discovery of diamonds?
   (e) Who were the 'Uitlanders'?
   (f) Why was Rorke's Drift important?
   (g) What was the Jameson Raid?
   (h) Why did Paul Kruger hate the British?
2. Give the reasons for the quarrel between the Boers and the British which led to the Great Trek.
3. The following is an extract of the evidence of General Sir Redvers Buller, V.C., G.C.B., G.C.M.G., before the Royal Commission on the War in South Africa, February 1903:

   At 9.15 in the evening of 30th October, 1899 I arrived at Cape Town. I then learned that the Boers had utilised to the utmost the advantages given to them by their greater readiness for war. The small garrisons of Mafeking and Kimberley were beleaguered. . . . All the bridges over the Orange River, except that known as Orange River Bridge on the Western Railway, were in the hands of the enemy. Further, the Boers had already occupied the northern border of Cape Colony with some 3,000 men, while reports from the Dutch districts in Cape Colony pointed to considerable disaffection to British rule. In Natal Sir George White had had several encounters with the enemy . . . it was evident that he had failed to check their advance. The military situation on the 1st November was as follows:— On the side of Cape Colony the enemy had invested Mafeking and Kimberley. . . . They had crossed Bethulie bridge with about 3,000 men and were marching on Colesberg; 3,000 Orange Free State Boers were reported to be on the Basuto Border. . . .

   (a) What did General Buller mean by 'the advantages given to them by their greater readiness for war'?
   (b) What effect did this situation described by General Buller have on his plan of operations?
   (c) What plan did General Buller carry out?
   (d) What was the effect of this plan?

12 : The Union of South Africa

South Africa After the War

BY the Peace of Vereeniging the two Boer Republics were to be annexed by Britain but were to receive responsible government as soon as possible. British and Boers were to be completely equal and both languages were to be official. The British Government were to assist in the reconstruction of the country damaged by the war and a grant of £3,000,000 was made to replace stock and repair damage on the farms. Further help was to be available in the form of loans. With this aid the farms were soon restored and the diamond mines were soon working again. It was more difficult to get the gold mines into operation again since there was a shortage of labour on the Rand. To help the mines to begin working at full stretch the British Government gave permission for the importation of Chinese indentured labour. The employment of some 50,000 Chinese coolies was looked upon with disfavour and aroused great criticism in Britain, where the charge of 'Chinese slavery' helped in the defeat of the Conservatives and the landslide Liberal victory in the General Election of 1906.

Sir Alfred Milner, who had become Lord Milner, was still High Commissioner and his conciliatory measures did something to bring to an end the bitterness which followed the war. The Conservative Government under Mr Balfour considered granting responsible government to Transvaal but were defeated before being able to put it into operation. The year the Liberal Government, under Sir Henry Campbell-Bannerman, took office, Transvaal received responsible government. At the same time the employment of Chinese coolies ended. The next year, in 1907, the Orange River Colony, as it had been known since the end of the war, was also granted responsible government. Thus South Africa consisted of four colonies with responsible government: Matabeleland and Mashonaland, or Rhodesia as it was now known, and the Bechuanaland Protectorate, Basutoland and Swaziland which were ruled directly by Britain.

Lord Selborne succeeded Lord Milner as High Commissioner and in 1907 suggested that the four colonies should unite. Their representatives met in a National Convention at Durban in 1908, and later

Lord Milner.

at Cape Town. The Convention agreed broadly on the principle of unity, and it was agreed that the colonies should surrender their independence and not adopt a federal constitution. Each colony would give up its own Parliament and become a province of the Union. The Convention drew up a Draft Constitution and after this had been submitted to the four Parliaments it was agreed, subject to amendments.

South Africa Act, 1909

The British Parliament passed the South Africa Act in 1909. Under it the four colonies were to become provinces of the Union of South Africa. There was to be a Governor-General, and a Council of Ministers who were to be responsible to the Union Parliament. In a desire to please both the British and Boer elements of the population the administrative capital of the Union was to be at Pretoria in Transvaal and the Parliament at Cape Town. Parliament was to consist of two chambers; a Senate of 64 members, 16 from each province, and a House of Assembly of 121 members. The Assembly was not to exceed 150 members. Great care was taken to protect the rights of the coloured voters in Cape Province. They were not to lose the right to vote without a combined vote of both Houses with a two-thirds majority. The clauses which laid this down were known as the 'entrenched clauses'.

In each province there was to be an elected Provincial Council with certain limited powers. Each province was also to have an Administrator appointed by the Union Government and responsible to it. English and Dutch were to be official languages. The Act came into force on 31 May 1910.

This far-sighted and just action only seven years after the end of a bitter war did much to make many Boers friends of the British. Indeed, the first Prime Minister of the new Union Government was General Louis Botha who had been one of the most able Boer leaders in the war and he proved a great friend. Yet the hatred which was rooted so deeply in the past could not easily die and although many Boers found new friendship with Britain easy and were to demonstrate it in the years to come, many others still looked for separation from the British Empire.

It is interesting to note that Bechuanaland, Basutoland and Swaziland did not become part of the Union. Their chiefs and peoples felt that they were more likely to receive fair treatment from the British than from the South Africans and they remained directly under British rule. They were known as the High Commission Territories and were administered by a High Commissioner who was also British Ambassador to South Africa. Their white population is negligible. In 1966 Bechuanaland became independent as Botswana and Basutoland became independent as Lesotho, both remaining in the Commonwealth.

South African Politics

The feelings of the Boer people towards a nation which had treated them generously so soon after defeating them in war were soon to be tested. When the First World War broke out the division which had shown itself at the time of independence appeared again.

Two main parties appeared in the Union Parliament at once. Dr Jameson, who had been Prime Minister of Cape Colony from 1904

General Botha (1914).

L. to R. Sir William Morris and General Hertzog outside International Motor Show, 1930.

General Smuts (*right*) and South African troops.

to 1908, led a party known as the Unionists which believed in the predominance of British race and ideas and close ties with Britain. The South African Party, embracing both British and Boers, stood for close co-operation between both races and an end to all rivalry and bitterness in the interests of the new Dominion as a whole. This party, led by General Botha, won power. Botha, and his associates Smuts and Hertzog, had fought against the British with distinction, but he and Smuts became extremely pro-British and outstanding Commonwealth statesmen. Hertzog left the South African Party in 1912 and formed the Nationalists who drew to them all the extreme Dutch elements based on traditional hatred of Britain and still looking for an independent republic.

When war began in 1914, Botha guaranteed to defend the Union and led the Union forces successfully against a pro-German rising under De Wet. He also sent an expedition against German South-West Africa and later in the war sent a considerable South African army to Europe while 50,000 South Africans under General Smuts defeated the Germans in East Africa. Except for a small minority, South Africans of both races were loyal to Britain. Although General Hertzog took no action against his Government or Britain, he criticised South African support of the British war effort. After the war the Union received the ex-German colony of South-West Africa under mandate from the League of Nations and has administered it ever since. It is one of the few mandated territories which have not been granted self-government. Because of the attitude of the Nationalists, the Unionists supported the South African Party, and on Botha's death in 1919, when General Smuts succeeded him as leader of the Party and Prime Minister, they joined with it and Smuts led a combined United party to victory in 1921. They remained in power until 1924 when Hertzog and the Nationalists won the election with the support of the Labour Party which had been gaining in strength. Although a section of the Nationalist Party wanted a republic, Hertzog gave no support to this view when Prime Minister and, in fact, pursued a moderate policy. Because of his success at the Imperial Conference of 1926, where the equality of status of the Dominions and Great Britain was declared, he was able to persuade his followers to support his policy. Hertzog remained in power until 1939 and except for a controversy over the subject of the South African flag it was a largely uneventful period. A compromise was reached whereby the Union Jack was to be flown beside a South African flag which included the Transvaal and Orange Free State flags together with the Union Jack. The Statute of Westminster of 1931 had confirmed the decision

South African troops, Second World War.

of the Imperial Conference of 1926, and the Union was now an independent country. This again quietened the extremists.

The Second World War again showed the loyalty of many South Africans. Yet Hertzog broke with Smuts over the question of participation in the war and advocated neutrality. Throughout the war there was a strong anti-war minority stimulated by Nazi propaganda in Afrikaans from one of their radio stations. The Nationalist party split into three factions led by Nicolaas Havenga, Daniel Malan and Oswald Pirow. There were organisations similar to Nazi storm-troopers known as the Broederbond and Ossewabrandwag or Sentinels of the Ox-Wagon. These not only advocated neutrality and secession from the Commonwealth but also a totalitarian form of government dominated by 'Afrikaaner Volk'. It is significant that many of these people formed the basis of the Nationalist Party after the war. Nevertheless, Smuts was able to muster the support of English-speaking South Africans and a great many of the Afrikaaners and South Africa played a significant part in the war. South African troops fought in East Africa and the Middle East and the South African Air Force flew beside the Royal Air Force, mainly in the Middle East.

The first general election after the war in 1948 resulted in a victory for the Nationalists under Dr Daniel Malan. Smuts led the United Party in opposition until his death in 1950. Mr J. G. Strauss succeeded him but retired in 1956 and Sir de Villiers Graaff led the party from then onwards. The Nationalists have retained power ever since, first under Mr Strijdom until 1958, and then under Dr Verwoerd, who was assassinated in 1966. He was succeeded by Mr Vorster.

Apartheid and Problems Today

Since the Second World War the interest of the world had been focused on South Africa.

South African troops surveying the land.

When the South Africa Act became law in 1910 it contained clauses which set up a Senate of 64 members, limited the size of the House of Assembly to 150 members, and guaranteed the rights of coloured voters in Cape Province. This was designed to ensure equality of representatives for the provinces, and fair treatment of coloured people in Cape Province at least. The Separate Representation of Voters Act of 1951 passed by the Union Parliament provided four members of the Assembly to represent coloured voters but all Bantu lost the right to vote completely, even for their own representatives, in November 1959. The Senate Act of 1960 also passed by the Union Parliament, reconstituted the Senate. It now contains 54 members, 11 appointed by the Government, and 43 elected, 14 for Transvaal, 11 for Cape Province, 8 each for Natal and the Orange Free State, and 2 for South-West Africa. The House of Assembly now contains 160 representatives, 52 from Cape Province, 16 from Natal, 68 from Transvaal, and 14 from Orange Free State, with 6 from South-West Africa. It will be seen that representation in both the Senate and the House of Assembly now favours the largely Afrikaans areas and consequently the Nationalist Party. This is undoubtedly one of the main reasons why the United Party has never won power again and the opponents of the Nationalists accuse them of so arranging the representation that they cannot be beaten. Certainly some of the main safeguards of the South Africa Act including the 'entrenched clauses' have been removed.

In October 1960 a referendum was held among white voters who decided by a very small majority on republican status, although still within the Commonwealth. The Union of South Africa became a republic on 31 May 1961 and withdrew from the Commonwealth largely because of pressure from other members at the Commonwealth Prime Ministers' Conference of March 1961.

There had long been criticism of South Africa's racial policies which under the Nationalist Government denied basic rights of citizenship to the Bantu. The Nationalist Party had long favoured a policy of Apartheid or segregation of the Bantu peoples from the whites. This involved the eventual establishment of Bantu states in which the Africans would develop naturally by themselves and certain such states of Bantustan have already been created. The policy of Apartheid in action had meant to the Bantu not only the deprivation of the right to vote but the Pass Laws restricting their right of movement and much more legislation denying basic human rights. The reaction that this policy has aroused among the Bantu has been ruthlessly suppressed and demonstrations have been dealt with by force.

Bantu children drawing water near Johannesburg.

Such an incident was the Sharpeville Massacre of March 1960, when 72 Bantu were shot in the back and killed by South African police while attending a demonstration against the Pass Laws. It was the reaction of some of the Commonwealth countries to these policies which brought about South Africa's withdrawal from the Commonwealth.

The United Party has always supported a policy of limited Apartheid but without the denial of rights to the Bantu of the Nationalist policy. The Progressive Party containing many moderate opponents of Apartheid has sought to unite people of all races but has never succeeded in gaining more than a very few seats in the House of Assembly. The Liberal Party has fought Apartheid wholeheartedly and this has resulted in many of its leaders suffering imprisonment or exile. The Pan-African Congress was formed in 1959 by Africans to protest against Apartheid by non-violent means.

The Nationalist Party has gained most of its supporters from Afrikaaner elements of the population and their attitude towards the Bantu has stemmed from the teaching of the Dutch Reformed Church that God had created white men superior to black. Other churches in South Africa have opposed the policy. Notable among the church leaders who have been opponents of Apartheid are Archbishop Joost de Blank of Cape Town and Bishop Ambrose Reeves of Johannesburg, who was forced to leave the country to escape arrest. The policy of Apartheid has resulted in segregation on sports grounds; no coloured man may play cricket for South Africa for example; in railway stations, theatres, cinemas, post offices, buses and trams. Intermarriage of white and black has been illegal since 1949. When the changes were made which violated the Act of 1909, the opponents of the Nationalists appealed to the South African Supreme Court who ruled against the Government. The Nationalist Government then created a High Court of Parliament to set aside the decisions of the Supreme Court. This and the alteration of membership of the Senate and the House of Assembly, to which reference has already been made, ensured the supremacy of the Nationalists.

Even before the crisis provided by the intensification of the Apartheid policy since the war, successive South African Governments have had difficulties with the Indian population many of whom had been encouraged to come during the nineteenth century and Mr Gandhi was prominent just after the First World War for his leadership of them. Segregation was enforced as a policy and the Indian Government protested particularly at conditions under which the Indians had to live. In spite of attempts to find a solution, relations between India, Pakistan and South Africa have deteriorated since the Second World War and complaints have been made to the United Nations at the treatment of Indians. Thus it will be seen that the racial question was not confined to the Bantu.

In spite of criticism of South Africa in the United Nations and pressure from other countries, particularly the newly emergent African nations, the country has continued to develop and is extremely prosperous. Out of a total population of nearly sixteen millions, over three millions are whites, nearly eleven millions Africans and the remainder Asian and coloured.

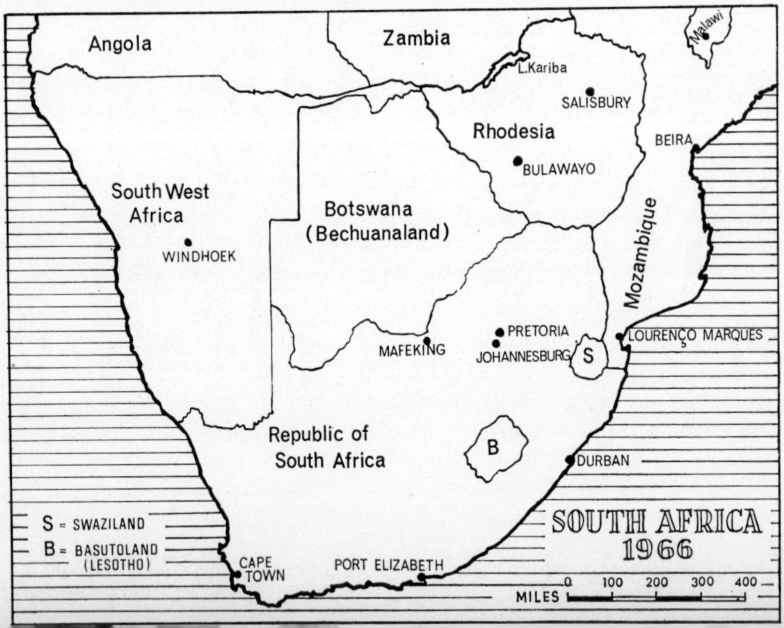

SUMMARY

South Africa After the War

Peace of Vereeniging (1902).—Transvaal and Orange Free State annexed by Britain.—Responsible government as soon as possible.—Equality of British and Boers; English and Dutch as official languages.—Financial assistance for reconstruction of country.—Chinese indentured labour.—Outcry against 'Chinese slavery'.—Responsible government for Transvaal (1906).—End of Chinese labour (1906).—Orange River Colony received responsible government.—Selborne plan for unity (1907).—National Convention of Durban and Cape Town (1908).

South Africa Act, 1909

Four colonies to become provinces of the Union, with a Governor-General and Council of Ministers.—Administrative capital at Pretoria; parliamentary capital at Cape Town.—'Entrenched clauses' to protect coloured voters in Cape Province; Provincial Councils.—Administrator for each province.—English and Dutch as official languages.—Act in force 3 May 1910.—Bechuanaland, Basutoland and Swaziland not part of Union, known as High Commission Territories. —Bechuanaland (Botswana) and Basutoland (Lesotho) independent within Commonwealth (1966).

South African Politics

Unionist Party under Jameson.—South African Party under Botha.—Hertzog left South African Party to form Nationalists (1912).—Small anti-British party in First World War.—South African and Unionist Parties joined under Smuts (1921).—Nationalists won power under Hertzog with support of Labour Party (1924).—Effect of Imperial Conference of 1926 and Statute of Westminster (1931).—Loyalty of Union in Second World War; Nazi-type organisations among Nationalists.—Nationalists won power under Malan (1948).—Remained in power under Strijdom and Verwoerd.—United Party as opposition under Smuts, Strauss and de Villiers Graaff.—Verwoerd assassinated and succeeded by Vorster (1966).

Apartheid and Problems Today

Separate Representation of Voters Act (1951) provided four members to represent coloured voter.—Bantu lost vote (1959).—violation of Act of 1909.—Reorganisation of Senate and House of Assembly to ensure Nationalist majority.—Referendum voted narrowly in favour of republic (1960).—South Africa left Commonwealth after Commonwealth Prime Ministers' Conference (1961).—Nationalists' extreme policy of Apartheid.—Idea of Bantustan states.—United Party's limited policy of Apartheid.—Opposition to Apartheid by Progressive Party, Liberal Party and Pan-African Congress.—Appeal to South African Supreme Court against violation of Act of 1909.—Supreme Court ruled violation of Act null and void (1952).—Nationalist Government passed High Court of Parliament Act (1952) setting up High Court of Parliament which could overrule Supreme Court.—Indian problem.—India's complaint to United Nations.

QUESTIONS

Answer the following questions briefly:

1. (a) List the main points of the Peace of Vereeniging (1902).
   (b) List the main points of the South Africa Act (1909).
   (c) What were the main political parties in South Africa up until 1914?
   (d) What are the main political parties today and what do they stand for?
   (e) What steps have the Nationalist Party taken to ensure that they retain power?
2. What is meant by 'Apartheid'?
   Why do you consider it has become a question of world controversy today?
3. In one of the last speeches that Cecil Rhodes made before his death in 1902, he said to the Loyalists of Cape Town:

   You think you have beaten the Dutch. It is not so. The Dutch are not beaten. What is beaten is Krugerism, a corrupt and evil Government, no more Dutch in essence than English. No! the Dutch are as vigorous and unconquered today as they have ever been: the country is still as much theirs as yours, and you will have to live and work with them hereafter as in the past.

   (a) What did Rhodes mean by Krugerism? Do you think it still exists today?
   (b) What evidence was there of Krugerism in the twenty years after the end of the Second Boer War?
   (c) What influence do you consider Smuts had on the relations between British and Dutch?
   (d) What are the attitudes of British and Dutch today in South Africa?

India: The Third Mysore War. The storming of Seringapatem, 1799.

13 : India Before the Mutiny

The Effects of the Seven Years War

THE end of the Seven Years War in 1763 left Britain the sole real power in India. Britain controlled Bengal and most of the Carnatic and the Circars while French influence had almost gone.

During Clive's absence in England, Mir Jaffir who depended upon British support had been overthrown and replaced by his son-in-law Mir Cassim. The wrath of the Indians had been aroused by the behaviour of many of the officials of the East India Company. Although the Nawab of Bengal nominally controlled the area he tended to be a tax-collector for the British and consequently was prepared to pay to make his position secure. This was a situation which demanded the utmost honesty from the Company's servants if it was not to be abused. Many of the officials were not completely honest and were prepared to make the most of their opportunities. It was not yet the time when British colonial officers saw a duty in caring for the welfare of their native peoples and they regarded their service in India as a chance to make a quick fortune. Since life in a tropical country with its cholera, fever and great heat took a heavy toll and a great many died on service, it is not really surprising that they were prepared to make what money they could. The salaries of the junior officials were extremely small, and all Company officers regarded it as their right to carry on private trade without paying normal customs dues. Since they often sold their right to native traders, this brought chaos to the finances of the state in which they served. Mir Cassim was prepared to pay for his position with gifts but not to see this private trade ruin the economy of the Bengal. He and his army attacked the British and massacred the Agent and merchants at Patna in 1763, but was soon overthrown by British and loyal Indian troops and Mir Jaffir was placed back on the throne. Mir Cassim then joined with the Nabob of Oudh, and the Mogul, or nominal Indian ruler, at Delhi and entered Bengal with a considerable army. He was decisively defeated at the Battle of Buxar by Munro in 1764.

Clive, now Lord Clive, returned to India as Governor of Bengal the next year with orders from the directors of the Company to

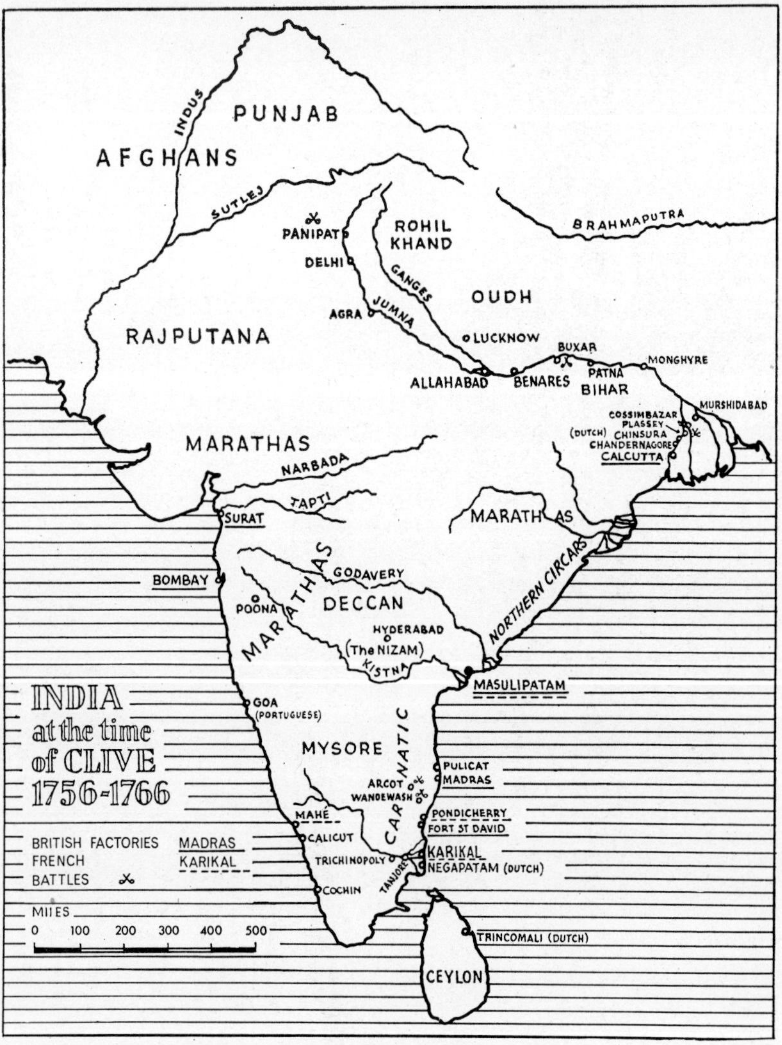

restore the situation. Although his health had been ruined by service in India, he answered their call.

The Achievements of Clive

Clive first signed the Treaty of Allahabad in 1765 with the Mogul. The Nabobs were restored, the Emperor recognised the Company's possession of their territory and their right to collect the revenues of Bengal, Bihar, Orissa and the northern Circars. The Company was to make grants to the Mogul and the Nabob of Bengal.

The next task was to tackle the corruption of the Company's

servants and the dishonesty of tax-collectors both Indian and British. Clive dismissed the dishonest council and replaced them with his own nominees. He made the Company's servants sign undertakings not to accept presents from natives. He ended the private trading system and took steps to improve the inadequate salaries of officials. He also took steps to reduce the large allowances of military officers and when they started a mutiny he suppressed it quickly. The mutiny itself was evidence of the bad state of affairs and Clive's strong measures brought angry resentment. Accusations were made that Clive had himself taken part in the corruption and he was recalled to England in 1767. The House of Commons appointed a committee to investigate the charges against him. The House passed a resolution that 'Robert, Lord Clive hath rendered great and meritorious service to his country.' Although he had been cleared of the charges against him, he was deeply affected by the scandal and committed suicide in 1774.

Between 1767 and 1772 the corruption in India continued and in 1770 there was a serious famine in Bengal and the situation was so bad that the Company had to send out a governor strong enough to deal with it.

Lord North's Regulating Act and Warren Hastings

Warren Hastings became Governor of Bengal in 1772. The events of the few previous years had made the British Government realise that all was not well with Company rule. In 1773 it passed what became known as Lord North's Regulating Act. It did not declare British sovereignty but it regulated the Company's functions and accepted that it would work under the British Government. The Governor of Bengal was to be styled Governor-General of India and he was to have a Council of four members to assist him. A Supreme Court of Justice with English judges was to be set up at Calcutta. English law was to apply to Englishmen, but Hindus and Mohammedans were to be judged by their own laws.

Warren Hastings was thus the first Governor-General and he had great difficulty with his Council from the beginning. He was a man of great ability who had served the Company in a subordinate position during the great days of Clive. It was unfortunate that three of the four members of the Council were opposed to him and led by Philip Francis who treated him extremely badly. They criticised his every action, reversed his wise decisions and made it impossible for him to carry out his policy. Only Barwell of the Council supported him, while Monson and Clavering joined Francis against him. This tended to make the Indians see Hastings as a man without power.

A wealthy Indian named Nuncomar produced a document which purported to show that Hastings had taken bribes. The Council received this with delight but almost immediately charges were brought against Nuncomar himself of forgery committed some time before and his document was shown to be forged. The Chief Justice, Sir Elijah Impey, sentenced him to death. Although the charges were proved and the sentence deserved, Hastings' enemies accused Impey of abusing his position. In 1776 Monson died, Clavering died the next year and Hastings was able to control the Council more easily, both Wheler and Coote, the newly appointed members, supporting him. Hastings was able to accuse Francis of dishonesty and in the duel with pistols which followed this, Francis was seriously wounded and returned to England.

Hastings was now able to proceed with his policy of tightening up administration and cleaning up corruption. He enforced the rules against private trading, checked corruption, and replaced the Indian tax-collectors with British.

In 1780 the relations with the Indians in the Ganges valley became difficult. When the Rajah of Benares refused to pay the money he owed to the Company, Hastings deposed him and in the same year, he seized the treasure of the Begums of Oudh because the Nabob refused to pay the sums due. Naturally, Hastings was criticised for this, but he felt it necessary to enforce the rights of the Company and also to collect sufficient revenue to defend India against the dangers which were now threatening.

Britain was at war with her American colonies and France joined the war in 1778. The French backed two of the native powers, the Mahrattas and the state of Mysore against the British. The Mahrattas were a warlike people from Western and Central India. They were led by three chieftains, Sindhia, Holkar and Bhonsla, who owed nominal allegiance to the Peshwar of Poona. The three chieftains attempted to overthrow the Peshwar and Hastings intervened to help him, realising that the Mahrattas could be a serious menace. Although his forces were small he crushed the Mahrattas in the First Mahratta War from 1779–82 and then turned his attention to Hyder Ali. Hyder Ali, the Rajah of Mysore, under French influence, invaded the Carnatic and threatened Madras. Hastings sent a force under Sir Eyre Coote to deal with him and there followed the First Mysore War from 1781–84. He defeated Hyder Ali at the battles of Porto Novo and Arni in 1781 and 1782. In the latter year Hyder Ali died and his son Tipu made peace in 1784 after the Treaty of Versailles of 1783 had brought the war with France to an end. A French fleet had

Warren Hastings.

arrived at Madras to support Hyder Ali and several battles had been fought with British naval squadrons.

Hastings had saved India from the French by his energetic action and the Mahrattas and Mysore had been halted although they were to cause much further trouble. During the fighting the French factories at Chandernagore, Pondicherry and Mahe had been captured by the British, but these were restored in 1783.

Pitt's India Act was passed in 1784 and Warren Hastings retired the next year. His enemies had been working against him and his old Council opponent, now Sir Philip Francis, turned the public against him in Britain. On his return he was impeached, being charged with instituting a false case against Nuncomar, of exceeding his authority against the Rajah of Benares and the Nabob of Oudh. He was also accused of exterminating a whole group known as the Rohillas. They were marauders who had swept down from the mountains and attacked Oudh. The Nabob appealed for military help and Hastings helped him to restore order. His trial lasted from 1788 to 1795 and cost him the whole of his fortune. He was acquitted on every charge and he was granted a pension from the East India Company which enabled him to live comfortably in retirement until his death in 1818. Hastings had been a great Governor-General and had served India and his country well, and the charges should never have been brought.

Pitt's India Act, 1784

The Regulating Act was not working as satisfactorily as had been hoped. In 1784, William Pitt, the Younger, introduced an India Act

Arthur Wellesley,
Duke of Wellington.

designed to remedy it. It was a sensible measure and was to last for well over fifty years. It separated the commercial and political functions of the Company. A Secretary of State was appointed to deal with Indian Affairs in London with a Board of Control to assist. The Board of Control was to be responsible for all political and military matters and for the appointment of the Governor-General and senior officials, although the officials were in theory appointed by the Company. Since the appointments needed the approval of the Board they were responsible for them. The Company was to continue its commercial functions but the real control of India passed into the hands of the Governor-General and the Secretary of State. Although the Council in India had power to overrule the Governor-General if their decision was unanimous, this was withdrawn in 1786 and the Governor-General became supreme.

The enhanced position of the Governor-General attracted men of great ability and it was fortunate for India that such fine administrators served her for so long. The first of these was Lord Cornwallis, who had distinguished himself in the American War of Independence. His term of office was from 1786 until 1793 during which he defeated Tipu, the son of Hyder Ali, in the Second Mysore War from 1790 until 1792. He carried out a series of reforms in Bengal known as the Permanent Settlement of the Bengal revenue. After five years under Sir John Shore, when trouble with the Mahrattas again began, the Marquis of Wellesley, the elder brother of the Duke of Wellington, became Governor-General in 1798. Britain and France were once more at war and the latter was anxious to challenge British power in India. French agents went to the courts of Indian rulers who were known to be willing to see the decline of British rule.

Development of British Rule

The first task of the new Governor-General was to defeat the allies of France and to make British rule secure. Tipu listened readily to the French agents and to show his sympathy with the Revolution called himself 'Citizen' Tipu and prepared for war against the British. The Nizam of Hyderabad was also preparing for war and he, too, had a large army trained and officered by the French. Wellesley took action at once. He gave both Tipu and the Nizam the alternative of dismissing their French officers and advisers and reducing their armies, or of fighting. If they agreed to the former they would pay subsidies to the Company and in return would receive military protection. Napoleon and his armies were in Egypt and Wellesley knew that they might soon be moving eastwards. The Nizam of Hyderabad accepted the terms since he was frightened of the Mahrattas and realised that a war against the British would weaken him. Tipu, however, would not accept the terms and the Third Mysore War resulted in 1798. Wellesley sent his younger brother, Colonel Arthur Wellesley, later to become the Duke of Wellington, against him at his capital of Seringapatem. The British stormed the city and captured it, Tipu dying in the breach. A descendant of the former ruler was placed on the throne in his place although some of the territory of Mysore was taken and divided between the Mahrattas, the Nizam of Hyderabad and the British. Wellesley also annexed the territories of Doab, Rohilkund, Tanjore and the Carnatic, the latter being added to Madras.

Wellesley had succeeded in extending British rule and influence and in suppressing the disorder and misrule in some Indian states. The Mahrattas were still a menace, although the chiefs were fighting among themselves. In 1802 the Peshwar fled to the British for protection and signed the Treaty of Bassein by which he accepted the guidance of the Company. Sindhia and Bhonsla thereupon joined to make war on the British and the Peshwar. General Arthur Wellesley commanded the British forces which invaded the Deccan in what was to be called the Second Mahratta War. He defeated the Mahrattas at the Battle of Assaye in September 1803, in spite of the fact that they had artillery, French officers and outnumbered the British by odds of ten to one. He won another victory soon afterwards at Argaum and General Lake captured Delhi and Agra and finally defeated the

Mahrattas at Laswaree. Sindhia and Bhonsla accepted British terms; some territory was surrendered and they entered into subsidiary alliances by which there was British supervision of their Government.

In 1804, however, one of the Mahratta chiefs, Holkar, whose forces had not been among those decisively defeated, declared war and after an initial disaster was beaten in 1806.

Wellesley's policy of extending British power and influence, eliminating the French and suppressing un-cooperative leaders, aroused considerable opposition in England and the rising of Holkar brought matters to a head. After disagreements Wellesley resigned in 1805. He had been one of the greatest Governors of India and in only seven years he had transformed India, making Britain the paramount power.

He was succeeded by Lord Cornwallis who returned for a second tour as Governor-General but died soon after arrival. Of Sir George Barlow and Lord Minto who were the next Governor-Generals little need be said except that Minto opened diplomatic relations with the Sikhs and with Afghanistan.

In 1813 the Company lost the monopoly of trade with India which was opened to all merchants. This marked its decline as a trading company and it ceased to function as such in 1833.

The Marquis of Hastings became Governor-General in 1813 and his ten years term was marked by vigorous action to maintain British prestige and power. He made war first upon the Gurkhas, the mountaineers from Nepal, who had been plundering the plains. After their submission they remained completely loyal to Britain and Gurkha soldiers have served in the British Indian Army ever since. The disbandment of native armies in Central India caused by Wellesley's policy had resulted in many soldiers finding themselves unemployed. They formed themselves into robber bands called the Pindaris, supported secretly by some Mahratta chiefs. Hastings took strong action against the Pindaris and suppressed them, but this caused the Mahrattas to rise once again. The Third Mahratta War was fought from 1817 to 1818 and the Mahrattas were finally crushed and their power was completely destroyed. The territory of the Peshwar was annexed and joined to Bombay and the Mahratta chiefs were strictly controlled. In the governor-generalship of Lord Amherst, Hastings' successor, the First Burmese War was fought from 1824 to 1826. Burma had been seriously ill-treating British traders and Amherst moved against the Burmese and annexed Assam, Arakan and Tenasserin.

Reforms and Further Development

Lord William Bentinck became Governor-General in 1828 and his seven years in office were marked by reforms which had far-reaching effects. For many years the Thugs, a band of murderers, had infested the roads of India and had attacked those who did not join with them in the worship of the goddess Kali. The Hindus had traditionally followed the custom of burning widows alive on the funeral pyres of their dead husbands. This was known as 'suttee'. Bentinck suppressed 'thuggee' and the Thugs who practised it and forbade 'suttee'. Although he received some Indian support, the suppression of 'suttee' was resented and it continued in secret to a certain extent. He also improved the facilities for the education of Indians, founding colleges for them, and ended newspaper censorship. These were sensible and necessary reforms but were probably introduced too quickly and were to be the cause of difficulties.

During his tour of office the Governor-General of Bengal officially became the Governor-General of India.

The North-West Frontier, famous as a place of almost constant fighting of some sort or another, began to become important in Indian history about this time. The ways through the mountains including the Khyber Pass were largely in the hands of the Afghans who had often in the past raided India. Between British India and the mountains were the independent states of Sind and the Punjab. The eyes of Russia were beginning to turn towards India and Russian influence was beginning to move towards Afghanistan. Not only Britain but other European countries were beginning to look upon the Russian menace as replacing that of France.

Lord Auckland, who had succeeded Bentinck as Governor-General in 1836, decided to support Shah Shuja who claimed the throne of Afghanistan, in order to ensure that British influence was supreme. He sent a force to invade Afghanistan in 1839 to depose Dost Mohammed, the Amir. Thus began the First Afghan War which was to last until 1842. The force was successful, but the proud Afghans resented the intervention of a foreign power and under the son of Dost Mohammed, Akbar Khan, they rose against Shah Shuja and the British troops supporting him. Shah Shuja had a British Resident and the latter was murdered in the rising. The British Commander at Kabul, the Afghan capital, agreed to evacuate the country and was promised safe conduct. The force of 4,000 soldiers and 12,000 civilians set off through the snow-covered mountain passes in December 1841 and was attacked by Afghan tribesmen. It was completely destroyed except for one survivor, Dr. Brydon, who struggled

Lord Dalhousie.

to the Fort of Jalalabad in January 1842 with the news of the massacre. Lord Ellenborough, who had just succeeded Auckland as Governor-General, sent a strong force into Afghanistan. They rescued prisoners and defeated the Afghans, but Shah Shuja had been killed and Dost Mohammed was Amir once more. The British had to accept his rule and the failure of the enterprise seriously damaged British prestige.

The chiefs of Sind had been allies of the Afghans and their allegiance to the Company was demanded. When they refused, a force under Sir Charles Napier conquered the state.

The next state of the Punjab had been ruled by Ranjit Singh who had been friendly with the British and had built up a fine, well-trained army. When he died in 1839 there was no one to succeed him and the Sikh chiefs quarrelled among themselves. After the loss of British prestige following the Afghan War, the Sikh chiefs saw an opportunity to use their splendid soldiers and to conquer Central India. They crossed the River Sutlej in 1845 and invaded British India. British forces under Sir Hugh Gough, heavily outnumbered, were defeated with heavy losses in several battles, but eventually beat the Sikh army at the battle of Sobraon in 1846 and took Lahore the capital of the Punjab. This ended the First Sikh War and a protectorate was declared over the Punjab with a British Resident at Lahore. Lord Hardinge, the Governor-General, who had taken office in 1846, did not want to annex the Punjab but peace was short-lived.

A year after Lord Dalhousie became Governor-General in 1849, the Sikhs rose again, and the Second Sikh War broke out after the murder of British officers. After initial setbacks, Sir Hugh Gough defeated the Sikhs at Gujerat and the war was over within a year. This time Dalhousie annexed the Punjab and it was ruled for the next few years with great ability and wisdom by Sir Henry and Sir John Lawrence. The Lawrences introduced a system of land settlement, reduced taxation, built irrigation works, roads and bridges and maintained law and order. Under them the Punjab prospered and became a loyal province.

In 1852 the Second Burmese War was fought and Indian troops fought outside the borders of their country. Some of the high-caste Sepoys felt that this degraded them in the eyes of their people and this was to contribute to future difficulties.

Dalhousie introduced many reforms, including public works, but it was his constitutional measures which led to the Mutiny.

The Causes of the Indian Mutiny

British troops were now at their weakest. Many had been withdrawn to serve in the Crimean War and the Persian War. This shortage was noticed by many of the discontented and it was also seen that losses caused by the Afghan and Sikh Wars had not been made good. Matters were made worse by the division of existing forces into the Company's Army and the Royal Army with two separate chains of command.

However, it was the too rapid introduction of western reforms, and the constitutional measures of Lord Dalhousie which caused the greatest discontent. He introduced the 'Doctrine of Lapse' which laid down that territories ruled by Indian princes should lapse to British rule if they should die childless. For years it had been the custom that in such a situation the princes would adopt an heir not necessarily related to them and when they died their title and property would pass to them. Dalhousie would not recognise this and when a prince died childless, annexed his land. He annexed five small states and some of the Mahratta lands which became the Central Provinces.

Dalhousie deposed the Nabob of Oudh in 1856 for gross incompetence and misrule. Although his people were oppressed and undoubtedly gained from the annexation, this added to the resentment of many Indians. Naturally this was greatest in the courts of the princes concerned with the 'Doctrine of Lapse' or danger of deposition.

All these factors contributed to the Mutiny, but it was a rising of soldiers and its basic causes were military. The Bengal army numbered

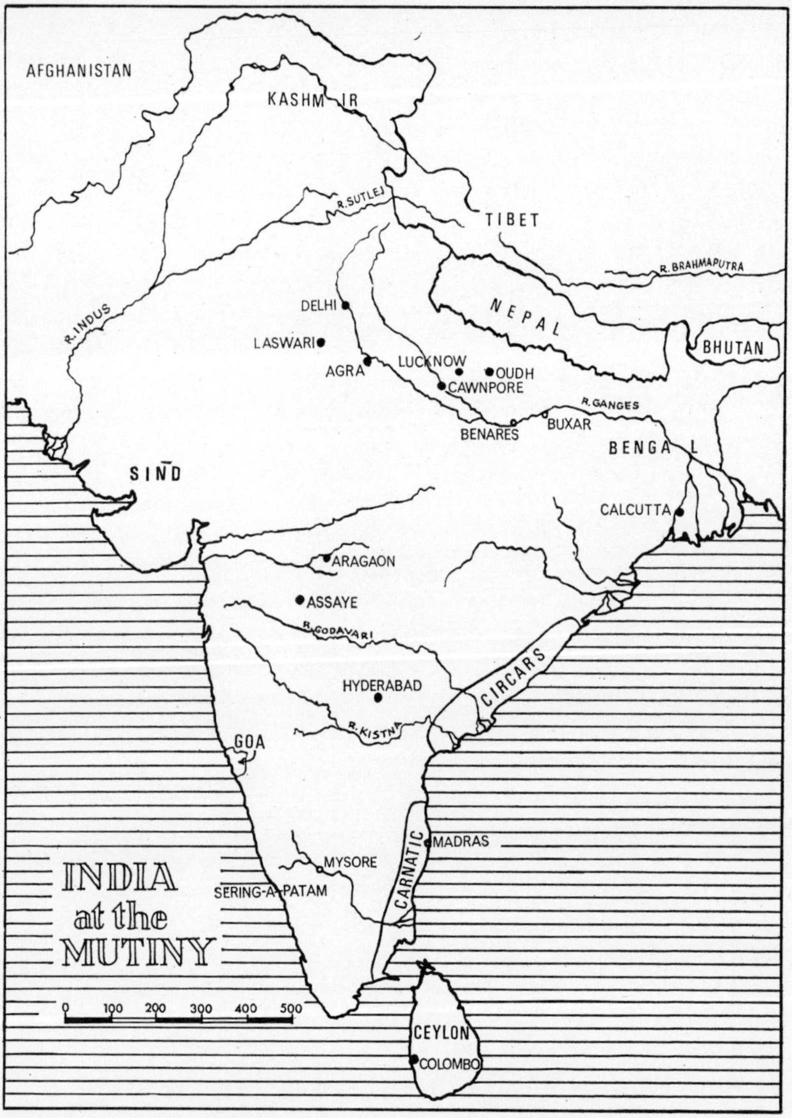

very nearly half the British Indian troops and many were recruited from Oudh. There were far too few British troops in the Ganges Valley and this weakness was apparent. By coincidence it was also the hundredth anniversary of the Battle of Plassey and to the superstitious Indians this was of note. Perhaps the main immediate cause of the rising was the introduction of the new Enfield rifle in place of the old smooth-bore musket. It was still a muzzle-loader and it was necessary

Cawnpore: The massacre.

for the soldiers to bite off the ends of the cartridges before pouring the powder into the barrel and ramming down the bullet. In order to preserve the cartridge it was greased, and a rumour travelled around that the grease used was animal fat. Since to the Hindu the cow was a sacred animal and to the Mohammedan the pig was unclean, the biter considered himself defiled by the grease. The rifles were withdrawn as soon as the situation was realised, but the damage had been done. Indian unleavened cakes, called 'chappattis' were passed from hand to hand, a traditional sign of trouble.

The Indian Mutiny, 1857

In May 1857 the regiments at Meerut murdered their officers and marched on Delhi. The mutineers proclaimed the ancient Mogul as emperor and the rising spread. It failed to raise Calcutta where the British were strong and the Punjab would not join the revolt, but most of the basin of the Ganges was involved.

Dalhousie had just returned to England and had been replaced by Lord Canning who had the Mutiny to suppress.

At Cawnpore, Nana Sahib, who was a dispossessed heir of the Peshwar under the 'Doctrine of Lapse', besieged some British officers, soldiers and civilians, with women and children. After twenty-one days siege, short of water, they surrendered on the promise of safe conduct down river to Allahabad where there was a British garrison. On their way to safety in July 1857 the whole party of some eight hundred were murdered by the mutineers on the orders of Nana Sahib.

At Lucknow, a small British force of soldiers and civilians including many women and children was besieged in the Residency under

The relief of Lucknow by General Havelock.

Sir Henry Lawrence of Punjab fame. They held out from 1st July for three months until General Sir Henry Havelock reached them with a relief column. Lawrence had been killed and Brigadier Inglis had succeeded him. Havelock's small force was not strong enough to raise the siege completely and joined the besieged for a further seven weeks, during which the heroic garrison defended itself against a force of 60,000 mutineers. On 14 November Sir Colin Campbell with a strong force relieved them.

This was virtually the end of the Mutiny, although it was well into 1858 before order was fully restored and the mutineers rounded up. Delhi had been recaptured in September, Oudh was recovered early in 1858 and Sir Hugh Rose's brilliant campaign crushed the mutineers in Central India during the same year.

The Mutiny had been confined to the Sepoys of the Bengal army and some of the troops in Central India. The Sikhs of the Punjab had remained completely loyal under the leadership of Sir John Lawrence and the greater part of India was loyal or neutral. Great assistance was given to the British by the Gurkhas of Nepal. It was an entirely military rising, the civilians generally taking little or no part. The ringleaders were severely punished, proved murderers being executed, but Lord Canning insisted upon pardoning those who were misguided. This won for him the rather contemptuous nickname 'Clemency Canning' from many of the British, but was to help greatly in the future when changes took place as the result of the Mutiny.

SUMMARY

The Effects of the Seven Years War

Decline of French influence.—Britain controlled Bengal, most of Carnatic and the Circars.—Corruption among Company's officials; Mir Jaffir deposed, and replaced by Mir Cassim in Bengal.—Mir Cassim attacked British.—Patna massacre (1763).—Joined with Mogul and Nabob of Oudh and invaded Bengal.—Defeated at Buxar by Munro (1764).—Clive returned to India as Governor of Bengal (1765).

The Achievements of Clive

Treaty of Allahabad (1765).—Stamped out corruption.—Ended private trading by officials.—Improved officials' salaries.—Accusations against Clive as result of resentment.—Recalled (1767) to face charges of corruption.—Committee of House of Commons.—Cleared of charges but committed suicide (1774).—With absence of Clive, corruption continued.

Lord North's Regulating Act and Warren Hastings

Warren Hastings as Governor of Bengal (1772).—Lord North's Regulating Act (1773).—Governor of Bengal to be Governor-General of India.—Company under Government with Council appointed to assist Governor-General.—Supreme Court set up.—Hastings' difficulty with Council.—Nuncomar incident; sentenced to death.—Changes in Council.—Deadlock ended.—Hastings' measures against corruption.—Deposition of Rajah of Benares (1780).—Seizure of treasure of Begums of Oudh.—War of American Independence.—France backed Mahrattas and Mysore.—First Mahratta War (1779–82).—Mahrattas crushed.—First Mysore War (1781–84).—Hyder Ali defeated by Coote at Porto Novo (1781) and Arni (1782).—Hyder Ali succeeded by son Tipu.—Tipu made peace (1784).—Pitt's India Act (1784).—Hastings retired (1785).—Impeached on return to Britain.—Trial lasted from 1788–95.—Hastings acquitted on every charge.

Pitt's India Act, 1784

Commercial and political functions of Company separated.—Secretary of State for India appointed.—Board of Control to assist.—Governor-General became supreme in India after 1786.—Cornwallis (1786–93).—Defeated Tipu in Second Mysore War (1790–92).—Wellesley (1798–1805).—French support for Indian rulers during French Wars.

Development of British Rule

'Citizen' Tipu's friendship with Revolutionary France.—He and Nizam of Hyderabad planned war against British.—Wellesley's strong action.—Nizam agreed to terms.—Third Mysore War (1798).—Colonel Wellesley, later Duke of Wellington, defeated Tipu at Seringapatem.—Tipu killed.—Second Mahratta War (1802–06).—General Wellesley defeated Mahrattas at Assaye (1803); and Argaum (1803).—Lake captured Delhi and Agra and defeated Mahrattas at Laswaree (1803).—Wellesley resigned because of criticism and disagreements (1805).—Company lost monopoly of trade with India (1813); ceased to function as trading company (1833).—Marquis of Hastings as Governor-General (1813–23).—War with Gurkhas of Nepal—suppression of Pindaris—Third Mahratta War (1817–18).—Mahratta power completely destroyed.—Lord Amherst, Governor-General (1823–28).—First Burmese War (1824–26).

Reforms and Further Development

Lord William Bentinck, Governor-General (1828–35).—Suppression of "thuggee" and "suttee".—Improved education.—End of newspaper censorship. —Reforms introduced too quickly and caused resentment.—Difficulties with Afghans.—Russian influence.—Lord Auckland, Governor-General (1836–41).—First Afghan War (1839–42).—British failure and damage to prestige.—Lord Ellenborough as Governor-General (1841–44).—Annexation of Sind (1842).—Lord Hardinge as Governor-General (1844–48).—First Sikh War (1845–46).—Lord Dalhousie as Governor-General (1848–56).—Second Sikh War (1849).—Punjab annexed.—Work of Lawrences in Punjab.—Second Burmese War (1852).—Dalhousie's reforms.

The Causes of the Indian Mutiny

Weakness of British troops owing to Crimean War and Persian War.—Loss of prestige in Afghan War.—Division of forces into Company's Army and Royal Army.—Dual command.—Dalhousie's reforms.—'Doctrine of Lapse'.—Annexation of states.—Deposition of Nabob of Oudh (1856).—Hundredth anniversary of battle of Plassey.—Greasing of cartridges.—Too rapid introduction of Western reforms.

The Indian Mutiny, 1857

Rising at Meerut (May 1857).—Lord Canning now Governor-General (1856–62).—Massacre at Cawnpore.—Siege of Lucknow.—Mutiny finally crushed (1858).—Mutiny confined to Ganges valley and some troops in Central India.—Military rising.—Few civilians involved.—Sikhs of Punjab and Mahrattas remained loyal.—Canning's clemency.

QUESTIONS

Answer the following questions briefly:

1. (a) List the achievements of Clive.
   (b) With what was Clive charged?
   (c) What early difficulties did Sir Warren Hastings have?
   (d) What was the effect of Pitt's India Act (1784)?
   (e) What were the main events during the governor-generalship of the Marquis of Wellesley?
   (f) Who were the Mahrattas? Why did they figure so prominently in Indian history?
   (g) What was the 'Doctrine of Lapse'?
2. What were 'thuggee' and 'suttee'?
   What measures did Lord William Bentinck take?
3. What were the causes of the Indian Mutiny?
4. Speaking of conditions in Oudh in 1856, the Governor-General, Lord Dalhousie, said:

   > The British Government would be guilty in the sight of God and man if it were any longer to aid in sustaining by its countenance an administration fraught with suffering to millions.

   (a) What did Dalhousie mean?
   (b) What action did he take?
   (c) Do you agree with his action?
   (d) What was its effect?

14 : India—From Mutiny to Independence

The Effects of the Mutiny

THE results of the Mutiny were far-reaching both to the British and the people of India. The prestige of Britain had been restored by the energetic suppression of the Mutiny and by the firm yet fair punishment meted out to the mutineers by Lord Canning. Steps were taken to remove the grievances which had been the causes of the rising and to ensure that progress for the common good should continue.

In 1858 the British Government passed the India Act. This ended the long rule of the East India Company by the abolition both of the Company and the Board of Control and by transferring its army to the Crown. A Secretary of State for India was appointed with headquarters and an Advisory Council of India in London. The Governor-General became Viceroy of India with an Executive Council to assist him. India was now wholly under the sovereignty of the Queen and at the same time the position of the Indian princes and their co-operation was secured by a proclamation by the Queen that there would be no further annexations of their territory, that no aggression by them would be allowed and their rights and dignity would be respected. The 'Doctrine of Lapse' was ended and from thenceforth much more consideration was given to the feelings of Indians before any reform was introduced.

For some forty years there was a period of peace and progress. The Indian Civil Service, which had replaced the officials of the East India Company, was a splendidly efficient body of dedicated men. The resources of the country were developed, disease, and famine were tackled, railways constructed, education improved and increased, and prosperity resulted.

Difficulties on the North-West Frontier

Yet the period was not without its difficulties. Further trouble developed on the North-West Frontier. Fears of Russian influence in the Afghan court, coupled with strained relations between Britain and Russia at the time, led to British forces invading Afghanistan in

North-West Frontier Rising: March of Roberts from Kabul to Kandahar during Second Afghan War.
(*By Louis Desanges.*)

Gurkhas descending a pass under fire.

A native cavalry charge in the Chitral campaign, 1895.
(*After a sketch by Lionel James.*)

1878 and resulted in the Second Afghan War of 1878–80. Shere Ali, the Amir, fled to Russia at that time and died there in 1879. In that same year a British force under General Sir Frederick Roberts and General Stewart invaded Afghanistan and the latter captured Kandahar. Once again Britain tried to place a friendly Amir upon the throne and insisted upon a British Resident, but the Afghans resented having a ruler imposed from outside. More fighting broke out, the British Resident, Sir Louis Cavagnari, was murdered and Roberts was sent with a further expedition to punish the culprits. He made his famous forced march from Kabul to Kandahar and defeated the rebels. Abdurrahman became Amir, came to terms with the British and the demand for a British Resident was dropped although Britain retained control of Afghanistan's foreign policy. Later, in 1893, the frontier between Afghanistan and British India was fixed and became known as the Durand Line. The North-West Frontier, as this area was also known, was a trouble spot until comparatively recent times, tribal risings by the Afridis, Chitrals and Pathans taking place and British troops being engaged there.

Concern over Russian intentions also led to an expedition into Tibet by Colonel Sir Francis Younghusband in 1904. This resulted in an agreement with Tibet and both Russia and Britain agreed to leave Tibet alone and agreed at the Anglo-Russian Convention in 1907 that Afghanistan should remain under British influence.

Burma became a province of India in 1886 when the Third Burmese War was fought.

Benefits of British Rule

After the Mutiny the greater part of India enjoyed peace, law and order of a measure it had never experienced before. At the same time a great deal was done to improve the lot of the people.

Communications improved immensely. New roads were built and the plans for an extensive railway system which Lord Dalhousie had drawn up before the Mutiny, were carried out.

The greatest menace facing the Indian people had always been famine. The success of their agriculture had depended, and still depends, upon the summer monsoon which brings the needed rain. If the rainfall was insufficient in one area the crops failed and the people starved. For many years nothing had been done to help these people and, indeed, no central government had been strong and efficient enough to do so until the British took over. After 1858 the British Government slowly but steadily attempted to tackle the problem of famine. One of the main factors was lack of transport. Often

Starving natives in famine-stricken India.

millions of people died of starvation in one area simply because surplus food in another area could not reach them as there were no transport facilities. The coming of the railways and better roads did much to counteract this. Serious famines in the North-West Provinces and Rajputana in 1860, Orissa in 1866 and Western India in 1868, caused a very heavy loss of life. The Government did a great deal to help, but with transport not yet sufficiently advanced, and possibly because of lack of real experience, the measures were insufficient.

In 1873 a failure of crops in Bihar threatened a serious famine but Government action was so vigorous and efficient that it was prevented. In 1876, however, a serious famine developed in the Deccan and although strong measures were taken they were not so successful and over five million people died. Great efforts were then made to deal with future situations and a policy known as the Famine Code was drawn up in 1883 as the result of a commission under Sir Richard Strachey. It decided that plans should be prepared in case of famine in order to save time when the catastrophe actually struck. In order to meet the cost a sum should be allocated annually from Government revenue to be known as Famine Insurance. This policy was tried out in action in the Deccan in 1896 and 1899 and worked well. Commissions under Sir James Lyall in 1898 and Sir Anthony Macdonell in 1900 reported favourably on the famines and the working of the Code. India continued to suffer from famines but the death-rolls were only a fraction of what they had been. It is worth noting that famine is still a major problem to independent India today.

The health of the people was the other great problem. The conditions under which the bulk of them lived, the bad housing, the poor food—particularly the famines—and bad sanitation had made them susceptible to diseases such as cholera, plague, smallpox and fever. The death-roll was high. By 1888 Sanitary Boards had been set up in every province with the task of introducing western ideas of sanitation and cleanliness. A School of Tropical Medicine was established at Calcutta and this did tremendous work in combating diseases of all kinds, but particularly cholera and leprosy. Malaria was attacked and measures taken to exterminate mosquitoes. There was opposition to all these efforts from the Indian peasants on religious grounds but steady progress was made.

In order that the evils of famine, disease and poverty could be overcome a great extension of education was necessary. Schools, colleges and universities were founded and many Indians were able to gain degrees. This sometimes led to difficulties as they then sought posts in government service and suitable employment was not always available which caused discontent and resentment. Nevertheless, great strides were made although the problem of illiteracy among the peasants has not been conquered even today.

The people of India had gained peace and order, famine relief, a transport system, improved agriculture, better public health in addition to the suppression of inhuman practices such as 'suttee'

The Maharajah of Jammu and Kashmir.

The Maharaja Holkar of Indore.

Member of the robber tribes.

and child-killing. Yet the great mass still lived a life of poverty and suffering.

Constitutional Progress

By the middle of the nineteenth century it had become British policy to associate Indians with the government of the country in various ways. Indians joined the Civil Service, became barristers and judges, and after the reorganisation of the Indian Army following the Mutiny the bulk of the officers gradually became Indian although senior command was by British officers.

Indians were also brought into the Legislative Councils. The Indian Legislative Council was first established in 1833 and the India Councils Act of 1861 reorganised the Legislative Council to consist of the Executive Council of four members and from six to twelve additional members, of whom at least half were to be non-official, that is to say would be appointed by the Viceroy from outside the Civil Service. Indians became eligible for appointment for the first time. This also applied to Provincial Legislative Councils. The Executive Council was directly descended from the Council which had been established by Lord North's Regulating Act of 1773. This system continued without change until the India Councils Act of 1892. This enlarged the Legislative Council by four members and allowed members to be recommended by the Calcutta Chamber of Commerce and by non-official members of the Provincial Councils. These, in turn, were enlarged and their members could be recommended by Universities, Chambers of Commerce and town councils, but in neither case was there direct election.

The India Councils Act of 1909, a part of the Morley–Minto reforms, provided elected members to the Provincial Councils for the first time as well as enlarging the Legislative Council once more and appointing an Indian member to the Executive Council. Mr John (afterwards Lord) Morley, was Secretary of State for India and Lord Minto was Viceroy. During their term of office the changes described above took place and two Indian members were appointed to the Council of India in London. These reforms were intended to bring Indians far more into Government in co-operation with the British, but both Lord Morley and Lord Minto were careful to point out that they were not to be considered as steps towards a parliamentary system and responsible government. They considered these to be unsuitable for Indians because India was not a nation, being divided by great differences of race, caste, language and religion.

However, it was precisely because many Indians, with sympathetic support from some British, felt that movement towards a parliamentary form of government was essential that the Indian National Congress had been formed in 1885. This gradually developed into a political party, the aims of which eventually became Indian independence. The Moslems, although taking part in the Congress for a time, formed the Moslem League in 1905. Thus from being an assembly, it eventually became a basically Hindu party—the Congress Party.

One of the great Viceroys was Lord Curzon whose term of office was from 1898 to 1905. He was a fine administrator who did great things for India and her people. However, since he had no time for political agitators and condemned them frankly with a caustic tongue, he built up a strong anti-British feeling among a minority of extremists. This was made worse by his decision to divide Bengal into two parts. He was succeeded by Lord Minto whose reforms have been described.

After King George V came to the throne in 1910, he and Queen Mary made a state visit to India. This was the first time that a reigning

Lord and Lady Curzon with the Nirzam and party.

monarch had visited India. A magnificent Durbar was held at Delhi, which had become the capital of India in succession to Calcutta. This was an occasion for a great show of loyalty to the Crown by the Indian princes and people, while this was to take a practical form soon afterwards with the outbreak of the First World War.

The First World War

Large numbers of British troops had to be withdrawn for service elsewhere, but instead of this providing an opportunity for risings and disorders it produced a great outburst of loyalty. A great many Indians rushed to enlist and Indian troops served overseas on the Western Front, in Mesopotamia and German East Africa. The Indian Legislative Council voted large sums of money to assist the British Government and the Indian princes, as well as providing soldiers, gave of their private fortunes to help. Nevertheless, when the news from the war fronts was bad the National Congress revived and put forward further demands for independence. This partly resulted in the Montagu Declaration of August 1917, when Mr Edward Montagu, Secretary of State for India, said the policy of the British Government was,

> the increasing association of Indians in every branch of the administration, and also the granting of self-governing institutions with a view to the progressive realisation of responsible government in India as an integral part of the British Empire. Progress towards this goal could be achieved by successive stages, and the time and extent of each stage must be determined by the British and Indian Governments in the light of the fitness shown by Indians to be entrusted with responsibility.

This statement, as well as virtually promising eventual self-government, also set the pattern by which it was to be achieved. He then visited India and with Lord Chelmsford, the Viceroy, drew up a report which resulted in the Government of India Act of 1919.

This set up an Executive Council and a Legislative Council to assist the Viceroy, but the Legislative Council was to be divided into two parts, a Council of State, and a Legislative Assembly. Of the Council of State members, 33 were to be elected and 27 nominated. The right to vote was given only to men of property or standing. Of the members of the Legislative Assembly 104 were to be elected and the remaining 41 nominated. There was to be a tax qualification for voting. The really big changes, however, were in the Provincial Legislative Councils. These were to have a majority of elected members and a principle known as Dyarchy was introduced. This meant that certain functions of Government were 'reserved' to the Executive Councils which were responsible to the Provincial Governors and thence to the Viceroy as previously. Other functions such as education, sanitation, public health, local government and public works were 'transferred' to ministers from the elected members of the Legislative Assembly. These ministers were responsible to the Assembly. The Provincial Governors had certain reserve powers. This meant that the Provincial Legislative Assemblies had a certain amount of responsible government but the dual control, or Dyarchy, thus established was not enough for the more extreme workers for independence. Nor was this a really good time for the introduction of such a cautious step forward. The British Government's intention was to train Indians for further responsibility later, but this was not realised. The more extreme members of Congress failed to remember that India would not even have been in a position to demand independence but for the unifying influence of English as the only language universally understood in India, and for the law and order and social progress which British rule had brought. In spite of this, there had been much disorder and Mr Justice Rowlatt had been sent to India to report on the causes. His report had resulted in the Rowlatt Acts which gave the Indian Government special powers to deal with any unruly situation. This provoked resentment.

The Non-Co-operation Movement

Although the Act of 1919 was the first real step on the road to independence the people of India did not regard it in that light. Their mood was bitter and they were ready for revolution. The war had made the cost-of-living high and the soldiers returned from the war were discontented. The leaders of the Indian National Congress denounced the new constitution. They claimed that it was unjust and attacked those Indians who co-operated with the British in working it. The Punjab was on the verge of revolution and this led to the Amritsar Massacre in which a force of British troops, heavily outnumbered and finding it difficult to maintain order, opened fire on the crowd, killing 379 people. Although the British Government condemned the action and dismissed the local military commander, the tempers of the Indians were roused.

It was at this time that Mohandas Gandhi became the leader of the Congress Party. He dedicated his life to the achievement of Indian independence. He was an unselfish man who devoted himself to his people who adored him and gave him the title of 'Mahatma' or 'great of soul'. He hated violence and taught his followers to practise non-violent civil disobedience or non-co-operation. Unfortunately, his followers did not always obey his instructions and his speeches often raised them to a pitch of excitement which led to disorder and violence. Although Gandhi was greatly grieved by the bloodshed, he did not alter his policy.

He gave instructions that Hindus were not to take any part in the Government, and were to boycott all British goods. This did not have universal support from the Indian people and many Indian Liberals put their loyalty to the Government first.

In 1924, a movement known as the Swaraj or Swarajists began to obtain control of the Congress Party. They stood for immediate self-government and were under the leadership of C. R. Das and Pandit Nehru. Gradually the Swarajists began to lose ground but Pandit Nehru remained as the real leader of Congress.

Because of the continued agitation and disorder, and the fact that the system of Dyarchy did not seem to be working well, the British Government at the end of 1927 appointed a Commission to investigate and report on the position of Indian Government.

The Simon Commission, 1927

Sir John Simon was appointed Chairman of the Commission which, in spite of the fact that it came to India to bring independence nearer, provoked hostility and disorder from the more extreme elements.

The Commission's terms of reference were clear. They were to investigate the working of the Government of India Act, to consider what changes were necessary and to report on the desirability and possibility of extending responsible government. It seems incredible

Gandhi arriving at 10 Downing Street, London, November 1931, for a conference.

today, but the Commission was entirely composed of British members and the fact that no Indians were appointed to it caused resentment, even among liberal and pro-British Indians.

The Commission's Report was published in 1930 and made the following recommendations:

(*a*) India to have a Federal Constitution to include the provinces and the princely states.

(*b*) Provincial councils were to be enlarged and the policy of dyarchy to end.

(*c*) There should be full responsible government in the provinces, and in the central government with the exception of certain matters such as defence.

(*d*) The Federal Assembly should take the place of the central Legislative Assembly.

(*e*) It should be possible for further steps towards independence to be made without an enquiry by the British Government.

The publication of the report was preceded by a statement by the Viceroy, Lord Irwin, describing Dominion status and suggesting that this was the British Government's aim and explaining that Round Table Conferences would be held after the report was published to ensure the greatest measure of agreement on the steps to be taken.

The Report was received with hostility by the Congress Party and new agitation was led by Pandit Nehru and Gandhi. Congress had put forward its own proposals for immediate Dominion status with votes for all men and women. It was their failure to suggest safeguards for minorities which prevented the plan receiving universal Indian support. The Moslems rejected it at once.

The first of the Round Table Conferencсs met at once in 1930 and was attended by British and Indian delegates but the Congress Party refused to send representatives. The Conference supported the Simon Report's main recommendations generally but recommended that the Viceroy should retain special powers with relation to defence, law and order, finance and the protection of minorities in the first instance.

A second Round Table Conference met in 1931 and at this the Congress Party was represented by Mr Gandhi who was released from prison for the purpose. The main problem was the animosity of the Hindus and the Moslems. The representation of the two groups failed to agree so the British Government decided that safeguards for minorities must be written into any legislation which resulted.

In 1932 a third Round Table Conference met largely to settle some points of the constitution and franchise. The British Government accepted the recommendations of the three conferences and published a 'White Paper'. This said that the provinces were to receive full responsible government. The Federal Legislature was to consist of representatives of the provinces and the princely states in 1933. A Joint Select Committee of both Houses of Parliament considered the White Paper and heard a great deal of additional evidence. Thus it will be seen that the British Government did everything within its power to enable India to move smoothly towards independence, and it cannot possibly be said that insufficient consideration was given to its problems.

In 1935 the Government of India Act was passed by the British Parliament, not without difficulty. A large number of Conservatives led by Winston Churchill opposed it on the grounds that it attempted to go too far, while the Labour Party considered that it did not go far enough. The Act provided for a Federal Constitution to include both provinces and the princely states. The central government was to be responsible to the Federal Assembly except for defence and foreign affairs. The provinces were to receive full responsible government. Two new provinces—Sind and Orissa—were established while Burma was separated from India. The Viceroy retained the power to intervene in the event of law and order or administration breaking down, and it was on this last point that the Act was most severely criticised by the Indians. There was not yet to be universal suffrage; some 36,000,000 or just over a quarter of the adult population were allowed to vote, about one-fifth being women. This was a great improvement on 1919.

The reception of the Act varied from province to province, some co-operating fully, others refusing to co-operate. The Indian princes, too, conferred and did not agree to join the federation until the end of 1937. When the Second World War broke out in 1939 the new constitution had not been brought into being. Consequently, the central government continued under the old 1919 constitution while the provinces adopted the new. In October 1939 the Viceroy announced that no further progress to bring the new constitution into operation could take place during the war but once more said that the intention of the British Government was to grant Dominion status. In spite of a further promise in August 1940, this was unsatisfactory to both the Congress Party and the Moslem League.

The Second World War

India played her part in the Second World War with even greater loyalty than in the first war. Apart from being threatened by invasion

Mohammed Ali Jinnah (*left*) with Sir Stafford Cripps (*right*).

the great burden of the war against Japan was shouldered in great part by Indian troops fighting alongside British. Indian troops fought in many theatres of war, notably the Middle East. While there was a small amount of subversive activity, the great mass of the Indian people played their part nobly.

In 1942 Winston Churchill sent Sir Stafford Cripps with a mission to India which virtually offered Dominion status at once, subject to a satisfactory constitution. This was to provide for the right of any province to withdraw if it wished to do so. It was also stated that until this came about, and during the war, the British Government must be fully responsible for the conduct of affairs in India. These proposals were unacceptable to both Hindus and Moslems, the Congress Party demanding that the British 'quit India at once'. In spite of the rejection of the terms many Indians notably some within the Congress Party were in favour of their acceptance.

In 1945, soon after the German surrender, the Viceroy re-affirmed that the Cripps' offer still stood and as a sign of Britain's desire to bring about Indian independence all the members of the Viceroy's Council would be Indian except for the Viceroy himself and the Commander-in-Chief. In spite of a conference at Simla with Indian leaders, including Gandhi for the Congress Party and Dr Jinnah for the Moslem League, no agreement was reached. The Moslems who were about a quarter of India's population feared Hindu domination and wished for a separate Moslem state. The problem was magnified by the Hindu caste system which looked upon the lowest caste as 'untouchables'.

Jawaharlal Nehru.

Mahatma Gandhi.

Independence

In 1946, Mr Attlee, who was now Prime Minister, stated that the British Labour Government intended to grant India independence. He sent three Cabinet Ministers, Sir Stafford Cripps, Lord Pethick-Lawrence and Mr A. V. Alexander, to discuss the question. Once again it was the impossibility of agreement between Hindus and Moslems which brought about failure.

The next year the British Government announced that it would withdraw from India by June 1948 and hoped that this would force a settlement. Lord Mountbatten, who had been Supreme Commander in South-East Asia with his headquarters in India during the war, was appointed Viceroy. This was an inspired move since he had gained great popularity in India and had built up good personal relationships with Indian leaders. There is no doubt that his leadership and the personal courage of both himself and Lady Mountbatten, who moved freely among crowds of demonstrators, did much to bring about successful negotiations for independence. At last both the British Government and the Congress Party accepted the principle of partition as the only solution, and on 15 August 1947 the two new Dominions of India and Pakistan were founded.

Lord Mountbatten was appointed the first Governor-General of

India, while Dr Jinnah became Governor-General of Pakistan. Mr Nehru was Prime Minister of the Government of India.

Unfortunately, the division into India and Pakistan was made mainly on a religious and racial, rather than a geographical or economic, basis. Pakistan consisted largely of Sind, Baluchistan and part of the Punjab in the west and parts of Bengal and Assam in the east, the two parts being separated by a thousand miles of Indian territory.

Independence brought tragedy and disorder. Although an attempt had been made to divide the land into Hindu and Moslem territories, each new state contained a minority of the other religion. Moslems were massacred in India and Hindus were massacred in Pakistan. It has been said that more people died in these massacres than in the whole of British rule. In 1948 Gandhi was assassinated by a Hindu fanatic. After a time order was gradually restored.

The New Dominions

The new constitution of India of 1949 provided for a union of states with a Parliament of two Houses, a Council of States and a House of the People. Each state was to have its own legislature. At the same time India became a republic with a President instead of a Governor-General. Eventually all the Indian princes surrendered their states to the Government of India. The Congress Party has been the ruling party since independence and there has been no strong opposition party. Delhi is the capital of India.

Pakistan was declared an Islamic republic within the Commonwealth in 1956 with the capital at Karachi, it having taken some years to work out a constitution. This constitution allowed for a President and a National Assembly. This did not work and corruption, intrigue and disorders followed resulting in a coup in October 1958.

Nehru and Lord Mountbatten.

Field-Marshal Ayub Khan, the Army Commander-in-Chief, seized power and the constitution was ended, martial law being declared. Soon after he was appointed President of Pakistan with a council of eleven to assist him until democratic institutions could be reinstated. A new constitution was instituted in 1962, Ayub Khan remaining as President with virtually dictatorial powers. Rawalpindi became the capital city in 1960. A National Assembly was set up with assemblies in the provinces but without responsible government.

Relations Between India and Pakistan, India and China

Apart from the racial and religious antagonism between the two countries, Pakistan as the smaller of the two has tended to fear domination by India.

Both India and Pakistan claimed Kashmir which had a Hindu ruler but predominantly Moslem population. The dispute was re-

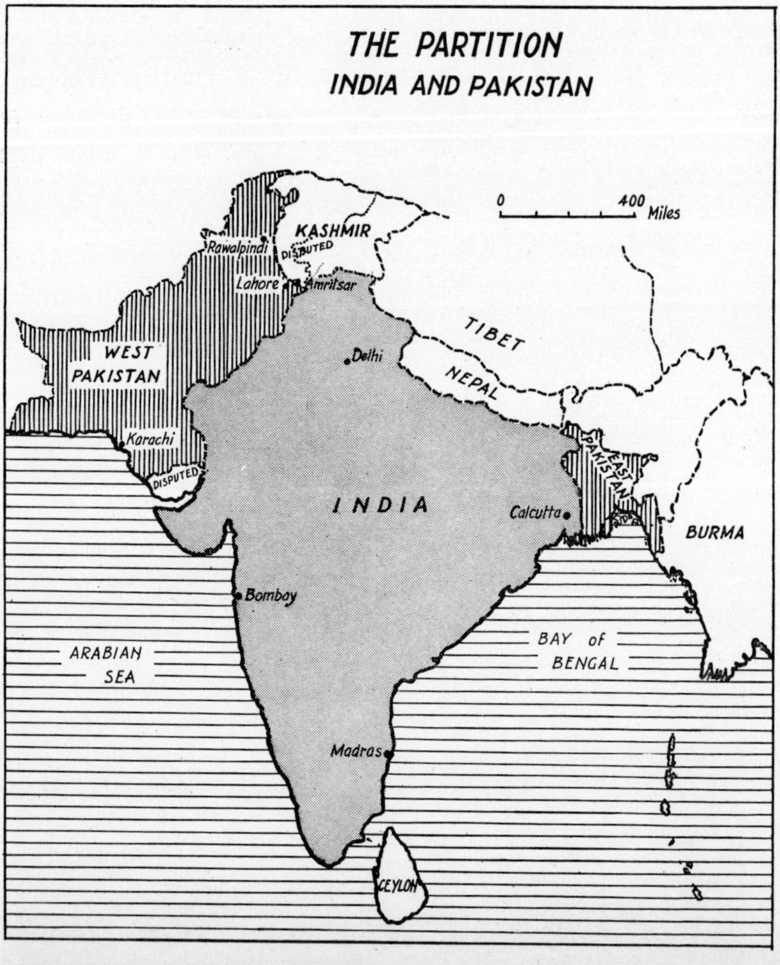

ferred to the United Nations who sent a commission to investigate. The commission recommended a plebiscite and the United Nations ordered that this should be carried out. The Indian Government refused to do this, knowing that the vote would be likely to be in favour of Pakistan, and the state has been divided between the two countries ever since. In September of 1965, Pakistan invaded the Indian sector of Kashmir and open war broke out between India and Pakistan, India retaliating by the invasion of Pakistan, and both countries indulged in air-raids. After a peace mission by U Thant, the United Nations' Secretary-General, and an offer of mediation by Mr Kosygin, the Russian Prime Minister, an uneasy cease-fire was agreed. The problem of Kashmir however, remained unsolved.

After early friendship with the People's Republic of China, India quarrelled with her when she invaded the northern mountain frontiers and serious fighting broke out in 1962. Although peace was restored after a few weeks China again threatened India during the war with Pakistan in 1965. The strained relations between India and Pakistan have led to Pakistan's friendship with China.

India was also involved with military operations in 1961 when her troops invaded the small Portuguese possession of Goa on her west coast. This was the last European possession in India, France having surrendered Chandernagore and Pondicherry by 1954 after negotiations.

Ceylon

Although so close to the continent of India, Ceylon had a completely separate history. Becoming British by the Treaty of Amiens in 1802 after having been captured from the Dutch in 1796, it had been an uneventful history.

From 1802, it was a Crown colony with a Legislative Council. In 1927, a Commission under the Chairmanship of Lord Donoughmore was appointed and as the result of their report a new constitution was granted in 1931 which gave a State Council of 50 elected, 3 officers and 8 nominated members. This did not work well and in 1937 a new system was considered. This was delayed by the Second World War and further development waited until peace. In 1945, Lord Soulbury was chairman of a commission which resulted in a new constitution in May 1946. This gave Ceylon responsible parliamentary government except for defence and foreign affairs. Full independence was granted by the Ceylon Independence Act of 1947 and came into force in February 1948. It has two Houses of Parliament, a Senate and a House of Representatives.

Burma

Burma, which had been separated from India by the Act of 1935, was completely occupied by the Japanese during the Second World War and reconquered by British Commonwealth forces in 1945.

In May 1945 the British Government offered Dominion status but this was refused by Burmese politicians who demanded independence.

The British Parliament passed the Burma Independence Act in 1947 and Burma became an independent country outside the Commonwealth in 1948.

SUMMARY

The Effects of the Mutiny

Restoration of British prestige.—Removal of grievances.—India Act of 1858.—End of East India Company.—Secretary of State for India.—Council for India in London.—Governor-General became Viceroy.—Executive Council to assist Viceroy.—Formation of Indian Civil Service.

Difficulties on the N.-W. Frontier

Fears of Russian influence.—Second Afghan War (1878–80).—Durand line as frontier between India and Afghanistan.—Troubles of N.-W. Frontier.—Younghusband's expedition into Tibet (1904).—Third Burmese War (1886).—Burma as province of India.

Benefits of British Rule

Peace, law and order.—Improved communications.—Famine relief.—Public health.—School of Tropical Medicine.—Education.—Suppression of inhuman practices.

Constitutional Progress

Gradual Indianisation of Army, Civil Service and legal system.—Indian Legislative Council established in 1833 and re-organised in 1861 with Indian members.—Morley–Minto Reforms.—India Councils Act (1909) elected members for first time.—Indian National Congress formed 1855; developed as Hindu-dominated Congress Party.

First World War

Loyalty of Indians.—Indian troops fought overseas.—Montagu Declaration (1917) promising self-government.—Montagu–Chelmsford Report.—Government of India Act of 1919.—Executive and Legislative Councils.—Provincial Legislative Councils.—Principle of Dyarchy.—Hostile reaction of Congress.—Disorder.—Rowlatt Acts (1919).

Non-Co-operation Movement

Bitter mood of many of Indian people.—Effects of war.—Congress denounced new constitution.—Amritsar Massacre (1919).—Gandhi as leader of Congress Party.—Policy of non-violent civil disobedience and non-co-operation.—Swaraj movement in Congress; immediate self-government demanded; Nehru as leader of Congress Party.

Simon Commission

Hostility from extremists.—No Indian members; in favour of Federal constitution and responsible government with some reservations.—Lord Irwin's statement on Dominion status.—Report of Commission published (1930).—Congress Party's proposals for immediate Dominion status; rejected by Moslems—First Round Table Conference (1930) boycotted by Congress Party.—Conference support for Simon Report.—Second Round Table Conference (1931).—Congress represented by Gandhi.—Third Round Table Conference (1932).—Government of India Act (1935) passed by British Parliament after difficulty.—Federal constitution of both provinces and princely states.—Responsible government except for defence and foreign affairs.—Full responsible government in provinces.—Viceroy's reserve powers.—Widened franchise.—Varied reception of Act.—Second World War halted further progress.—Viceroy's promise of ultimate Dominion status (1939); reaffirmed (1940).—Congress and Moslem League dissatisfied.

Second World War

Indian loyalty.—India's part in war with Japan.—Indian troops fought in many theatres of war.—Cripps Mission (1942).—Failure of Hindus and Moslems to agree.—Viceroy reaffirmed Cripps' offer (1945).

Independence

Mr Attlee sent Cabinet mission (1946).—Hindus and Moslems still failed to agree.—Announcement of independence in 1947 and British withdrawal by 1948.—Mountbatten as Viceroy.—Dominions of India and Pakistan founded (August 1947); disorder and massacres.

The New Dominions

Indian constitution of 1949.—Union of states; Parliament of two Houses.—India became a republic with a President.—Pakistan became an Islamic republic in 1956.—President and National Assembly.—Corruption and disorder resulted in coup of October 1958.—Ayub Khan as President.—New constitution 1962.—Dictatorial powers for President.

Relations Between India and Pakistan, India and China

Racial and religious antagonism.—Pakistan's fear of Indian domination.—Dispute over Kashmir.—Moslem majority and Hindu ruler.—U.N. Commission and recommendation for plebiscite; India refused; Pakistan invaded Indian sector of Kashmir (Sept. 1965).—War between India and Pakistan.—U.N. and Russian mediation led to cease-fire; problem of Kashmir unsolved.—India's early friendship with China.—Dispute over northern frontier; fighting (1962).—Chinese threat to India during Pakistan war.—Pakistan's friendship with China.—India seized Goa (1961).

Ceylon

Became British (1802).—Crown colony.—Donoughmore constitution (1931).—State Council partly elected.—Further constitutional progress delayed by Second World War.—Soulbury constitution (1946).—Responsible parliamentary government.—Ceylon Independence Act (1947).—Fully independent as Dominion (1948).

Burma

Separated from India by Act of 1935.—Occupied by Japanese in Second World War.—Re-conquered 1945.—Dominion status offer refused by Burmese who demanded independence.—Burma Independence Act (1947).—Burma became independent country outside Commonwealth in 1948.

QUESTIONS

Answer the following questions briefly:

1. (a) What effect did the Mutiny have on Indians and British opinions of each other?
   (b) What was the main result of the Mutiny?
   (c) Why did the Second Afghan War break out?
   (d) List what you consider to be the main benefits of British rule in India.
   (e) When did Indian members first become eligible to join the Legislative Council?
   (f) What was the Indian National Congress?
   (g) What was the importance of the Montagu Declaration of 1917?
   (h) What was the Amritsar Massacre (1919)?
   (i) Who were the Swarajists?
   (j) Why did some of the Indians object to the Simon Commission?
   (k) Who was Gandhi?
   (l) Why was there difficulty between the Hindus and Moslems?
2. Describe the problems of famine in India and say what was done in the nineteenth century to solve them.
3. What part do you consider the following played in India's eventual achievement of independence:
   (a) Gandhi, (b) Nehru, (c) Jinnah, (d) Cripps, (e) Mountbatten.
4. Dadabhai Naoroji, the President of the second National Congress towards the end of the nineteenth century, said:

   > new light has been poured upon us, teaching us the new lesson that kings are made for the people, not peoples for their kings; and this lesson we have learned amid the darkness of Asiatic despotism only by the light of free English civilization.

   (a) This shows that, in spite of demands for responsible government, there was understanding of the debt India owed to Britain. Why did the Congress change?
   (b) In what way do you consider that the problems of the Congress reflect the problems of India as a whole?
   (c) How important is the Congress Party today?
5. Give your reasons for the disagreements which have arisen between India and Pakistan.

15 : Britain and the Empire in the Nineteenth Century

Changes in Attitudes to Empire

THE mercantilism which had been the background of the Old Colonial System was not yet dead at the beginning of the nineteenth century. The supporters of mercantilism argued that the lesson of the loss of the American colonies was not that control of colonial trade was wrong, but rather that colonies with British settlers were too troublesome and that new colonies in the tropics should be obtained. Thus the first part of the century was given largely to the development of the Indian trade and the colonies in the West Indies.

Nevertheless the opposition to mercantilism was growing. Adam Smith's *Wealth of Nations* was published in 1776, and his idea of Free Trade was beginning to win support. In addition the development of both agricultural and industrial revolutions was changing the view of overseas trade. Some of the free traders were against the possession of colonies altogether. The nineteenth century was notable for its reforms and behind most of these were the humanitarians. They looked upon any sign of the exploitation of the native peoples of the colonies as cruel and unjust.

Later in the century there grew up a more general feeling against Empire before the second half brought a new imperialism which was to lead to a great expansion of the Empire.

The Agricultural and Industrial Revolutions

The great changes in agriculture with the introduction of machinery and new methods of scientific stock-breeding and cultivation of crops had resulted in enclosure on a large scale. By the middle of the nineteenth century most of the old open fields had become enclosed farms. This had a devastating effect upon the population of the countryside. The old peasant class was uprooted from the soil, some remaining landless labourers, but large numbers drifting to the new industries.

At the same time the advances in industry had led to a change from domestic industry to the factory system. The new machines needed factories and money to finance them and industry which had been spread over the whole land began to flock to the new industrial towns. This, too, led to a great movement of population and ill-paid, under-nourished industrial workers living in over-crowded and unhealthy conditions.

The two revolutions were to add to the problems being created by the ever-increasing population.

Growth of Population

The population of England and Wales grew from six and a half millions in 1750 to almost eighteen millions in 1850 and thirty-two millions in 1900.

This great increase in population was not matched by an increase in work for them. As has been noted above, the agricultural and industrial revolutions deprived people of their work and forced them to move into badly-paid jobs and live under bad conditions. With this and the vast increase in the rate of unemployment, there grew up a population of surplus workers discontented and without any real hope for the future. Is there any wonder that their thoughts and hopes turned towards emigration? Between 1820 and the end of the century well over ten million people left Britain, some four millions to the United States but the remainder to the Empire. It will be seen how important the changes in Britain and the increased population were in their effects upon the development of colonial territories.

The Humanitarians

The work of John Wesley in the previous century had changed the views of many people as to their responsibility for others, not the least in their attitude to colonial peoples. This was seen in the trial of Warren Hastings, for the charges against him were that he had exploited subject peoples. He was not guilty and so the Humanitarian efforts were here misguided.

The effects of Humanitarianism were varied, but one of the main objects of the movement was the abolition of the slave trade. For years William Wilberforce, supported by others such as Fowell Buxton and Thomas Clarkson, had laboured against tremendous odds, first to end the slave trade and secondly to abolish slavery itself. It was estimated that there were some 750,000 slaves in the British Empire. It took twenty years from 1787 to 1807 to abolish the slave trade, and in 1833 slavery and all the suffering and brutality associated with it and the 'Middle Passage' ended within the Empire. The Government and the British taxpayer paid twenty million pounds in compensation to the slave owners. There had also been a considerable loss of trade to places like Bristol, London and Liverpool. The ending of the slave trade and slavery was one of the most altruistic acts by any government and ample evidence of the power of the Humanitarian movement.

Much the greatest reason for this power was the work of the missionaries. There were missions to almost every part of the Empire, but particularly to Africa and the Pacific Islands. Not only did they work to take the Gospel to the native peoples but they also sought to improve their conditions and save them from oppression. They wrote letters home which were read in the churches and these had great influence. This was noticeably so in the case of letters from colonies using slaves and did much to build up public opinion against slavery. The Clapham Sect, to which Wilberforce belonged, had great influence at this time. Their efforts sometimes led to trouble, notably with the Boers in South Africa, but gradually a body of opinion grew up in Britain which regarded duty to the native peoples of the colonies as an overriding feature in policy towards them. The reports of missionaries such as Livingstone later in the century led to the view that it was the duty of Britain to take over territories with primitive peoples in order to protect them from exploitation and to assist those peoples to develop.

The Radical movement was growing in England at the beginning of the century with such men as Joseph Hume, Charles Buller, Sir William Molesworth, George Grote and Lord Durham, all advanced Liberals, concerning themselves with reforms of all kinds. They then began to turn their attention to the colonies. One of their number, Edward Gibbon Wakefield, produced his views on Systematic

William Wilberforce.

Colonisation and with others formed the Colonisation Society in 1830 to promote colonies along these lines. Lord Durham, or 'Radical Jack' as he was known, lent weight to this movement and was able to put forward some of the ideas in his famous Report on conditions in Canada in 1839.

The developments in the colonies in the early part of the century demanded their attention. The new settlers who were going out to the colonies were mainly working men, many of them Radicals or Chartists themselves, with their own ideas of how a new colony should develop. The colonial governors of the period were often soldiers, men of high character and ability, devoted to their tasks but out of sympathy with the ideas of many of the new settlers. A gulf grew between them and the settlers developed a dislike of governors and officials and wrote home to provide ammunition for the Radical Imperialists.

They attacked the Colonial Office for what they considered to be corruption, ignorance and complete indifference to the needs of the colonists. Their attacks were particularly directed at Sir James Stephen, the Colonial Secretary. These attacks were not altogether deserved and were exaggerated although they did some good. Stephen, in particular, was a high-minded man, who worked hard for what he believed to be a just development of the new territories.

At least the work of the Radical Imperialists awakened an interest in the colonies at home which was to help the development of the Empire. They saw their task as being the development of the possessions across the seas to receive the surplus, poverty stricken population of Britain and to reproduce British society in them, but a new society, free, democratic, self-governing and without the social divisions existing at home.

Free Trade and the Manchester School

The struggle between the ideas of Adam Smith and those of Protection came to a climax about the middle of the century.

A group of manufacturers in Lancashire known as the 'Manchester School' and led by Richard Cobden and John Bright had succeeded in ending the Corn Laws in 1846. They were wholeheartedly for the end of Protection and for trade being allowed to proceed freely. They were all for cutting the bonds which linked Britain with the Empire. In fact, they regarded colonies as quite useless, expensive and the chief cause of war. They received considerable support leading to moves towards independence for some colonies designed to rid this country of their burden.

Richard Cobden.

John Bright.

The combination of the work of the Radical Imperialists and the Manchester School, coupled with Gladstone's particular preoccupation with home affairs, led to the Liberal Party adopting a policy of Free Trade and opposition to adventures overseas. This tended to develop into a policy of anti-colonisation. Those who held these views became known as 'Little Englanders' because their attention was purely upon Britain herself.

Even Disraeli was not free from the mood of pessimism as to the value of colonies at first and in 1852 described them as 'millstones around our necks', but his view changed greatly.

The New Imperialism

With the increase of emigration and the cheapness and ease of postage making it simple for the new settlers to write to their relatives at home about the new lands, interest in the Empire was growing by about 1870. Newspapers took up the tale and a new feeling grew up between the Mother Country and the colonies.

Disraeli was quick to sense this change and in 1874 he made a speech which really launched the New Imperialist Policy. He called for a new attitude to Empire, 'responding to those distant sympathies which may become the source of incalculable strength and happiness to this land'. Although the policy of Disraeli's government did not do much to put these ideas into practice, they were in such direct opposition to the Gladstone Liberals, the Manchester School and the pessimists that they had great effect. They suited the mood of the country and paved the way for the New Imperialists like Sir J. R. Seeley, J. A. Froude, Sir Charles Dilke and, at the very end of the century, Joseph Chamberlain.

Joseph Chamberlain.

Benjamin Disraeli.

Disraeli died in 1881 but his ideas bore fruit. One of them, that there should be a council for the whole Empire, led to the setting up of the Imperial Federation League in 1884. It came to nothing because the general movement in the colonies was towards self-government, but later the Imperial Conferences provided a meeting point for all colonial representatives. They first met as the Colonial Conference in 1887.

Imperialism was at its height at the end of the century. The Humanitarians, the missionaries, the Radical Imperialists and the New Imperialists all played their part in stimulating the interest in the colonies and the care for the well-being of their people. The Manchester School and the pessimists—the 'Little Englanders' of the middle of the century—had little real lasting effect.

SUMMARY

Changes in Attitudes to Empire

Mercantilism.—Development of trade with India and West Indies early in century.—Adam Smith's *Wealth of Nations*.—Free trade.—Reforms through Humanitarians.—Feeling against Empire.—New imperialism.

The Agricultural and Industrial Revolutions

Changes in agriculture.—Unemployment among countryfolk.—Drift to industry.—New factory system.—Industrial towns.—Bad conditions.

Growth of Population

Great increase in population from 1750–1900.—Unemployment.—Increase in emigration.

The Humanitarians

Influence of John Wesley.—New attitude to coloured peoples.—Abolition of slave trade and slavery.—Work of missionaries.—Desire to protect and advance coloured peoples.

The Radical Imperialists

Growth of Radical movement.—Discontent among new settlers and distrust of officials.—Action of Radical Imperialists.—Colonial Office attacked.—Desire to develop colonies to receive surplus population from Britain.

Free trade and the Manchester School

Lancashire manufacturers.—Manchester School.—Cobden and Bright.—feeling against colonies.—Gladstone and Liberal policy.—'Little Englanders'.

The New Imperialism

Increase in emigration.—Easy postage.—New interest in Empire by 1870.—Disraeli's adoption of New Imperialist policy.—Effect on Imperialism.—Colonial Conference (1887).

QUESTIONS

Answer the following questions briefly:

1. (a) Why was the main emphasis on trade with India and the West Indies early in the nineteenth century?
   (b) What was the effect of the agricultural and industrial revolutions on the colonies?
   (c) In what way did the growth of population contribute to emigration in the nineteenth century?
   (d) Who were the Humanitarians?
   (e) What was meant by Radical Imperialism?
   (f) How did the ideas of Free Trade influence the Manchester School?
2. Give an example of the practical effect of the work of the Humanitarians in the British Empire.
3. In 1874 Disraeli, calling for a new attitude to Empire said:

   > This issue is not a mean one. It is whether you will be content to be a comfortable England . . . or whether you will be a great country, an Imperial country, a country where your sons, when they rise, rise to paramount positions, and obtain not merely the esteem of their countrymen but command the respect of the world.

   Richard Cobden declared that colonies were the chief cause of war and ought to be cast off.
   (a) What were the chief differences in their views of the Empire between Disraeli and Cobden?
   (b) How do you think that the Radical Imperialists influenced their views?
   (c) Why do you think that the doctrines of the New Imperialists prospered at the end of the nineteenth century?

16: Africa

Early European Settlements in Africa

THE voyage in 1487 of Bartholomew Diaz to the Cape of Good Hope blazed a trail for the seamen who were to sail and explore the coast of West Africa. Ten years later Vasco da Gama sailed around the Cape to India, and the coast of East Africa was open to exploration. Before this Europeans knew little of Africa, and as Jonathan Swift said:

> Geographers, in Afric maps,
> With savage pictures filled their gaps,
> And o'er unhabitable downs
> Placed elephants for want of towns.

The Portuguese were the first to take an active interest in the west coast of Africa but the English had visited Gambia in the sixteenth century and a trading settlement had been established by the early seventeenth century. Both Dutch and English visited the Gold Coast which became the centre of the slave trade in the seventeenth century. Eventually fortified posts were established.

The Portuguese, too, showed some interest in East Africa, particularly Zanzibar and nearby, and later Mozambique.

Although slaves and gold attracted European seamen and traders and there were a few settlements, some of them temporary, it was the nineteenth century before the real scramble for Africa began. Then the main contestants were Britain and France, moved by commercial rivalry, particularly the battle for the profitable trade in palm oil.

WEST AFRICA

Gambia

As has been said, English traders visited the Gambia River in the sixteenth century and a settlement was founded in 1618. A fortified post, known as Fort James, was built in 1663 and this became an important centre of the slave trade. After the end of the slave trade in 1807 it appeared that Gambia would lose its importance but trade in palm products gradually developed and in 1816 a settlement, Bathurst, was founded on St Mary's Island in the mouth of the river.

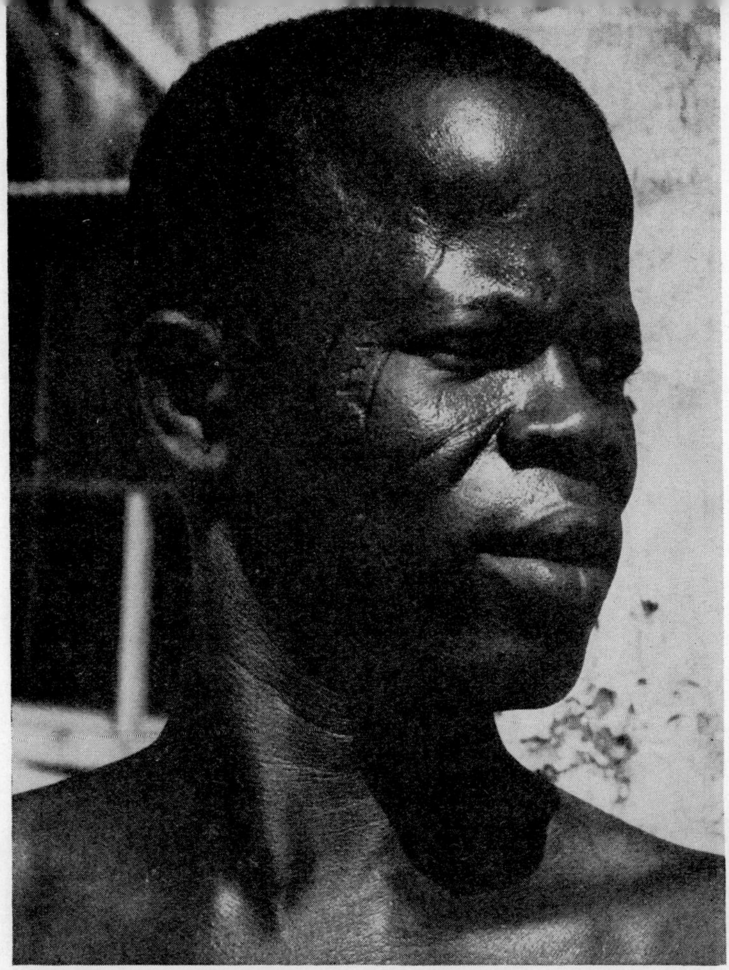

Member of one of the tribes in Ghana, with facial tribe markings.

The Royal African Company which had been founded in 1672 had been responsible for all trade with West Africa, including the slave trade, but it was dissolved in 1821, its forts and posts becoming part of the West African Settlements. For twenty-one years, from 1845, Gambia was a separate colony, when once again it became part of the West African Settlements until 1888. The next year an Anglo-French agreement recognised the British Protectorate extending each side of the river for two hundred and forty miles and the colony at the mouth.

There was little difference between the government of the colony and the Protectorate, the governor and Executive and Legislative Councils of the colony governing the Protectorate through the African chiefs. Gradually more members of the Legislative Council were elected and in 1965 Gambia was granted her independence within the Commonwealth.

Early view of Sierra Leone.

Sierra Leone

Although both Portuguese and British traders had visited and used Sierra Leone, and its name owes its origin to the Portuguese 'head of a Lion', probably based on the shape of its mountain, its foundation as a colony was unique. In 1772, Lord Chief Justice Mansfield pronounced his famous judgement in 'Summersett's Case', that slavery was illegal in England and any slave entering the country immediately became free. This meant the immediate liberation of the few slaves in England and any which West Indian and American planters had brought with them. A group of philanthropists who had been working with William Wilberforce to end the slave trade founded a settlement for them at Sierra Leone in 1788 which became known as Freetown. The new colony had many early difficulties; it was raided and sacked by the French in 1794, but recovered and became a Crown colony in 1807. After the end of the slave trade its population was added to by many more freed Negroes taken from slave-ships captured by the Royal Navy, while after the end of slavery more came from slave areas. Agreements with native chiefs led to the foundation of a Protectorate over territory which extended inland for one hundred and eighty miles. The chiefs ruled their own tribes under three Commissioners, while the colony had Executive and Legislative Councils, the governor being responsible for both colony and Protectorate.

After the Second World War, representatives of African tribes and a majority of elected members in the Legislative Council were gradually introduced and in 1953 African ministers were brought into the Government. Sierra Leone became an independent member of the Commonwealth in 1961.

Ghana

Ghana was originally known as the Gold Coast and British interest in the area dates back to the seventeenth century, when it was the centre of the slave trade. Dutch, Danish and English merchants engaged in this trade and they maintained fortified posts in which to keep the slaves which had been bought from African slavers. There was no desire to colonise at this time. The Royal African Company, which had been granted a charter in 1672 by Charles II, owned these forts. When the slave trade was abolished in 1807, the importance of the Company declined and it was abolished in 1821, the Crown taking over the forts which together with Gambia and Sierra Leone formed the West African Settlements. Because illegal slave trading went on, the British Government under pressure from the Humanitarians at home, bought out the Danish forts in 1850 and the Dutch forts in 1871, and exercised a much stricter control over the area. Gradually British influence spread into the interior, up to the border of Ashanti.

The Ashanti were a warrior people who had probably originally come from the area of the Sudan and who now had formed a strong kingdom in the interior. They had been the main providers of slaves and were disgusted because the trade had ended. They had established a dominion over the Fanti on the coast by early in the nineteenth century and threatened the British. In 1826 they invaded the coastal strip, killing Sir Charles McCarthy in battle and afterwards using his skull as a royal drinking cup. Captain George Maclean defeated the Ashanti the same year and signed a treaty with them, establishing the Ashanti boundary as the Prah river.

The Ashanti continued to menace the coastal tribes and a serious invasion took place in 1874. A considerable British force under Sir Garnet Wolseley defeated them in the Ashanti War of 1873–74. Although British prestige was restored, the Ashanti were not subdued and a second Ashanti War broke out in 1896. The capital, Kumasi was captured and a British Resident and a garrison were left there. The British demanded that the Ashanti Golden Stool should be surrendered. They regarded it purely as the King's throne and failed to understand its significance. The Ashanti regarded it as containing the soul of the nation and upon the British demand further fighting broke out. Kumasi was besieged and not relieved for more than three months. The Ashanti were finally defeated later in the year. Ashanti was annexed as a British colony in 1901. In the same year the area to the north of Ashanti, known as the Northern Territories was annexed as a Protectorate.

Joseph Chamberlain, the Colonial Secretary, in 1899, passed an Act enabling colonies to borrow money at low interest rates to build railways and harbours. The Gold Coast took advantage of this and communications were much improved, the colony becoming a prosperous country of small farmers. Europeans were not allowed to buy land, so there has been no problem of white settlers.

After the Second World War in 1946, a new constitution was granted. The governor had the help of an Executive Council with a Legislative Council of thirty members, eighteen of which were elected. This African majority set the colony on the road to responsible government which was granted in 1954. The Gold Coast, Ashanti and Northern Territories became a fully independent country within the Commonwealth in 1957, taking the name of Ghana, a legendary African empire of the past. Ghana declared itself a Republic, still remaining in the Commonwealth, in 1960.

Although the first constitution after independence was democratic, the President, Dr Kwame Nkrumah, became more and more a dictator, some of his supporters calling him the Messiah and hailing him as a god-like creature. In 1960, the Ghana Government passed a Preventive Detention Act which authorised imprisonment, without trial, of any whose activities were considered to be against the state. This had enabled Dr Nkrumah to imprison most of his political opponents. This and censorship of the press, including the deportation of foreign journalists, gave much concern to people in this country who were anxious to see ex-colonies develop as independent nations on democratic lines.

Ghana in 1958 agreed with Guinea and Mali to co-operate economically with the intention of forming eventually a Union of West African States. Although nothing further came of this, Dr Nkrumah took the lead in encouraging co-operation between newly-independent African states.

President Nkrumah tightened his one-man control of Ghana in August 1965 when he dismissed Major-General Otu and Ankrah as Chief and Vice-Chief of his General Staff. He declared himself Commander-in-Chief of the armed forces, and appointed two of his chief supporters, Major-Generals Aferi and Barwah, to replace the dismissed generals. He also announced sweeping Cabinet changes designed to strengthen his own position.

For some time tension had been growing between Ghana and the former French colonies of Ivory Coast, Cameroons, Niger, Togoland and Upper Volta. They accused Ghana of harbouring and encouraging exiled opposition groups and referred their complaints to the Organisation for African Unity.

Early in 1965 the matter of Nkrumah's treatment of political detainees had been raised with the United Nations and this and the changes of August 1965 brought to a head the dissatisfaction which

Dr Kwame Nkrumah. (*Photo: John Bulmer.*)

was beginning to show itself in Ghana. It is likely that plotting to overthrow Nkrumah started soon after.

In February 1966. President Nkrumah and some of his senior ministers and officers went on an official visit to Communist China. While he was away there was a *coup d'état* which won control of the country. A National Liberation Council was set up under the Chairmanship of Major-General Joseph Ankrah, one of the generals dismissed in August 1965. The leader of the military *coup*, Colonel Kotoka, said, 'the myth surrounding Nkrumah has been broken'. Nkrumah and his ministers were dismissed and his party, the C.C.P., dissolved. Ankrah was promoted Lieutenant-General and declared Commander-in-Chief with Kotoka now a Major-General as Army Commander.

Kwame Nkrumah, unable to return to Ghana, was welcomed by President Touré of Guinea. It had been agreed in 1958 that Guinea and Ghana should unite, though this did not take effect, and Touré now made Nkrumah co-president of Guinea.

Since the coup, most political prisoners have been released and the situation has been comparatively peaceful. The National Liberation

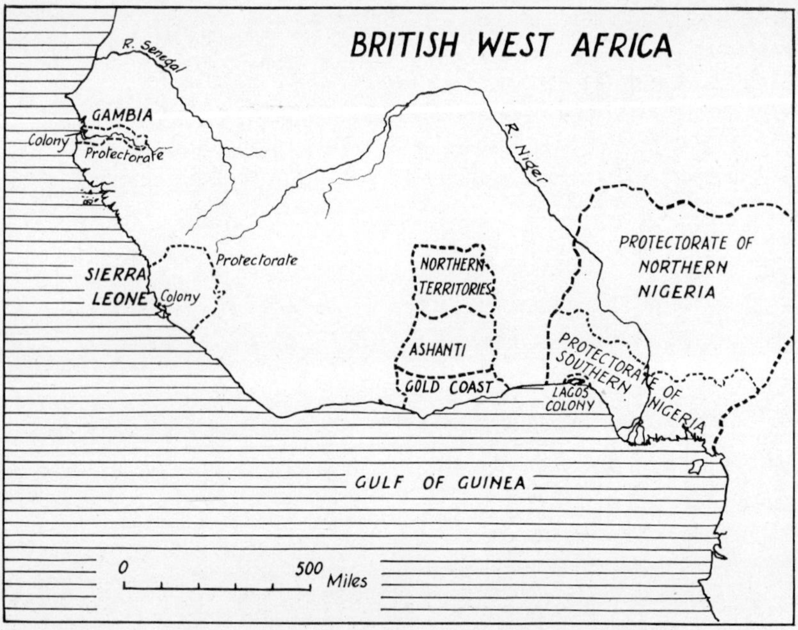

Council has declared its intention of holding free elections and bringing about full democratic rule as soon as possible.

A great deal has been done since independence to improve Ghana's economy. A new harbour has been built at Tema, capable of taking ocean-going ships, while roads and railways have been constructed in the interior. The River Volta project is providing her with hydro-electric power and irrigation.

Nigeria

It was well into the second half of the nineteenth century before any real attempt was made by British merchants to penetrate Nigeria. There had been some earlier connections but the poor climate and hostile natives had hindered any progress.

In 1879 the National African Company was formed by several trading groups and made agreements with African chiefs to trade with the area. The British Government founded the Oil River Protectorate in 1884 to cover the area along the Niger and the Oil Rivers.

Largely due to the work of Sir George Goldie, the National African Company became the Royal Niger Company, with a Royal Charter, in 1886, authorised to administer any territory it could obtain.

For thirteen years the Company carried out its task with energy and made treaties with chiefs to acquire considerable areas. As it advanced up the River Niger it came into contact with warrior peoples who had come across Africa from the Sudan. They were Moslems and were ruled by Emirs. Their subject peoples were treated harshly and there was much slave-trading, raids being made on the people to the south for this purpose.

In 1899 the Crown took over the area ruled by the Royal Niger Company as the Protectorates of Northern and Southern Nigeria and Colonel Frederick Lugard, later Lord Lugard, was appointed High Commissioner. Lugard had to take military action against the Hausa emirates of Kano and Sokoto in the north. A system of indirect rule was established in the north with the general administration left to the native rulers with the aid of British Residents. In the south, since there were no strong native rulers, a system of rule by District Commissioners was used.

In 1906, Lagos, which had been a British possession since 1861, was added to the Protectorate of Southern Nigeria. Lord Lugard returned in 1914 to become the first governor of the new colony and Protectorate of Nigeria, formed from Northern and Southern Nigeria and later the mandated territory of the ex-German Cameroons.

Gradually, roads and railways were built and the production of rubber, cotton, ground-nuts, cocoa and palm-oil increased. Tin and coal mines were developed.

After the Second World War the advance to independence began. There was a great deal of mutual distrust between the three regions of Northern, Eastern and Western Nigeria. The Northern peoples, particularly the Hausas who had long formed the soldiers and police of West Africa, looked with a certain amount of contempt on those of the South. The two Southern regions with tribes such as the Ibos, Yorubas and Aros providing most of the more educated and intelligent of the population, looked with some contempt on the North. The memories of the slave-raiding of the North remained, too. It was felt, therefore, that independence must come as a federation. Eastern and Western Nigeria became self-governing in 1957 and Northern Nigeria in 1959. The Federation of Nigeria consisting of these three regions became an independent member of the Commonwealth on 1 October 1960 and a republic in 1963. One of the most famous figures in Nigerian politics, Dr Azikiwe became its first President with Sir Abubakar Tafawa Balewa from the North as its first Prime Minister. There has been a tendency for the Northern Region with its greater population to dominate affairs and this has brought resentment from the other regions. Chief Awolowo, former Prime Minister of the Western Region, was charged with plotting against the Government and imprisoned in 1962, an English barrister being refused permission to defend him at his trial. In 1963 Chief Enahoro fled to Britain seeking political asylum. On being refused permission to stay, he returned to Nigeria and imprisonment, once again British legal aid being refused. Many others opposing the Government have also been imprisoned.

In the General Election held in January 1965 there was a clash between the Prime Minister of the Western Region, Chief Akintola and the Federal Prime Minister and there was much boycotting of voting booths making the Election in many ways farcical and producing a temporary constitutional crisis. A second Election was held in October 1965 which also provided criticism of the arrangements, including that of rigging the elections, and there was considerable disorder.

Many people in Britain with knowledge and experience of Nigeria had forecast such difficulties, and their forebodings were to be proved tragically right.

In January 1966 there was a *coup d'état* by young army officers, mainly of the Ibo tribe, who feared the dominance of the Hausas of the North. The Prime Minister, Sir Abubakar Tafawa Balewa, was assassinated, together with other ministers. To prevent the situation getting further out of hand, the Army Chief-of-Staff, Major-General Aguiyi-Ironsi, also an Ibo, took control and set up a military government. In the disorder brought about by the rising, Chief Akintola was also killed. Chiefs Enahoro and Awolowo were released from captivity, as were other political prisoners.

It soon became clear that it was largely a struggle for control of the country between the Ibos of the south-east and the numerically superior Hausas of the North. The latter's dominance had long been resented by the rest of the country.

Because of tribal feelings between Ibos, Hausas and Yorubas of the south-west, Nigeria had been made a federation on becoming independent. General Ironsi now sought to dissolve the federation and set up a military form of government with strong central control.

This and the tribal feelings provoked a later *coup d'état* in July 1966 when a further rising of Hausa officers, led by Lieutenant-Colonel Gowon, overthrew General Ironsi's government, many Ibo officers being killed including General Ironsi himself.

EAST AFRICA

Somaliland

This territory on the Gulf of Aden was of little importance until after the completion of the Suez Canal in 1869. In 1884 the area of Somaliland was divided between Britain, France, Italy and Abyssinia as a part of what became known as the 'scramble for Africa'. British

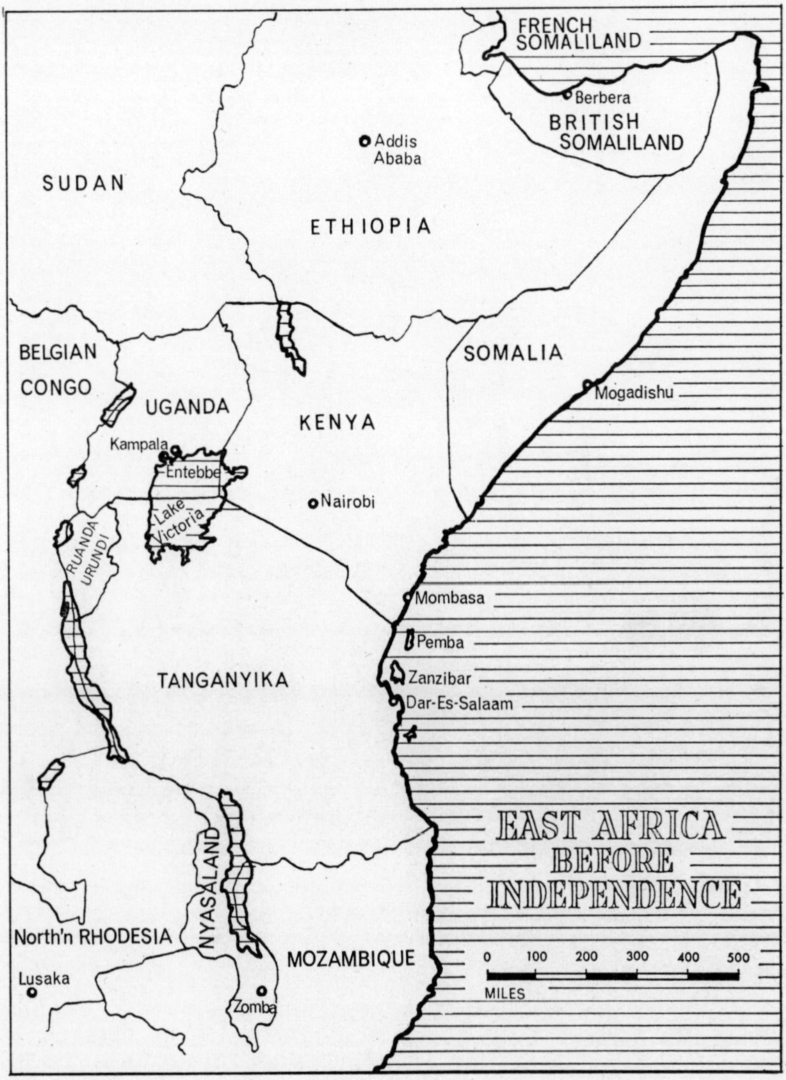

Somaliland had certain strategic importance. After the Second World War and temporary Italian occupation a slow move towards independence was begun. In 1960 it was granted independence and at once united with ex-Italian Somaliland to form the independent state of Somalia outside the Commonwealth. There has been some disagreement with Kenya about the border between the two countries as some Somalis are within Kenya.

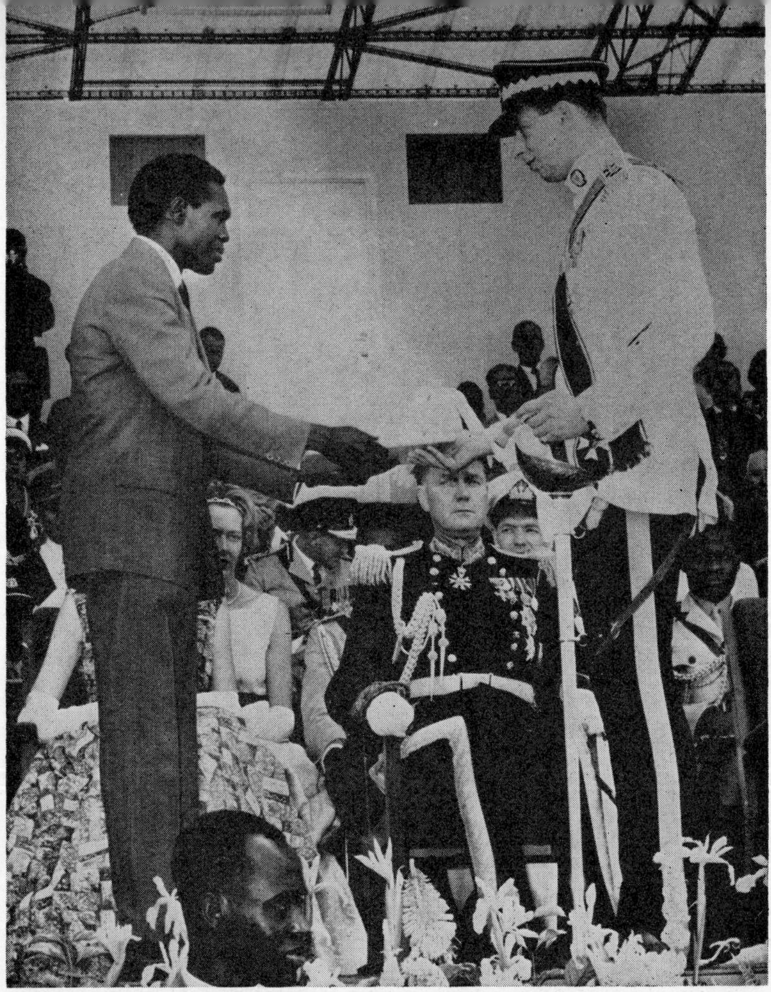

Uganda's Independence: Duke of Kent hands over constitutional documents to Dr Milton Obote.

Uganda

The British explorers, John Speke and James Grant, visited Uganda in 1862, Sir Samuel Baker followed in 1864 and Henry Stanley in 1875. Missionaries followed, particularly up to 1879. One of the provinces of Uganda, Buganda, was ruled by a Kabaka or King, Mutesa I. He was friendly to the Christian missionaries but when he died in 1884 his successor, Mwanga, was hostile and many missionaries were murdered. As a result the Imperial East Africa Company, which had been founded in 1878 by Sir William Mackinnon, was given control of Uganda together with other British territories in Africa considered to be within the British 'sphere of influence'. The 'sphere' was agreed by the Anglo-German agreement of 1886 which arose from the Germans joining the 'scramble for Africa' rather late. Captain Frederick Lugard, later Lord Lugard, was sent to restore order and to establish the Company's authority in Uganda. With the help of Captain Williams and never more than a handful of Sudanese soldiers he succeeded in restoring order and establishing British rule, as well as preventing the Protestant, Catholic and Moslem missionaries from quarrelling. The Company considered giving up Uganda because of the cost of maintenance, but in 1894, as the result of an appeal by Lugard supported by the missionaries, the British Government established a Protectorate over Buganda, soon extending it to the remainder of Uganda.

A 'Union Agreement' was arranged between British officials and African chiefs in 1900. Gradually, Africans were introduced into the Government. Uganda did not find movement towards independence easy consisting as it did of four kingdoms and the small province of Busoga. Buganda at one time wanted complete independence from the remainder of the territory, since it was a monarchy. After the Second World War progress towards independence continued, a new constitution was inaugurated in March 1962, and in October 1962 Uganda became an independent member of the Commonwealth. It became a republic within the Commonwealth in October 1963, with the King of Buganda, the Kabaka, as its first President.

Dr Milton Obote, the Prime Minister, resented the attempts of Buganda to run its own internal affairs and relations with the Kabaka, Sir Edward Mutesa, became strained. The Kabaka in his turn viewed Dr Obote's efforts with suspicion, believing that he wished to make Uganda a one-party dictatorship.

These suspicions were proved sound, when in February 1966 Dr Obote assumed full dictatorial powers and imprisoned five Cabinet ministers. This action followed immediately upon opposition accusations of corruption directed against several ministers and Dr Obote himself.

Sir Edward Mutesa, as President, disputed Dr Obote's right to take such measures and requested that foreign troops should be brought in to maintain order until the situation improved. This was refused and when Buganda objected to the new constitution which placed all power in the hands of the central government and ended Buganda's right to govern its own internal affairs, Dr Obote used troops to enforce it. This was in May 1966, and after desperate fighting between Buganda's royal troops and those of the central government the Kabaka fled the country.

Kenya

When in 1878 Sir William Mackinnon obtained concessions on the mainland from the Sultan of Zanzibar, these included the territory today known as Kenya. The British Government were disinterested and disavowed the agreement but when rivalry between Britain and Germany led to the Anglo-German Agreement of 1886, Kenya was to be within the British 'sphere of influence'. The Imperial British East Africa Company administered the new territory, but the British Government took it over in 1895 as the British East Africa Protectorate.

In 1901 a railway was completed from Mombasa to the shore of Lake Victoria, which opened up the East African Highlands. Because of their suitability for agriculture and temperate climate they became attractive to European settlers and became known as the White Highlands. Much of the best land was reserved for white settlers and this was resented by the Africans who regarded it as tribal property. Many settlers from South Africa, both British and Dutch, and from Britain arrived from then onwards. The British Government still seemed reluctant to develop the territory and in 1905 a considerable part was offered to the Zionists as a national home for the Jewish people. This offer was refused.

Because of demands by the white settlers, Executive and Legislative Councils were set up in 1906.

After the First World War, in 1920, it became Kenya Colony, so named after Mount Kenya, although the coastal strip still remained a Protectorate.

In 1923 the British Government published a White Paper which spoke of Kenya as being held in trust for its native peoples and of its eventual independence. This produced a reaction from the white settlers and their leader, Lord Delamere, said that such an idea was unacceptable in a territory suitable for white settlement. The attitude of the white settlers slowed down the pace at which Africans were trained to share in government. This led to a feeling among many Africans and their leaders that insufficient was being done on their behalf.

After the Second World War there was a general move towards independence in British colonies, but nothing approaching the Mau-Mau rising in Kenya had been seen before.

The report by the all-party Parliamentary Delegation to Kenya of January 1954 stated that Mau-Mau was a secret society largely confined to the Kikiyu tribe which began to attract attention about

1950 and grew and erupted during the following years. It described Mau-Mau as:

> a conspiracy designed to dominate first the Kikiyu tribe, then all other Africans and finally to drive out all other races and seize power in Kenya . . . it uses terrorism to secure obedience where it cannot command willing support and compliance. . . . Mau-Mau has progressed from the political oath with which it began, through successive oaths each more violent than its predecessor. . . . Mau-Mau intentionally and deliberately seeks to lead the Africans of Kenya back to the bush and savagery, not forward into progress.

It published a description of the oaths and ceremonies in an Appendix, which was only available to Members of Parliament since it was too obscene and bestial for the public to see. A Czech psychiatrist, asked by the delegation to prepare a report, said:

> A very clever man, a man knowing the psychology of his peoples, their superstitions, their fear of witchcraft, must have made the plan. The Killing Oath was the answer. . . . It forces a man or woman to kill when called upon to do so, or it kills the man or woman upon breaking the oath. . . . It has been possible to transform the human being into a new frame of mind unknown and never met by me before. After having taken three or more oaths the personality of the oath-taker has changed. . . . These people do not hesitate or think any more . . . they just kill on being instructed to kill—their own mother, their own baby. . . .

In fact large numbers of the Kikiyu rejected Mau-Mau and so the police and many British troops were able to suppress it by 1955. The Parliamentary delegation had reported critically on a number of things in Kenya, including brutality and corruption within the police force and the attitude of many of the white population. This made some progress towards eventual independence very necessary. Mr Jomo Kenyatta, who was leader of K.A.N.U. (Kenya African

Jomo Kenyatta.
(*Portrait: Baron Studios.*)

National Union), was said to have been implicated in Mau-Mau and was imprisoned from January 1954 to August 1961.

Kenya was granted new constitutions in 1951 and 1960, each of which granted more African representation, the second giving an African majority and in 1963 a transitional constitution was granted with internal self-government with reserve powers for the governor for external affairs, defence and internal security. Mr Kenyatta became the first Prime Minister. Full independence as a republic within the Commonwealth was given on 12 December 1963.

In January 1964 mutinies within the Kenya army led to Mr Kenyatta asking for British troops, who soon restored order. Since then all British troops have left Kenya.

The chief opposition party led by Mr Ngala, K.A.D.U. (Kenya Africa Democratic Union) voluntarily amalgamated with K.A.N.U. late in 1964, making Kenya a one-party state. Mr Kenyatta became the first President of the Republic. Mr Ngala was later elected Vice-President of K.A.N.U. replacing Mr Oginga Odinga by 72 votes to 6. This was a significant move since Mr Odinga, strongly pro-Communist, had been challenging for power. This challenge had been opposed by Mr Jomo Kenyatta who, to the surprise of many who had remembered his supposed association with Mau-Mau, had proved himself a fine President. His moderate and statesmanlike guidance of his country marks him as outstanding among the leaders of the new Africa.

In April 1966 Mr Odinga resigned from K.A.N.U. and formed his own opposition party. The thirty Members of Parliament who joined him were forced to resign their seats and seek re-election. They were heavily defeated at the polls in May and this proved a resounding victory for Mr Kenyatta.

Many people believe that the white settlers have not been treated fairly, since they have been unable to obtain good prices for their farms if they decided not to remain in Kenya under an all-African government. Those who have stayed have settled well and appear to be satisfied with the situation.

There has been unrest among the peoples of northern Kenya who have shown a desire to join the Republic of Somalia.

Tanzania

This was formed by the union of Tanganyika and Zanzibar in April 1964.

Tanganyika became a Protectorate known as German East Africa in 1890. After the First World War it was given to Britain to administer as a mandated territory. Government was carried on largely through African chiefs, although a Legislative Council was set up in 1926.

After the Second World War gradual moves were made towards self-government. In March 1961 a conference was held at Dar-es-Salaam to agree upon a constitution and Tanganyika became independent within the Commonwealth on 9 October 1961 and a Republic exactly one year later. Her first Prime Minister, Julius Nyerere, who later became President both of the Republic and the Union, is generally regarded as one of the most statesmanlike and moderate of African leaders, and Tanganyika's move to independence was both gentle and reasonably uneventful. There was a certain amount of difficulty, in which the President called for the aid of British troops, early in 1964, but Tanganyika appeared to recover and united with Zanzibar soon afterwards.

Julius Nyerere and Malcolm MacDonald.

Zanzibar was under Portuguese overlordship until 1698, but was then captured by Arabs and came under the rule of the Sultan of Oman. In the eighteenth and early nineteenth centuries Zanzibar was a centre for the slave trade, but Treaties of 1873 and 1875 declared the trade to be illegal, although it was the end of the century before it was stopped. Zanzibar was separated from Oman in 1861.

It was from the Sultan of Zanzibar that Sir William Mackinnon obtained his concessions on the mainland in 1878. In 1890 the Sultan asked for British protection and a Protectorate was declared. The British Government ruled through the Sultan with a British Resident to assist and after 1926 Executive and Legislative Councils also.

In 1961 the Legislative Council received elected members and Zanzibar received internal self-government in June, 1963.

There was considerable Communist activity in the island, inspired by Red China, and there was a plot to take over the government. This led to a rising in 1964, when the Sultan was deposed, but afterwards Zanzibar entered into a union with Tanganyika and the Communists' influence and activity gradually declined. The new union became known as Tanzania.

East African Federation

In 1947 an East African High Commission was established to provide common services such as defence, customs, postal services, railways, shipping and research.

As the territories moved towards independence the Commission was replaced in 1962 by the East African Common Services Authority. Tanganyika, Uganda and Kenya became members. In 1964 these states almost reached agreement over the formation of an East African Federation, but with Tanzania drifting away it failed to come into being and was abandoned in 1965.

CENTRAL AFRICA

Rhodesia

Cecil Rhodes, Prime Minister of Cape Colony, had a great vision of a map of Africa with British 'pink' from Cairo to the Cape and certainly a railway linking those two places.

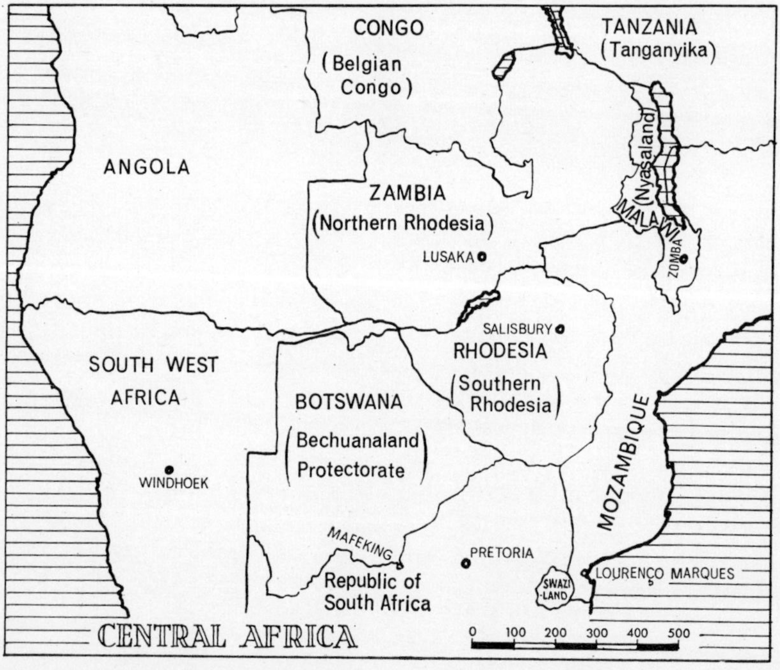

Sir Roy Welensky.
last P.M. of Central
African Federation.

In order to forestall a move from the Boers in the Transvaal, northwards across the River Limpopo, he entered into negotiations with the chiefs of the Mashonas and the Matabele. The latter race were a warrior people who had invaded the area, suppressing the Mashonas they conquered. In 1888 he obtained concessions from Lobengula, King of the Matabele, who later complained that he had been tricked by Rhodes, and fighting resulted; the Matabele were defeated.

In 1889, Rhodes founded the British South Africa Company which was granted a charter by the British Government to trade with and develop the new area. Britain proclaimed a Protectorate over both Mashonaland and Matabeleland in 1891. The Administrator of the territory was Dr L. S. Jameson, who was to become famous for his raid into the Transvaal in 1895. The British Government then intervened and appointed a Commissioner and a Military Commander. The area under the Commissioner between the Limpopo and Zambesi Rivers became known as Southern Rhodesia in 1895.

After the First World War the Legislative Council of Southern Rhodesia asked for responsible government. General Smuts, Prime Minister of South Africa, invited the territory to become a part of the Union, but the invitation was refused. In 1923 Britain formally annexed the territory and responsible government was granted

When the Second World War, in which Rhodesia had played a great part, ended, ideas which had been held for some time of co-operation between the Central African countries came to fruition. The Central African Federation was formed in 1953. When the federation finally broke up in 1963, and Northern Rhodesia and Nyasaland became independent as Zambia and Malawi, Southern Rhodesia became known simply as Rhodesia.

There had long been a difference in attitude to the Africans and their future between the white peoples in Great Britain and in Rhodesia. The white settlers held that since the Africans were a simple and primitive people who would never be able to take a full

Ian Smith.

share in government, white supremacy must be maintained at all costs. They were also in fear of losing the very high standard which they had built up, far higher than they could have hoped for in Britain. When the Rhodesian Government demanded independence from successive British Governments it was refused until some sign that rights of citizenship would be granted to the Africans.

After conferences in London and Salisbury, the capital of Rhodesia, a new constitution was announced in 1961. There were to be two electoral rolls. The upper roll would elect fifty members to the Legislative Assembly. There was to be no formal colour bar and Africans could be on the upper roll if they were qualified. Qualifications, both property and educational, would mean in practice that few Africans would be on the upper roll and it would be white-dominated. The lower roll, all of Africans, would elect fifteen members to the Assembly. The qualifications for this meant, also, that a comparatively small proportion of the African population would receive the vote. The Constitution also included safeguards for the Africans to prevent racial discrimination.

In fact the 1961 Constitution has never been fully in operation. In May of 1963, Mr Winston Field, Prime Minister and leader of the Right-Wing Rhodesian Front, demanded independence, but the British Government refused to grant it without some further concessions to the Africans. Mr Field was replaced as Prime Minister by Mr Ian Smith. Because the Rhodesian Government which was very Right-Wing and now led by Mr Smith, refused to go farther than this, a constitutional crisis arose within the Commonwealth. Legally, Rhodesia could only become independent by an Act of the British Parliament, but a referendum was held in which the Rhodesian white people voted for a declaration of independence unilaterally, without the British Government's agreement. This crisis reached serious proportions by 1965. For some time the main African leaders, Mr Nkomo and Mr Sithole, had been detained in restricted areas and an ex-Prime Minister, a Liberal, Mr Garfield Todd, was put under restrictive detention when he wished to fly to Britain to oppose Mr Ian Smith's point of view. Mr Smith had visited London for talks and, on negotiations breaking down, Mr Harold Wilson, the British Prime Minister, flew to Rhodesia. Suggestions were made for a Royal Commission to report on what was best for the future of the colony and the British Government also suggested a referendum in which all Rhodesians, Europeans and Africans should express their opinion on the future steps. Mr Smith had been threatening a unilateral declaration of independence, U.D.I. as it came to be called.

Independence was declared unilaterally in November 1965. This was immediately condemned by the British Government as an illegal act, which it undoubtedly was since Rhodesia was still a British colony. African members of the Commonwealth demanded that force should be used to make Rhodesia submit, but the British Government did not wish to do this. The United Nations asked for sanctions against Rhodesia and many countries broke off all trading relations with the rebel colony as a result. Britain also put severe economic restrictions into operation. At the request of Mr Kaunda, Zambian President, Royal Air Force fighter planes were stationed in his country, but his request that British troops should take over the Kariba Dam on the Zambesi was refused. The African states threatened to leave the Commonwealth if Britain did not take firmer measures.

Sir Humphrey Gibbs, the Governor-General, remained loyal to the Queen and refused to recognise the declaration of independence. He was virtually isolated in his official residence and Mr Smith attempted to make his own nominee, Mr C. W. Dupont, Governor-General in his place. The Queen refused to accept this nomination and Mr Smith then declared Mr Dupont to be Acting Official Administrator.

The application of oil sanctions by the British Government led to the interception by Royal Navy frigates, in April 1966, of tankers carrying oil to Rhodesia. Exploratory talks to attempt to find a solution were agreed in April, and these went on for some time.

In July the University College of Rhodesia was closed temporarily and several lecturers were arrested because of opposition to the Rhodesian Government's policy.

In October the British Government declared that if a settlement had not been reached by December the United Nations would be asked to agree to mandatory sanctions. Further talks followed but no agreement was concluded and sanctions were applied by the United Nations.

Kenneth Kaunda.
(*Photo: Baron Studios.*)

Zambia

The territory north of the Zambesi River, which had been settled at the end of the nineteenth century, was divided into North-West and North-East Rhodesia in 1900. In 1911 the two provinces were united as Northern Rhodesia and in 1923 the British South Africa Company ceased to be responsible for it, the territory becoming a colony under a governor with Executive and Legislative Councils the following year.

When the Central African Federation came into existence in 1953, Northern Rhodesia was a part of it, but African fears at the effect of the Federation were shown by the strikes and violence which followed.

At a constitutional conference in London in December 1960 and January 1961 it was impossible to find agreement on whether Africans should receive a majority. Much argument and discussion followed and there were outbreaks of violence among the workers in the copper mines, on which the colony's economy was largely based.

After a resumption of talks in 1962, a new constitution was announced for Northern Rhodesia in March 1962. The Legislative Council was to consist of 15 European, 15 African and 15 members who would be chosen from either, with 1 seat for Indians. The General Election of November resulted in an African majority and an African Government was formed, which demanded the right to leave the Central African Federation. Northern Rhodesia became independent in October 1964 taking the name of Zambia, with Mr Kenneth Kaunda as Prime Minister, and it has chosen to remain a member of the Commonwealth. There was a dispute with the British South Africa Company over compensation for the copper mines taken over by the Zambian Government but this was resolved at the end of October 1964.

Zambia has been deeply involved in the Rhodesian dispute and her economy has been in jeopardy. Mr Kaunda, his hand probably being forced by the more extreme elements, has expressed dissatisfaction with Britain's failure to resolve the situation and there have been threats that Zambia would leave the Commonwealth.

Malawi

The area around Lake Nyasa was first visited by David Livingstone in 1859. Many other missionaries followed, and in 1861 the Universities Mission to Central Africa set up a station in the territory. The hostility of the natives drove them out, but they returned in 1881. In the meantime a Church of Scotland Mission had been established to the west of the lake and a Scottish Free Church Mission at Blantyre to the south.

The African Lakes Company was formed in 1878 to develop trade in the region and after agreeing the boundary between the territory and Mozambique, with the Portuguese in 1891, it became the British Central African Protectorate. In 1907 its name was changed to the Nyasaland Protectorate and it was placed under a governor with Executive and Legislative Councils.

Africans were introduced into both these Councils later, and after the Second World War in 1953 it became a part of the Central African Federation. This provoked considerable criticism from the Africans and their leaders who consistently demanded that Nyasaland should secede from the Federation, and that it should receive independence. A conference to consider constitutional changes was held in London in the summer of 1960 and agreement was reached. There were to be two electoral rolls and a Legislative Assembly of 28 members, 8 elected by the higher roll and 20 by the lower. The constitution came

Dr Hastings Banda.

into force in 1961 and Dr Hastings Banda's Malawi Party won all 28 seats, Dr Banda becoming Prime Minister. He immediately demanded right of secession from the Federation. Fully responsible government was granted in February 1963 and it became independent in July 1964, with the name of Malawi, as a republic within the Commonwealth. There have been certain internal disturbances since and Dr Banda has found it necessary to take action against some of his political opponents by imprisoning them.

Dr Banda has proved himself a statesmanlike leader and has been one of the more moderate of the African heads of state during the Rhodesian crisis.

The Central African Federation

The first proposal for the federation of Northern Rhodesia with Nyasaland had come as early as 1927. In 1938 the British Government appointed the Bledisloe Commission to report on the future of the Central African territory. Its report in 1939 recommended closer co-operation and possibly union in the future. The Second World War held up any progress towards this but the question was reopened after the war.

In 1948 the victory of the Afrikaaner-dominated Nationalist Party in South Africa made many people in Southern Rhodesia desire federation as quickly as possible. After considerable discussion and negotiations, the Rhodesia and Nyasaland Federation Act was passed in 1953.

This Act set up a Federal Assembly under a Governor-General, each territory retaining its existing status. An African Affairs Board was established to safeguard the position of the African people. The whole constitution was to be reviewed in 1961.

There was much criticism of the Federation from all sections of opinion both in Africa and in Britain. Many people felt that it was a means of ensuring white domination and the Africans certainly feared this. They were very disappointed at the very small advance towards a share in government. It was said that the Africans had not been consulted on their views towards the Federation.

Because of the expression of criticism and the need for revision of the Act in 1961, the British Government appointed a Commission under Lord Monckton in 1959.

The Commission reported in October 1960 that the Federation should continue with increased African representation. It also said that racial discrimination should be illegal and that a Bill of Rights should be included in the constitution. Territories should have the right to secede if they so wished.

Southern Rhodesia disagreed with the right of secession and the Africans were disappointed that the Commission had not recommended independence with African majorities. The conference in December 1960 which met to consider revision had little success and as Northern Rhodesia and Nyasaland received their new constitution and demanded their right to secede, it became evident that the Federation would break up. It was formally ended after Mr R. A. Butler had supervised the negotiations and arrangements in 1963.

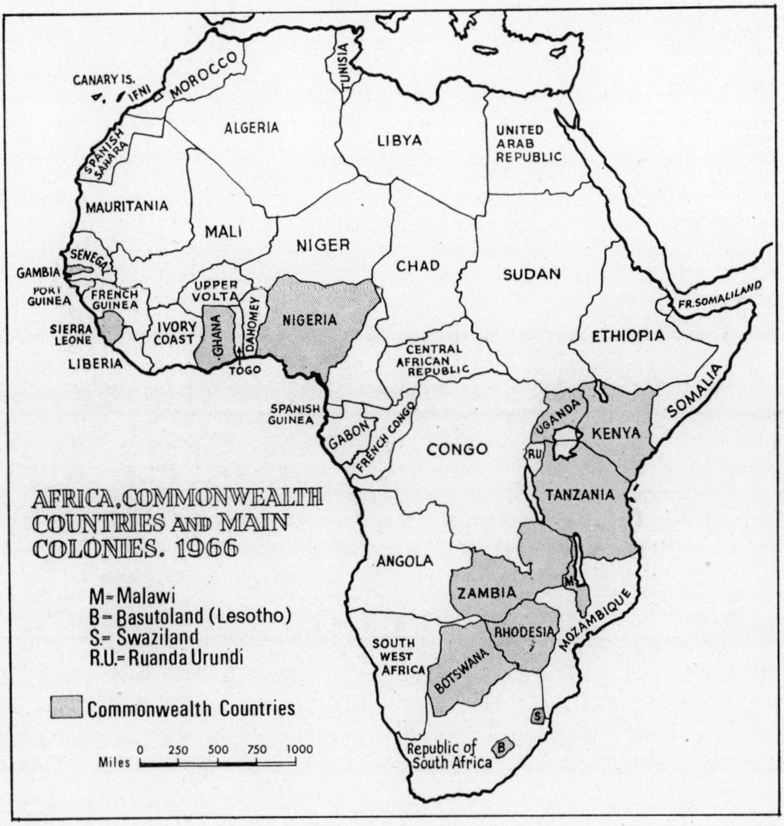

SUMMARY

Early European Settlements in Africa

Diaz' voyage to Cape (1487).—Da Gama's voyage (1497); Portuguese interest in West Africa.—Early English interest in Gambia.—Dutch and English interest in Gold Coast; centre of slave trade.—Portuguese early interest in East Africa.

WEST AFRICA

Gambia

Settlement in 1618.—Fort James (1663), centre of slave trade.—Bathurst (1816). —Royal African Company (1672) dissolved in 1821.—West African Settlement. —British colony and Protectorate (1889).—Independence within Commonwealth (1965).

Sierra Leone

Early visits by Portuguese and British.—Settlement for freed slaves (1788) at Freetown.—Crown colony (1807).—Protectorate.—Responsible government (1953).—Independence within Commonwealth (1961).

Ghana

British interest in Gold Coast in seventeenth century.—Dutch, Danish and English slave trade.—Royal African Company (1672) dissolved 1821 after abolition of slave trade.—West African Settlement (1821).—Ashanti Wars (1826, 1873–74, 1896).—Ashanti annexed (1901).—Northern Territories as Protectorate (1901).—New constitution (1946).—Responsible government (1954).—Independent within Commonwealth as Ghana (1957).—Republic (1960).—Nkrumah overthrown by *coup* (1966).

Nigeria

British merchants' interest in second half of nineteenth century.—National African Company (1879).—Oil River Protectorate (1884).—National African Company became Royal Niger Company (1886).—Moslems in north.—Slave trade.—Protectorates of Northern and Southern Nigeria (1899).—Lagos added to Southern Nigeria (1906).—Colony and Protectorate of Nigeria formed (1914). —Distrust between Northern, Eastern and Western Nigeria after Second World War.—Responsible government to Eastern and Western Nigeria (1957); to Northern Nigeria (1959).—Nigeria independent as federation within Commonwealth (1960).—Republic (1963).—Government overthrown by military *coup* (Jan. 1966).—Balewa assassinated.—Further military *coup* (July 1966).

EAST AFRICA

Somaliland

Divided between Britain, France, Italy and Abyssinia (1884).—British Somaliland.—Independence granted (1960); united with ex-Italian territory as Somalia outside the Commonwealth.

Uganda

Speke and Grant explored area in 1862.—Baker in 1864.—Stanley in 1878.—Missionaries.—King of Buganda's action against missionaries (1884).—Imperial British Africa Company founded in 1878.—Given control of Uganda.—Anglo-German Agreement (1886) determined 'spheres of influence'.—Captain Lugard sent to restore order.—British Protectorate (1894).—'Union Agreement' between British officials and African chiefs (1900).—October 1962 independent within Commonwealth.—October 1963 Republic within Commonwealth.—Constitutional crisis.—Kabaka fled (1966).

Kenya

Sir William Mackinnon obtained trading rights (1878).—Anglo-German Agreement (1886) determined 'spheres of influence'.—Imperial British East Africa Company.—British East Africa Protectorate (1895).—European settlers.—Executive and Legislative Councils (1906).—Kenya Colony (1920).—Mau-Mau.—New constitutions give more African representation (1951, 1960, 1963).—African majority.—Internal self-government (1963).—Independence as Republic within Commonwealth (Dec. 1963).

Tanzania

Tanganyika Protectorate as German East Africa (1890).—Mandate under League of Nations given to Britain (1920).—Constitutional conference (1961).—Independent within Commonwealth (Dec. 1961).—Republic within Commonwealth (Dec. 1962).—Zanzibar as British Protectorate (1890).—Internal self-government (June 1963).—Tanganyika and Zanzibar united as Tanzania (April 1964).

CENTRAL AFRICA

Rhodesia

Cecil Rhodes concessions from Lobengula (1888).—British South Africa Company (1889).—British Protectorate over Mashonaland and Matabeleland (1891).—Area between Limpopo and Zambesi as Southern Rhodesia (1895).—Invitation to join South Africa (1922).—British colony with responsible government (1923).—Central African Federation (1953).—On break-up of federation became Rhodesia (1963).—New constitution (1961).—Africans' demand for greater representation.—Demands for independence.—Constitutional crisis.—U.D.I. (Nov. 1965).—Sanctions.—Negotiations (1966).—Meeting on Tiger—U.N. sanctions (1966).

Zambia

North-West and North-East Rhodesia (1900).—Northern Rhodesia (1911).—British colony (1923).—Central African Federation (1953).—London Conference (1960–61).—New constitution (1962).—African majority.—Demand to secede from Federation.—Independent within Commonwealth (1964) as Zambia.

Malawi

Area of Lake Nyasa visited by Livingstone (1859).—Further missionaries.—African Lakes Company (1878).—British Central African Protectorate (1891).—Nyasaland Protectorate (1907).—Central African Federation (1953).—London Conference (1960).—New constitution (1961).—Responsible government (1963).—Demanded secession from Federation.—Independent as republic within Commonwealth as Malawi (July 1964).

The Central African Federation

First suggested (1927).—Bledisloe Commission reported in favour of closer co-operation (1939).—Rhodesia and Nyasaland Federation Act (1953).—Criticism of Federation, particularly from Africans.—Monckton Commission (1960) reported in favour of continuance.—Zambia and Malawi desired to secede.—End of Federation (1963).

QUESTIONS

Answer the following questions briefly:

1. (a) Why were European countries interested in West Africa in the seventeenth century and earlier?
   (b) How did Gambia develop as a colony?
   (c) What was unusual about Sierra Leone's development as a British possession?
   (d) Why was the Royal Niger Company formed?
   (e) Which African countries were first opened up by missionaries?
   (f) What was the importance of the Anglo-German Agreement of 1886?
   (g) What do we mean by the 'scramble for Africa'?
   (h) What was the 'great vision' of Cecil Rhodes?
   (i) What were the original names, as British colonies, of Zambia, Malawi, Ghana and Tanzania?
   (j) Why did the Central African Federation meet with so much criticism?
2. Describe the progress towards independence of any new African nation.
3. 'A conspiracy of evil.' How do you consider this describes the Mau-Mau rising in Kenya? Give an account of the rising.
4. Mr Harold Macmillan, then Prime Minister of Great Britain, speaking in Ghana in February 1960, said:

   > The wind of change is blowing through Africa and the rapid emergence of African countries to nationhood represents a new development in the world. . . . We share the strong tide of feeling among Africans that this is a time of destiny.

   (a) What do you think Mr Macmillan meant by 'the wind of change'?
   (b) Do you agree with his last sentence?
5. The Rhodesian Prime Minister, Mr Ian Smith, in his reply to Mr Wilson's message to him on 3 November 1965 after his visit to Rhodesia, said:

   > Undoubtedly, advocacy of the British Government's proposals (at the Royal Commission which had been suggested) would become a potent and distracting factor. Its effect would simply be to convert it into a constitutional conference, and in dealing with emergent and, in some cases, primitive peoples, through an interpreter, the confusion of thought caused could provide no significant answer at all. . . .

   (a) What did Mr Smith mean by the first sentence?
   (b) Do you agree that 'dealing with emergent and, in some cases, primitive peoples, through an interpreter, the confusion of thought could provide no significant answer at all'?
   (c) What does the quotation in (b) above show of the Rhodesian Front's attitude to the crisis?
   (d) How did the crisis develop?

17 : The West Indies

THE West Indies are in four main groups, the Antilles, the Bahamas, the Venezuelan Coast Islands and the Bermudas. The Antilles may be subdivided into the Greater and Lesser Antilles and the latter, once again, into the Leeward and the Windward Islands. Some of the islands are French, Dutch or American possessions, while some are independent, but most are British.

It was Spain which opened up the Caribbean in the great days of the Spanish Main. England was first interested when adventurous English seamen attempted to challenge Spain's supremacy and later when Virginia was settled. The first group of islands to be settled was the Bermudas when after Sir George Somers was shipwrecked in 1609, they were annexed by the Virginia Company. However, just before in 1604 and 1609, settlements had been made on the Guiana coast by Charles Leigh and Robert Harcourt. One of Sir Walter Raleigh's officers, Captain Roger North, established a settlement at the mouth of the Amazon in 1619 and founded the Amazon Company. Charles I gave a Royal Charter to the Guiana Company in 1627. These mainland settlements all failed, but were to lead to settlements of the islands.

Barbados and St Kitts

These two islands are in the Leeward group. Thomas Warner, one of the original settlers from North's Amazon colony, landed on St Christopher, or St Kitts as it is usually known, with a party in 1624. The settlers spread to Nevis, Montserrat and Antigua. Barbados was settled in 1627. Tobacco and sugar were the main crops and they prospered. The plantations needed labour and slaves were soon brought in from Africa in considerable numbers.

Bermuda

After the settlement following Sir George Somers' shipwreck in 1609, it was taken over by the Virginia Company until the Bermuda Company was founded soon afterwards. The Company continued until 1684.

Jamaica

Admiral Penn and General Venables seized Jamaica in 1655 after an unsuccessful attempt to capture the Spanish headquarters of Hispaniola. Spain recognised that the island was a British colony in 1670. The Cayman Islands were captured soon after Jamaica and ruled from there. In the late seventeenth and much of the eighteenth century, the island was a haunt of pirates, one of the most famous being Sir Henry Morgan who was governor from 1674 until 1682. Since the pirates operated mainly against the Spanish Government, the British made little effort to deal with them. The island's main product was sugar and slave labour was used extensively.

Bahamas

One of the islands was occupied by settlers from Bermuda in 1646 and a charter was given to the Elizabethan Company in 1649. The Bahamas were also a centre of piracy. The famous pirate Blackbeard, Edward Teach, used one of the islands as his headquarters. Little was done to deal with the pirates until the reign of George I. Cotton became one of the main products when Empire Loyalists came to the islands after the American War of Independence.

Trinidad

Trinidad was originally Spanish. It was captured and sacked by Sir Walter Raleigh in 1595. During the Revolutionary War, the island was captured from Spain by Sir Ralph Abercromby in 1796. It became British by the Treaty of Amiens in 1802.

Tobago

The first settlement was in 1639 and after changing hands several times, it became British during the Napoleonic War in 1803. This was confirmed by the Treaty of Paris in 1814.

Guiana

There were Dutch and English settlements by the early seventeenth century. Sugar, coffee and cotton were introduced by British settlers from Barbados. In 1796, during the Napoleonic War, the settlements were captured by the British and although restored to the Dutch by the Treaty of Amiens in 1802, they were recaptured in 1803. Those which were retained under the Treaty of Paris in 1814 were to be known as British Guiana.

Honduras

Both Spain and England made settlements here by the middle of the seventeenth century. A British settlement was established in 1739 and there was much trouble between the British and the Spanish. The last Spanish attempt to capture the settlement was in 1798.

Lesser Antilles

This large group of islands were settled by English and French in the seventeenth century. In the wars between Britain and France and Spain many of the islands frequently changed hands. Those known as the Leeward and the Windward Islands remained British.

The Slave Trade

Although early settlers in the West Indies grew tobacco a world glut destroyed the trade and they began to grow sugar, which proved to be very successful. The white population remained comparatively small and the need for labour which could work in sub-tropical conditions led to the importation of Negro slaves from Africa. In fact the slave traffic itself became a vital part of British overseas trade. The Portuguese, the Dutch and the French were rivals to the British in the trade in slaves. Many of the colonies in the Caribbean were Spanish and the right to trade in slaves was known as the Asiento. After the Treaty of Utrecht in 1713 it was granted to Britain and the South Sea Company held it until 1739 and from 1748 to 1750. The slave trade was organised largely by the Royal African Company up until 1689 when all British merchants were allowed to share in it.

This fearful trade in human lives grew during the decades which followed. At its height, over one hundred thousand slaves crossed the Atlantic every year. The 'middle passage', as the sea voyage was called, took a terrible toll. The slaves were packed and chained together and it is little wonder that many died on the voyage. This was in addition to the cruelty of the hunting and capturing the slaves in Africa and the brutal and rough treatment they received on reaching America or the Indies. They were sold at slave auctions in the same way as cattle and families were often broken up and separated. The British slave trade was carried on from the ports of London, Bristol and Liverpool, although Liverpool's share was some 85 per cent.

A movement against the slave trade began early in the eighteenth century. The Quakers were the first in England to protest against it and in Pennsylvania their members were forbidden to take any part in it. In England, Thomas Clarkson's book awoke an interest in the problem and in 1787 a Society for the Abolition of the Slave Trade

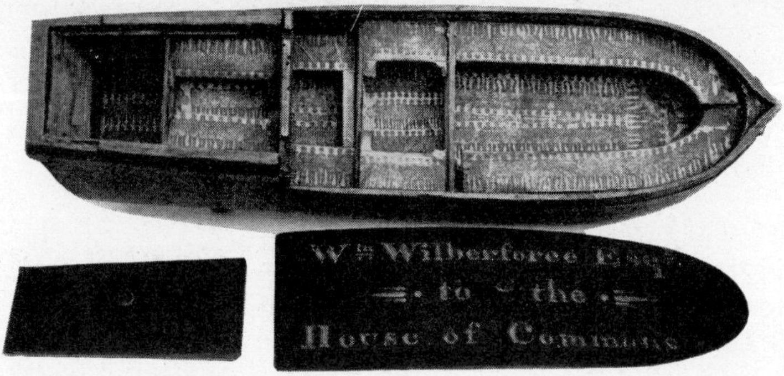

Slave ship model used by Wilberforce in his fight to end the slave trade.

was formed. Among its members were, in addition to Clarkson, William Wilberforce, Zachary Macaulay, Granville Sharp and Josiah Wedgwood. In the face of great opposition from the traders who claimed that the slave-trading ports would be ruined and England's economy seriously affected, under Wilberforce's leadership they eventually won through. In 1807, Parliament passed an Act for the Abolition of the Slave Trade. A further hard struggle was necessary before slavery itself was ended by the Act of 1833 just after Wilberforce's death.

The slave-owners received compensation, but there was much criticism of the amount of payment and the way it was paid. The economy of the West Indian islands was seriously hit. Their production and sale of sugar was in competition with Cuba, Puerto Rico and Brazil and other areas which still employed slaves. It was difficult, if not impossible, to match their prices and many planters were ruined. Sugar-beet sugar produced in Europe also competed for the world's markets. After the abolition of slavery the Negroes were disinclined to work and there was a really serious labour shortage. An attempt to combat the situation was made by bringing in Chinese coolies and Indian labour, and this accounts for Chinese and Indian sections of the population in some of the West Indies today.

The whole situation brought about by the end of slavery underlined the weakness of an economy based upon one main product, sugar. The introduction of Free Trade principles during the nineteenth century also meant that the West Indian sugar producers lost the protection and preference they had enjoyed. The French Government among others paid a bounty, or subsidy, to beet-sugar exported and this enabled it to compete with other sugar. Much of this cheap sugar went to Britain and this further damaged the West Indies trade.

It was many years before the West Indies recovered and they suffered from an enormous depression for most of the nineteenth century and much of the twentieth.

However, the introduction of other crops assisted recovery, and by the efforts of Joseph Chamberlain the bounty-system was brought to an end in 1902. In 1897, Canada had granted a 25% preference on West Indies sugar and the market in the United States grew. A Royal Commission was appointed to enquire into the West Indies trade in sugar in 1897 and as a result a regular service of steamships was commenced early in the twentieth century between the islands and Canada which greatly increased trade. Imperial Colleges of Tropical Agriculture were founded at Trinidad and Barbados to study insect pests and the best kinds of crops. These, too, were largely through Chamberlain's efforts, and the economic recovery continued.

Development of Government

The pattern of constitutional progress was very similar in most of the colonies. During the early stages of development many of the colonies received representative assemblies. During the nineteenth century, some of these were surrendered, but in the twentieth century Barbados, Leeward Islands, Windward Islands, Jamaica, Bahamas, Bermuda, Trinidad and Tobago, British Guiana and British Honduras all received representative assemblies and a measure of responsible government.

During the 1930s the West Indies were badly hit by economic depression once more and housing, education, medical services and general public works were half-a-century behind the times. It must be remembered that these islands were British colonies and responsibility for their neglect must be borne by the British people and their Governments. This resulted in much discontent and in 1938 a Royal Commission under Lord Moyne was sent to investigate. Its report was not ready until after the outbreak of the Second World War and consequently some action had to be delayed. However, an Act was passed in 1940 enlarging the Colonial Development Fund and setting up a West Indian Welfare Fund.

After the War steps were taken to unite the West Indies in a federation.

The West Indies Federation

There had been earlier suggestions for a federation in 1897 and 1932, but the proposals had been dropped because of insufficient support. In 1947 a conference was held at Montego Bay, Jamaica, at which a constitution for a federation was drawn. up. The report was published in 1950 and provoked a mixed reception. Public opinion in favour of federation increased and in 1956 the British Caribbean Federation Act was passed by the British Government. The Federation of the West Indies came into being in January 1958, consisting of the Leeward Islands, Barbados, Jamaica, Trinidad and Tobago, and the Windward Islands. In the case of the Leeward and Windward Islands the islands which belonged to them were each separate colonies within the Federation. British Guiana, British Honduras, Bermuda, Bahamas and the Virgin Islands did not immediately join, although they had the right to do so should they desire.

There were difficulties from the beginning and there were arguments about the site of the capital of the Federation. It was at first suggested that it should be on Barbados but later this was changed to Trinidad. There was then disagreement between Jamaica and Trinidad, the latter being fearful lest the new Federation should be dominated by Jamaica. It was found impossible to reconcile the differences and the great conception of an independent West Indies Federation, independence having been promised for 1962, came to an unhappy end. The Federation ceased to exist early in 1962.

Jamaica became an independent state within the Commonwealth in August 1962 and Trinidad and Tobago followed suit three weeks later. The West Indies Act of 1962 gave the British Government power to administer the remainder of the West Indian colonies. At a conference in May 1962, it was agreed to set up a new West Indies Federation consisting of Barbados, Leeward Islands (Antigua, St Kitts, Nevis, Montserrat) and Windward Islands (Dominica, Grenada, St Lucia, St Vincent)—eight member states. At a second conference in 1964 it was agreed that all the member states should obtain self-government before the Federation should be formed. Grenada did not attend this conference as she hoped to join Trinidad and Tobago. The remaining West Indian colonies of British Guiana, British Honduras, Bermudas, Bahamas and the Virgin Islands are ruled as Crown colonies.

During the first part of 1966 conferences were held which agreed that Antigua, Dominica, Grenada, St Kitts, Nevis, St Lucia and St Vincent should become 'Associated States'. This meant that each should become an autonomous state in association with the United Kingdom, being fully responsible for all internal government, Britain retaining responsibility for foreign affairs and defence. Barbados did not wish to follow this lead and asked for complete independence within the Commonwealth. This was granted in November 1966.

British Guiana has had a troubled history since the war, her main problems being the difference between those of Negro and Indian stock. After constitutional discussions, it became independent in May 1966 as Guyana. Mr Forbes Burnham is Prime Minister and the hope is held that he will be able to bring together the Asian and Negro elements in the population and build a peaceful future.

Guatemala has laid claim to British Honduras and this has led to troubles in recent years.

In September 1961 the Governments of France, the Netherlands, the United Kingdom and the United States established the Caribbean Organisation to advise on social, cultural and economic matters.

SUMMARY

The West Indies
Four main groups: The Antilles, consisting of Greater and Lesser Antilles; The Bahamas; The Venezuelan Coast Islands; The Bermudas.—Some French, Dutch or American, some independent, most British.—Early Spanish activity in sixteenth century.—Early British settlements in seventeenth century.

Barbados and St Kitts
First settlement on St Kitts (1624).—Spread to other islands.—First settlement on Barbados (1627).—Slave labour.

Bermuda
Settlement following Somers' shipwreck (1609).—Virginia Company and Bermuda Company.

Jamaica
Seized by Penn and Venables (1655).—Recognised by Spain as British colony (1670).—Pirate lair during seventeenth and eighteenth centuries.—Sugar.—Slave labour.

Bahamas
First settled by colonists from Bermuda (1646).—Elizabethan Company (1649).—Cotton brought by Empire Loyalists.

Trinidad
Originally Spanish.—Captured by Raleigh (1595).—Spanish again.—Captured by Abercromby (1796).—Ceded to Britain by Treaty of Amiens (1802).

Tobago
First settlement (1639).—Changed hands several times.—Captured by British (1803).—Ceded to Britain by Treaty of Paris (1814).

Guiana
Dutch and English settlements by early seventeenth century.—Sugar, coffee and cotton introduced from Barbados.—Settlements captured by British in Napoleonic War, ceded by Treaty of Paris (1814).—Known as British Guiana.

Honduras
Spanish and English settlements in seventeenth century.—British established (1739).—Trouble between British and Spanish.

Lesser Antilles
Group of islands settled by English and French in seventeenth century.—Many islands changed hands frequently.—Leeward and Windward Islands remained British.

The Slave Trade

Originally tobacco as main product.—Replaced by sugar.—Introduction of slave labour.—Importance of slave trade to Britain.—Asiento.—Treaty of Utrecht (1713).—Right to supply slaves granted to Britain.—Horrors of slavery and slave trade.—Movement to abolish trade and slavery.—Society for Abolition of the Slave Trade (1787).—Slave trade ended (1807).—Slavery ended (1833).—Economic decline.—Causes.—Competition with slave-owning sugar producers.—Free Trade in Britain.—Bounty-aided sugar.—Chinese and Indian labour.—Introduction of new crops.—Trade with Canada.—Introduction of steamships.—End of bounty system (1902).—Royal Commission (1897).—Colleges of Tropical Agriculture.

Development of Government

Early representative assemblies.—Some suspended in nineteenth century.—Twentieth century most colonies had representative assemblies and some responsible government.—Economic depression in 1930s.—Discontent.—Royal Commission (1938).—West India Development Fund (1940).—Steps towards federation.

The West Indies Federation

Early suggestions of federation (1897 and 1932).—Conference at Montego Bay (1947).—Report published with federal constitution (1950).—Mixed reception.—British Caribbean Federation Act (1956).—Federation of West Indies came into being (Jan. 1958): Leeward Islands, Barbados, Jamaica, Trinidad and Tobago, and Windward Islands.—Remainder of West Indian islands not members.—Difficulties from start.—Rivalry between Trinidad and Jamaica.—Federation ceased to exist (1962).—Jamaica and Trinidad and Tobago independent within Commonwealth (1962).—West Indies Act of 1962.—Conference.—New federation, to consist of Barbados, Leeward Islands and Windward Islands.—Conference (1964).—Self-government to be obtained first.—Grenada's desire to join Jamaica.—Remainder of West Indies as Crown colonies.—Caribbean Organisation set up by France, Netherlands, United Kingdom and U.S.A. (1961).—Associated States (1966).—British Guiana independent as Guyana (1966).—Barbados independent (1966).

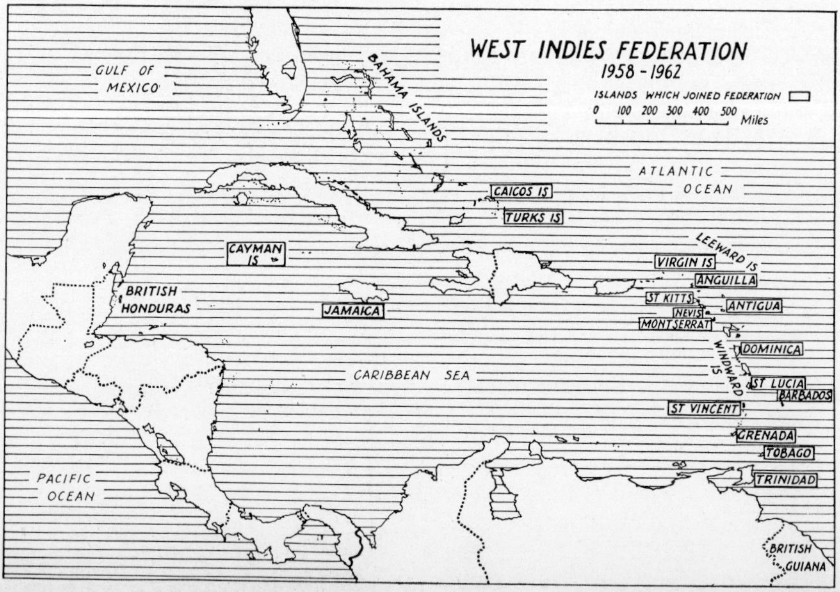

QUESTIONS

Answer the following questions briefly:

1. (a) What main groups of islands make up the West Indies?
   (b) Who were Sir Henry Morgan and Edward Teach?
   (c) What was the original main crop in the islands?
   (d) How were slaves first introduced?
   (e) Describe how any three of the West Indian islands became British.
   (f) What was the Asiento?

2. In 1823 Fowell Buxton introduced a motion into the House of Commons which condemned slavery 'as repugnant to the principles of the British Constitution and the Christian religion'. At that time there were some 750,000 slaves in the British Empire.
   Describe the effect of the abolition of the slave trade (1807) *and* the abolition of slavery (1833) on the West Indies and tell how they recovered from it. Say what you think of Fowell Buxton's comment and whether you consider the problem was handled correctly.

3. Sir Grantley Adams, the Prime Minister of the Federation of the West Indies, protested against the British Government's action at a press conference on 5 March 1962, at which he strongly criticised not only Mr Maudling but also Mr Macmillan and Mr Iain Macleod. Declaring that 'we must shame the British Government out of doing the blackest thing in British history,' Sir Grantley claimed that it was unprecedented for a federal treaty to be broken simply because 'a small percentage of one unit' wished to secede. The Federal Constitution deliberately contained no clause under which any territory could secede, but the British Government in its 'indecent haste' to 'placate and accommodate Jamaica', now intended to dissolve the whole Federation. There had at no time been any consultation with the Federal Government or Parliament, or any other unit territory, and he himself had only just received a copy of the Bill. In his (Sir Grantley's) opinion, the reason for this treatment might lie in the fact that Jamaica was only 90 miles from Cuba, and that the British Government wished 'to please Jamaica for fear of Communist infiltration'. The Federal Government had acquiesced in the Jamaican referendum on Federation membership (even though the Federal Constitution did not provide for it) partly because they did not expect a majority for secession; but it followed that at the very least the British Government should insist on a referendum, or some other procedure, to test majority opinion in Trinidad, which he believed was still pro-Federation.
   (a) Why was Sir Grantley Adams so angry at Jamaica leaving the Federation?
   (b) What do you consider to be the reasons for Jamaica and Trinidad leaving the Federation?
   (c) Do you agree with Sir Grantley Adams's reasons?
   (d) What do you think the future of the West Indies may now be?

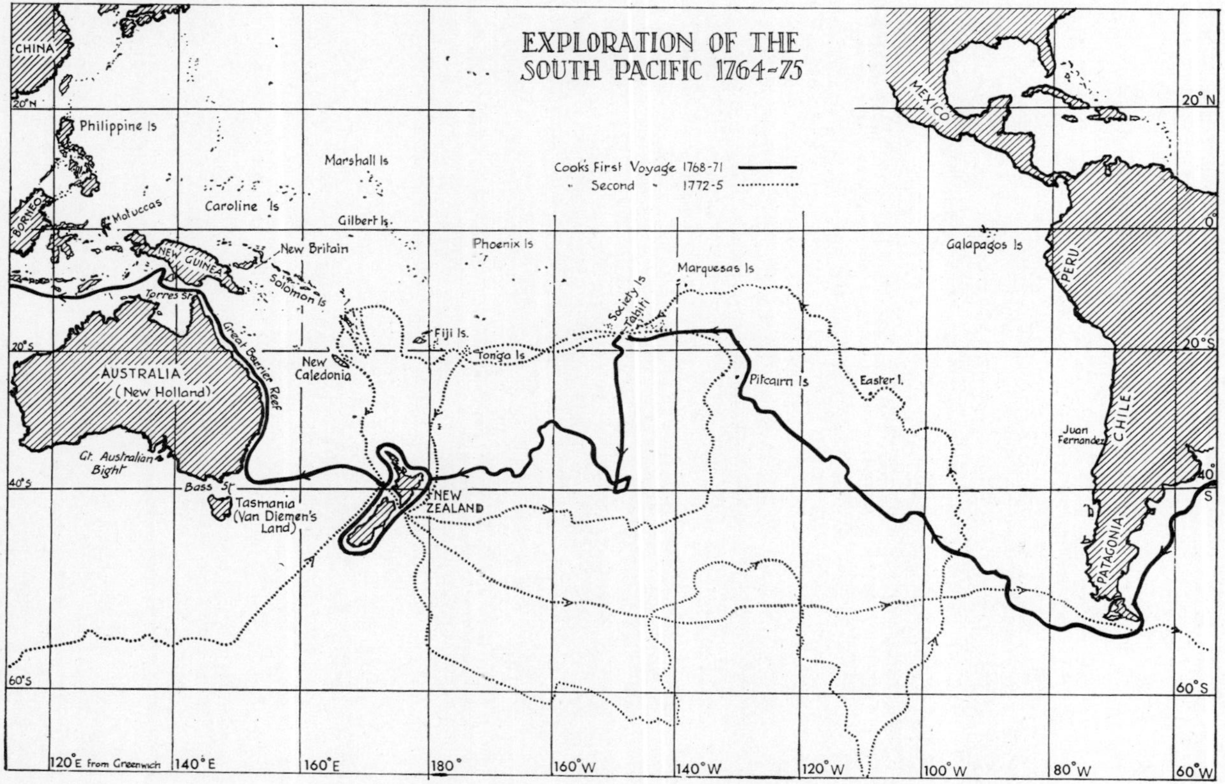
EXPLORATION OF THE
SOUTH PACIFIC 1764-75
Cook's First Voyage 1768-71
" Second " 1772-5
CHINA
Philippine Is
BORNEO
Moluccas
Caroline Is
Marshall Is
Gilbert Is.
NEW GUINEA
New Britain
Solomon Is
Torres St
Great Barrier Reef
AUSTRALIA
(New Holland)
Gt. Australian Bight
Bass St
Tasmania
(Van Diemen's Land)
New Caledonia
Fiji Is.
Tonga Is
Phoenix Is
NEW ZEALAND
Society Is
Tahiti
Marquesas Is
Pitcairn Is
Easter I.
Galapagos Is
MEXICO
PERU
CHILE
Juan Fernandez
PATAGONIA
20°N
0°
20°S
40°S
60°S
120°E from Greenwich
140°E
160°E
180°
160°W
140°W
120°W
100°W
80°W
60°W

18 : Malaysia, Pacific and the Far East

The East India Company

EUROPEAN countries were particularly interested in developing trade with the fabulous east after the route round the Cape had been shown them by Vasco Da Gama. The Portuguese and the Dutch were particularly energetic in this respect but England took a hand by founding the East India Company in 1600. They were soon trading with the islands of the East Indies but rivalry with the Dutch soon forced them out. The Amboyna Massacre in 1623 virtually drove the English to India except for the peninsula of Malaya where some uneasy trade continued. However, it was not until the end of the eighteenth century that Britain became established in the area.

Malaya

In 1786, the East India Company acquired the island of Penang and established a post there for trade with China. In 1800, Province Wellesley, on the mainland opposite, was obtained and used as a penal settlement for a time. Malacca was captured from the Dutch during the French Wars. Although it was returned to the Dutch at the Treaty of Paris in 1814, it was ceded to Britain in 1825. Java had also been captured from the Dutch during the Napoleonic War and after it had been returned to Dutch rule the Governor of Sumatra, Sir Stamford Raffles, persuaded the Sultan of Johore to cede Singapore Island to the British in 1819. In 1824, Penang, Malacca and Singapore were united under one governor as the Straits Settlements. These new settlements were governed by India until they became a Crown colony in 1867. The Dindings became a part of the colony in 1874, and the Cocos or Keeling Islands were taken by Britain in 1857 and became part of the Straits Settlements in 1886. Christmas Island became a part of the Settlements in 1900. Labuan, in Borneo, annexed in 1846 as a separate colony, came under the Straits Settlements Government in 1907.

For most of the nineteenth century conditions in the Malay peninsula were terrible. The people were under the tyrannical rule of feudal lords who fought with each other and devastated the country. They were terrorised by robber bands in the interior and pirates along

the coasts and many Malays were forced to be slaves. Already Chinese were beginning to come into the country and law and order had virtually disappeared.

The contrast between these areas and the Straits Settlements under British control was so evident that in 1874 the British governor persuaded the Sultans of Perak, Selangor and a part of Negri Sembilan to accept British protection and British Residents, and in 1888 the rest of Negri Sembilan and Pahang followed suit. In 1895, the states became a federation as the Federated Malay States, receiving a federal council in 1909. Gradually, under British influence, conditions improved. Law and order were restored, slavery and feudalism ended, and education, public health and transport services were inaugurated. New methods of agriculture were introduced and in 1884 railways were started, followed later by new roads. The tin mines which had originally attracted the Chinese were now organised by Europeans and became the main source of Malaya's wealth. Rubber plantation began in the twentieth century and eventually rivalled tin as a main product.

In 1885 Johore accepted British protection although the Sultan did not receive a British adviser until 1914. In 1909 the states of Kedah, Perlis, Kelantan and Trengganu, which had been in close co-operation with Siam, accepted British protection and British advisers, while Siam renounced any claim to them by Treaty. These were known as the Protected States.

The Japanese overran Malaya during the Second World War in 1942. British prestige, not unnaturally, declined, since the states had looked to Britain for protection. In 1943 the British Government issued a statement declaring its intention of granting self-government to Malaya after the war.

An attempt was made to bring the states of Malaya together in a union in 1946, although Singapore was omitted, but this provoked so much opposition that the idea was abandoned. Two years later, in 1948, the Federation of Malaya was founded, consisting of the four Federated Malay States and the five Protected States, nine in all, Singapore still not being a member. The Sultans were restored to their positions as monarchs, but ruled constitutionally and not absolutely. A Federal Legislative Council was established.

The Chinese population did not approve of the Federation and were a splendid breeding-ground for Communist agents who infiltrated from the northern border. Terrorism began and assumed serious proportions by 1950. Large numbers of British troops were involved in suppressing the rising and large-scale military operations were necessary. Field-Marshal Sir Gerald Templer was appointed High Commissioner and Commander-in-Chief of Malaya in January 1952, and he realised that political measures must accompany the military operations. Colonel Young of the City of London Police, who was seconded to Malaya in 1952, re-organised the Malayan Police and made them respected friends of the Malayan people and this with re-settlement of many villagers who suffered from the terrorists provided the climate for the successful suppression of the Communists. In 1955 an amnesty was offered to all terrorists who surrendered, but the more fanatical remained. The terrorism was virtually wiped out by 1958. It was important that political advances should accompany the suppression of the terrorists and in 1957 Malaya was granted independence within the Commonwealth. The new state was to be a monarchy with the ruler being elected for a period of five years by the Sultans of the states. It was to have a Senate and a House of Representatives.

Singapore, which had not been a member of the Federation, was given full internal self-government in 1959 also with an elected

Legislative Assembly. Britain remained responsible for defence and external affairs.

Island of Borneo

Approximately one-third of the island of Borneo became British or under British protection during the nineteenth century.

The island was originally known as Brunei and was ruled by a Sultan. It was largely under Dutch influence in the early part of the century. It was a haunt of pirates and the Sultan found difficulty in maintaining order.

Sarawak

In 1839 an East India Company Army officer, James Brooke, went to North Borneo and assisted the Sultan to restore order. In gratitude the Sultan created Brooke Rajah of Sarawak and gave him the province. Brooke, or the White Rajah as he became known, spent the remainder of his life developing Sarawak and was knighted by the Queen. On his death in 1868, he was succeeded by his nephew, Sir Charles Brooke, whose son, Sir Charles Vyner Brooke, became Rajah in 1917. It had become a British Protectorate in 1888, but continued to be governed by its white rajahs until after the Second World War. It was occupied by the Japanese from 1942–45. In July 1946 Sir Charles Vyner Brooke ceded Sarawak to Britain and it became a Crown colony.

During his rule Sir James Brooke and the British Navy suppressed the Malay and Dyak pirates and in 1846 the island of Labuan was taken over by Britain as a naval base. After being taken over by the Straits Settlements in 1907, Labuan eventually became a part of British North Borneo in 1946.

British North Borneo (Sabah)

North Borneo was developed by trade. Adventurous merchants who obtained grants of land on the coast after 1870, formed the British North Borneo Company, which received a Royal Charter in 1882. It became a British Protectorate in 1888. The Company governed the territory under British protection until the Second World War when it was occupied by the Japanese from 1942 to 1945. In 1946, North Borneo became a Crown colony with Labuan joined to it; and was given Executive and Legislative Councils in 1950.

Brunei

This was the rest of the Sultanate of Brunei after the cession of Sarawak and North Borneo. The Sultan accepted the protection of the British Government in 1888 and received the help and advice of a British Resident in 1906. Brunei continued to be ruled in this way until 1959. In that year Executive and Legislative Councils were set up and the British Resident was replaced by a Chief Minister. Defence and external affairs remained a British responsibility.

Malaysia

In 1961, Tunku Abdul Rahman, the Prime Minister of Malaya, presented to the British Government a plan for a federation to include Malaya, Singapore, Sarawak, North Borneo and Brunei. Since one of the states was independent, one had responsible government, two were Crown colonies and one was a Protectorate there were certain difficulties. Britain was anxious, too, to safeguard her rights to military bases in order to carry out her membership of the South-East Asia Treaty Organisation.

A Commission was sent to Sarawak and North Borneo in 1962 to sound popular feeling on the proposed federation. The report was in favour of federation and the Sultan of Brunei also approved the suggestion. However, the people objected and there was considerable disorder. After approval at the Commonwealth Prime Ministers' Conference of September 1962, the Federation of Malaysia came into being on 16 September 1963, consisting of Malaya, Singapore, Sarawak and North Borneo, or Sabah as it is now known. Brunei did not

join. Tunku Abdul Rahman, who was largely responsible for the idea of the new Federation, became its first Prime Minister.

Singapore withdrew from the new Federation in August, 1965 and is now a separate independent state within the Commonwealth. Lee Kuan Yew is the Prime Minister.

The new Federation of Malaysia has been threatened by Indonesia and considerable fighting has been going on in the Island of Borneo, while some Indonesian landings have been made on the Malayan mainland.

After a constitutional crisis and government changes in Indonesia produced a change in policy, an agreement was reached in August 1966 to end the confrontation between the two countries.

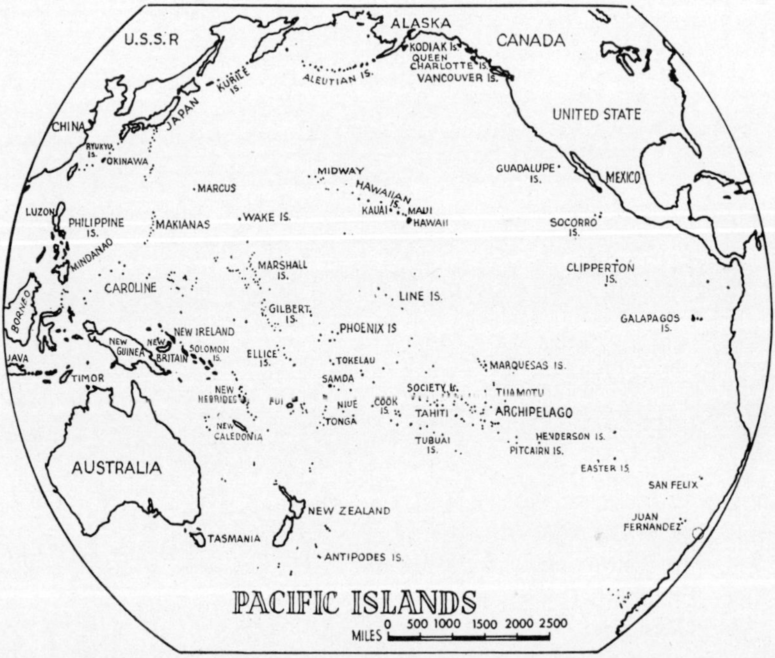

The Pacific

Very little interest was shown in the islands of the Pacific until the nineteenth century. Captain Cook had visited Tahiti in his first voyage in 1769, and in his second in 1773 he visited Easter Island, the Marquesas, Tonga, New Hebrides, New Caledonia and Norfolk Island. On his third voyage in 1777 he rediscovered Hawaii and visited a number of smaller islands, before he was killed by natives in 1779.

In 1797 the London Missionary Society sent representatives to the

Society Islands. The natives asked to become a part of the British Empire in 1836, but strangely the request was refused and the islands were taken over by France. France began to acquire other islands including New Caledonia in the second half of the century when imperialism was beginning to become popular.

Shortage of labour in Australia, particularly Queensland, led to a trade in workers from the Solomon Islands and the New Hebrides. They were sold, virtually as slaves, wherever the need was greatest. The traders were cruel and vicious men, concerned only with profit and their methods included violence and kidnapping. This aroused the indignation of the missionaries. The natives, too, naturally objected and were inclined to hit back at any white man. When in 1871 Bishop Patteson of Melanesia was murdered by natives in revenge for the traders' violence, the British Government intervened and the Pacific Islanders Protection Act was passed in 1872.

Fiji Islands

This group, first visited by missionaries in 1835, was offered to Britain in 1859. It was annexed in 1874 and became a Crown colony. Today Fiji is ruled by a governor with an Executive Council and there is a Legislative Council consisting of European, Fijian and Indian members, mostly elected. The Indian population who came in originally as labourers now outnumbers the Fijians. Negotiations have been going on for further constitutional advance with a fully elected assembly and internal responsible government.

Tonga or Friendly Islands

These islands were visited by missionaries in 1826 and a missionary acted as adviser to the native king. They became a British Protectorate in 1900. Queen Salote, who became the ruler in 1918, created a great impression when she came to London for the coronation of Queen Elizabeth II and has been particularly friendly to Britain. She died in December, 1965 and was succeeded by her son as King George III. A new treaty of friendship, which further recognised British protection, was signed in 1958. There is an elected Legislative Assembly and women have the vote.

Western Pacific High Commission

This was created in 1877 and includes the Gilbert and Ellice Islands, which accepted British protection in 1892 and were annexed during the First World War in 1915, and the Solomon Islands, which became a British Protectorate in 1893. There are also some smaller islands known as the Central and Southern Line Islands and the New Hebrides. The New Hebrides became a joint Anglo-French Protectorate in 1887 and are now a British and French condominium.

Australian Islands

After Germany became a nation in 1871, she annexed a number of Pacific islands. After the First World War under League of Nations mandate some of these, Norfolk Island, British New Guinea, German New Guinea, Bismarck Archipelago and some Solomon Islands came under Australian trusteeship, some of them under mandate as ex-German colonies. Australia also administers Nauru, (jointly with Britain and New Zealand), Cocos (Keeling) Islands and Christmas Island.

New Zealand Islands

New Zealand administers several groups of Pacific Islands. These are the Cook Islands, Tokelau Islands, the Ross Dependency, Kermadec Group and some other smaller islands. Western Samoa was administered by New Zealand, but became the first fully-independent Polynesian State in 1961 as a member of the Commonwealth.

South Pacific Commission

This body was formed in 1948 to provide an advisory and research body concerned with the well-being of the people of the Southern Pacific territories. The member nations are Australia, France, New Zealand, the United Kingdom and the United States of America. Its headquarters are in New Caledonia, one of the French islands.

China

The East India Company began trade with China in the seventeenth century. The Chinese nobles, or mandarins, regarded all outsiders as 'foreign devils' and considered them as inferiors and that they should show respect to the Chinese Emperor. Tea was the main item of trade and the best exchange for it appeared to be opium grown in India. The Chinese Government forbade the importation of opium although many of the mandarins were happy for it to continue provided that the bribes were large enough. Canton was the main headquarters of the East India Company in China and when the Chinese authorities destroyed a quantity of opium there in 1839, the first of the Opium Wars broke out between Britain and China. The British forces defeated the Chinese and by the Treaty of Nanking in 1842, the island of Hong Kong which had been annexed by Britain in 1841, was ceded and five ports, known as the 'treaty ports', were opened to British trade. These ports were Canton, Amoy, Foochow, Ningpo and Shanghai.

A second Opium War broke out in 1856 and lasted until 1860. This was over a minor incident involving the seizure of a small Chinese-owned, but technically British, vessel by the Chinese authorities.

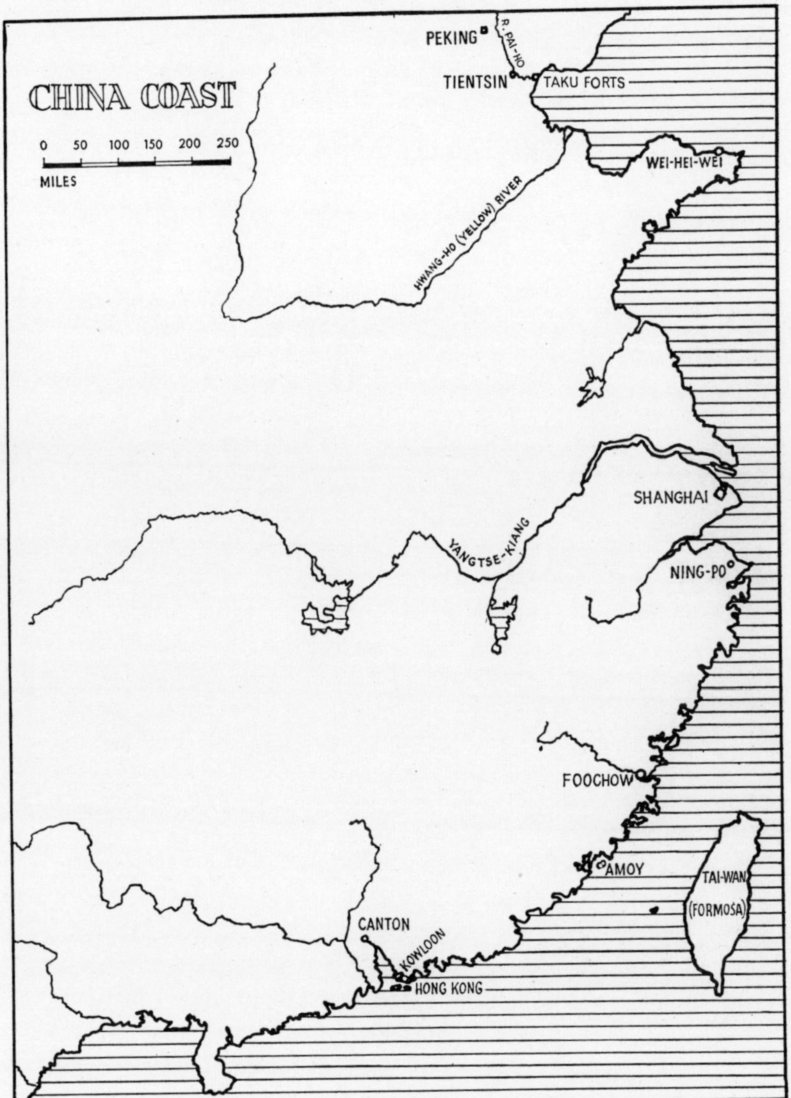

France, using the murder of a French missionary as an excuse, joined Britain in the war. The real reason for the war was the increased interest in trade by the western powers owing to the industrial revolution and the continuing Chinese resentment of foreigners and refusal to recognise them as equals. After considerable fighting, involving the capture by British and French forces of the Taku forts on the Peiho River, a treaty emerged. This was the Treaty of Tientsin in 1858 which promised the residence in Peking of foreign representatives, freedom for Christian missionaries, freedom of navigation for foreign vessels on the Yangtse-Kiang, and several additional ports to be opened for trade. The Chinese violated the Treaty the next year and fighting continued. The Treaty was enforced in 1860 and the Chinese then had to agree to open Tientsin to trade, to allow foreign ministers permanent residence in Peking and to cede the peninsula of Kowloon opposite Hong Kong to Britain.

Further troubles, including the Taiping Rebellion in 1864 occurred and in 1899 the Boxer Rebellion broke out. The Boxers, or Righteous Harmony Fists, a partly religious, partly political, Chinese movement aimed at the expulsion of foreigners, besieged Peking and a combined European force had to march to relieve it.

In 1898, Britain leased Wei-hai-wei, consisting of an island and a small coastal strip from China. Britain ruled the area until 1930 when it was returned to China.

Hong Kong

A larger area, known as the New Territories, was added to the original Hong Kong and Kowloon in 1898, when it was obtained from China on a 99-year lease. This formed the colony of Hong Kong.

Hong Kong has developed as a great centre of trade and has become relatively prosperous. It was captured and occupied by the Japanese in the Second World War. Its close proximity to the new China has made its position between the Communist and non-Communist world even more important. Refugees have poured over the border and Hong Kong has had to absorb them. Britain keeps a considerable garrison there.

Hong Kong is a Crown colony ruled by a governor, with an Executive Council and a Legislative Council. Much has been done to improve the living conditions of its people and to add to educational facilities, but the increasing population has made this much harder.

SUMMARY

The East India Company

Early interest in the East Indies.—Amboyna Massacre (1623).—Concentration of trade largely in India.—Some trade in Malaya continued.

Malaya

Penang acquired (1786).—Province Wellesley acquired (1800).—Malacca ceded (1825).—Singapore ceded (1819).—Sir Stamford Raffles.—Penang, Malacca and Singapore united as Straits Settlements (1824).—Governed by India until becoming Crown colony (1867).—Dindings, Cocos (Keeling) Islands.—Christmas Island.—Labuan (annexed 1846) joining Straits Settlements (1907).—Conditions in Malayan peninsula.—Perak, Selangor and part Negri Sembilan under British protection (1874), Pahang (1888).—Federation (1895).—Federal council (1909).—Tin and rubber.—Chinese labour.—Prosperity.—Johore as Protectorate (1885)—Kedah, Perlis, Kelentan, Trengganu as Protectorates.—Protected States (1909).—Japanese occupation (1942–45).—Federation of Malaya (1948).—Chinese Communist agents.—Terrorism (1948–58).—Independence within Commonwealth (1957).—Singapore not member of federation; given full internal self-government (1959).

Island of Borneo

One-third of island came under British rule.—Originally ruled by Sultan.—Haunt of pirates.

Sarawak

James Brooke helped Sultan of Brunei to restore order (1839).—Rajah Brooke of Sarawak.—Succeeded by Sir Charles Brooke (1868); Sir Charles Vyner Brooke (1917).—British Protectorate (1888).—Japanese occupation (1942–45).—Ceded to Britain and became Crown colony (1946).

British North Borneo (Sabah)

Developed by trade.—British North Borneo Company with Royal Charter (1882).—British Protectorate (1888).—Occupied by Japanese (1942–45).—Crown colony (1946).—Labuan joined North Borneo.

Brunei

Sultan accepted British protection (1888).—British Resident (1906).—Executive and Legislative Councils (1959).

Malaysia

Plan for federation (1961).—Commission to investigate (1962).—Federation of Malaysia (Sept. 1963).—Malaya, Singapore, Sarawak, North Borneo (Sabah).—Singapore withdrew (1965).

The Pacific

Cook's voyages (1769, 1773, 1777).—Early interest of missionaries.—Native labour for Australia.—Abuses.—Murder of Bishop of Melanesia (1871).—Pacific Islanders Protection Act (1872).

Fiji Islands

Missionaries (1835).—Crown colony (1874).—Today, Governor with Executive and Legislative Councils.

Tonga or Friendly Islands

Missionaries (1826).—British Protectorate (1900).—New treaty (1958).

Western Pacific High Commission (1877)

Gilbert and Ellice Islands, Solomon Islands, Central and Southern Line Islands. —New Hebrides, under British and French condominium.

Australian Islands.

Norfolk Island, British New Guinea, German New Guinea, Bismarck Archipelago, some Solomon Islands, Nauru, Cocos (Keeling) Islands, Christmas Island.

New Zealand Islands

Cook Islands, Tokelau Islands, Ross Dependency, Kermadec Group.—Western Samoa, originally under New Zealand, became independent (1961) as member of Commonwealth.

South Pacific Commission (1948)

Advisory and research body: Australia, France, New Zealand, United Kingdom, United States of America.

China

Early trade by East India Company.—Chinese distrust of 'foreign devils'.—Opium and tea trade.—First Opium War (1839).—Treaty of Nanking (1842).—Hong Kong ceded (annexed 1841).—Five treaty ports.—Second Opium War (1856–60).—Treaty of Tientsin (1858).—Foreign representatives at Peking.—Freedom for missionaries.—Freedom for vessels on Yangtse.—Chinese violated Treaty.—Treaty enforced (1860).—Tientsin opened for trade.—Ministers in Peking.—Kowloon ceded to Britain.—Taiping Rebellion (1864).—Boxer Rising (1899).—Wei-hai-wei leased (1898).—Returned to China (1930).—New Territories added to Hong Kong (1898).

QUESTIONS

Answer the following questions briefly:

1. (a) How did Britain first take an interest in Malaya?
   (b) How did the Straits Settlements come into being?
   (c) Who was Sir Stamford Raffles?
   (d) What were the Federated Malay States?
   (e) How did Sarawak become British?
   (f) Who was largely responsible for the idea of Malaysia? What states form it today?
   (g) How did Britain acquire most of her small Pacific Islands?
   (h) What is the Western Pacific High Commission?
2. Describe how British influence in China began and increased and say what difficulties developed.
3. The instrument which set up the Federation of Malaysia included the following articles:

Article 1

The colonies of North Borneo and Sarawak and the State of Singapore shall be federated with the existing States of the Federation of Malaya as the States of Sabah, Sarawak, and Singapore . . . and the Federation shall thereafter be called Malaysia.

Article 6

The Anglo-Malayan defence agreement of 12 October 1957 shall apply to all territories of Malaysia, and any reference in that agreement to the Federation of Malaya shall be deemed to apply to Malaysia subject to the proviso that the Government of Malaysia will afford to the Government of the United Kingdom the right to continue to maintain the bases and other facilities at present occupied by their Service authorities within the State of Singapore, and will permit the Government of the United Kingdom to make such use of these bases and facilities as that Government may consider necessary for the purpose of assisting in the defence of Malaysia, and for Commonwealth defence and for the preservation of peace in South-East Asia.

(a) Who was mainly responsible for the conception of the Federation of Malaysia?
(b) What other state joined the Federation later?
(c) In what way has Britain carried out the terms of Article 6?
(d) What changes have taken place in the Federation recently?

Tunku Abdul Rahman.

19 : Egypt, the Mediterranean and the Middle East

Egypt: Early British Interest

ENGLISH merchants had been interested in the Levant or the Turkish territory at the eastern end of the Mediterranean from the fifteenth century. By the end of the eighteenth and the early nineteenth century reasons of strategy were quickening that interest. British communications to the newly-won empire in India and to the Far East were partly dependent upon Egypt and the narrow piece of land which divided the Mediterranean from the Red Sea. It was this conviction which led Napoleon Bonaparte to make a bid for Egypt in 1798 and it was Nelson's victory of the Battle of the Nile which foiled his plans.

Because of this route to the East, Britain had an obvious interest in Egypt, but it was as much her involvement with European politics which eventually led to her active participation in Egyptian affairs. During the Greek War of Independence (1821–29), one of the revolutions of the tangled Eastern Question, Mehemet Ali of Egypt sent a fleet and troops to help Turkey suppress the rebels at the request of the Sultan.

Mehemet Ali, the ruler of Egypt, was an Albanian-born adventurer and he wanted Syria as his reward for helping the Sultan. Egypt, in theory, was one of the Sultan's dominions, but, in practice, was virtually independent under Mehemet Ali's rule. When the Sultan forgot his promised reward, Mehemet Ali sent his son, Ibrahim Pasha, to invade Syria. Because France backed Mehemet Ali, Britain intervened and through Lord Palmerston forced Mehemet Ali's withdrawal from Syria by the Treaty of London of 1841, rewarding him with the hereditary position as Pasha of Egypt. From Mehemet Ali was descended the Egyptian Royal family which ended with King Farouk. Britain was concerned with Egypt from this time onwards.

In 1869 the Suez Canal was opened after fifteen years of work under Ferdinand de Lesseps, a French engineer, and with French money. It was Napoleon himself who had conceived the idea of such a canal. When the Khedive Ismail, the extravagant ruler of Egypt, was on the verge of bankruptcy, he realised his only assets by selling his shares

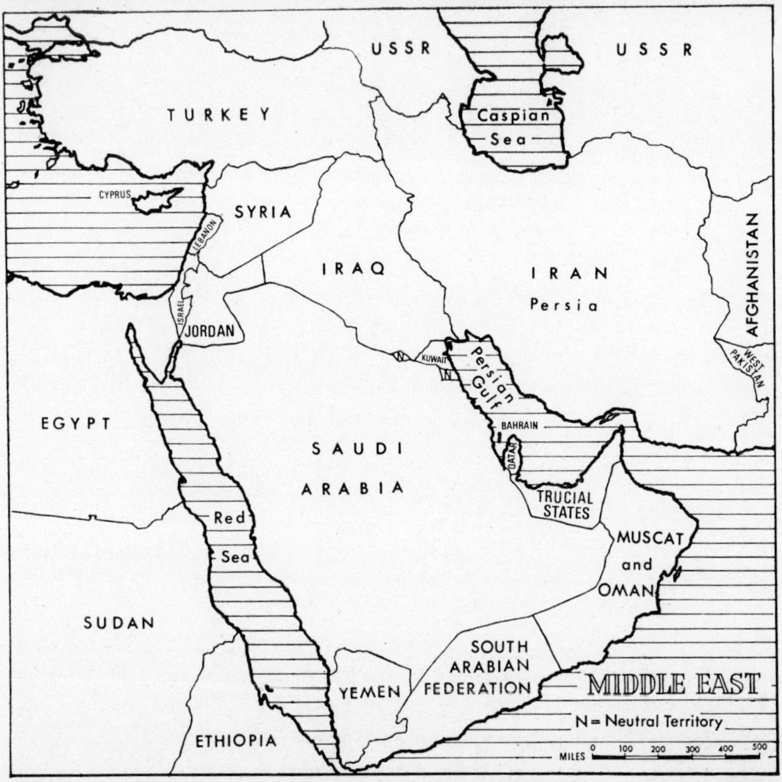
USSR
USSR
TURKEY
Caspian Sea
CYPRUS
SYRIA
LEBANON
IRAQ
IRAN
Persia
AFGHANISTAN
ISRAEL
JORDAN
N
KUWAIT
N
Persian Gulf
WEST PAKISTAN
EGYPT
BAHRAIN
QATAR
SAUDI ARABIA
TRUCIAL STATES
Red Sea
MUSCAT and OMAN
SUDAN
SOUTH ARABIAN FEDERATION
YEMEN
MIDDLE EAST
N = Neutral Territory
ETHIOPIA
MILES 0 100 200 300 400 500

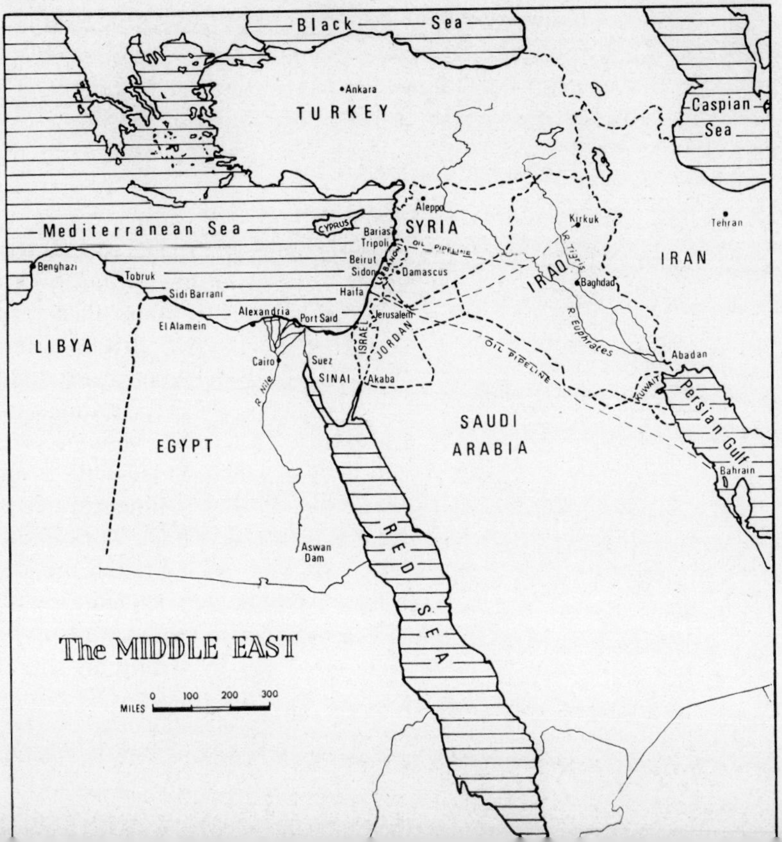
Black Sea
Ankara
TURKEY
Caspian Sea
Aleppo
Kirkuk
Tehran
Mediterranean Sea
CYPRUS
Banias
Tripoli
SYRIA
OIL PIPELINE
IRAN
Benghazi
Beirut
Sidon
Damascus
IRAQ
Baghdad
R. Tigris
Tobruk
Sidi Barrani
Haifa
LEBANON
Alexandria
Port Said
Jerusalem
El Alamein
R. Euphrates
ISRAEL
JORDAN
OIL PIPELINE
Abadan
LIBYA
Cairo
Suez
SINAI
Akaba
KUWAIT
Persian Gulf
R. Nile
SAUDI ARABIA
EGYPT
Bahrain
Aswan Dam
RED SEA
The MIDDLE EAST
MILES 0 100 200 300

in the Suez Canal. Disraeli's master stroke purchased them for Britain for £4,000,000 in 1875. This did not save Ismail who was still unable to pay his debts. Britain and France, as the chief creditor countries, intervened and set up the Dual Control of Egypt. Ismail made difficulties and in 1879 he was deposed and his son Tewfik was made Khedive in his place.

The Franco-British control was resented by many Egyptians and in 1882, Arabi Pasha, a colonel in the Egyptian army and leader of the military party, led a rebellion with the cry of 'Egypt for the Egyptians'. Many Europeans were killed and Arabi occupied Alexandria. Fearing a possible attack from Germany and because the French Parliament would not vote money for the operations, after so much had been spent in Tunisia, France withdrew from Egypt. Britain determined to act alone. The Mediterranean fleet under Admiral Seymour bombarded Alexandria and a British force under General Sir Garnet Wolseley was landed. Wolseley defeated Arabi's forces at the battle of Tel-el-Kebir and occupied Cairo. Arabi was captured and exiled. This action aroused controversy and it was suggested that had Britain been prepared to co-operate with Arabi Pasha the future history of Egypt might have been less troubled. In any event, Britain was in a difficult position. She had no real legal right in Egypt which was still technically a Turkish possession and under the overlordship of the Sultan. France now regretted her withdrawal from the Dual Control and was critical of British action. Yet it was British action which had restored order, and although Mr Gladstone the British Prime Minister emphasised that British occupation of the country was temporary, the situation was such that it had to continue. So for the next thirty years Britain took full responsibility for the control and administration of Egypt's finances, and law and order. British officers were appointed to reorganise and train the Egyptian army, and British officials were appointed to advise the Khedive. Their director was Sir Evelyn Baring, afterwards Lord Cromer, and although they had no legal authority, other than as employees of the Egyptian Government, their influence was immense. Although no protectorate was proclaimed until 1914 this was virtually the position. Sir Evelyn Baring continued in his office with great skill from 1884 until 1907 and extortion, slavery, forced labour and flogging were eliminated while education and justice were improved and Egypt became relatively prosperous. Irrigation was improved, reservoirs were built and agriculture developed. Public health was reorganised and epidemics dealt with. Above all, the administration and financing of the country were overhauled.

South of Egypt lay the Sudan, a province which had been conquered by Mehemet Ali, and in 1883 a religious rising took place. Mohammed Ahmed, who called himself the Mahdi, or prophet-deliverer, led a revolt of fanatical men called Dervishes. The Egyptian force sent to deal with the rising was defeated, their British general, Hicks Pasha, being killed. The British Government under Gladstone decided to abandon the Sudan to the Mahdi. General Gordon was sent out to Khartoum to withdraw the remaining Egyptian officials and garrisons, but after arriving there, decided to stay on in the hope that the British Government would be compelled to relieve him, defeat the Mahdi and continue to occupy the Sudan. Gordon was besieged in Khartoum and after much delay and argument, the British Government sent a relief force in 1885 under Sir Garnet Wolseley. It reached Khartoum two days after Gordon had been murdered by the Dervishes. The Sudan was under the Dervishes control for some twelve years and the people suffered great hardship.

The British Government then decided to reconquer the Sudan, to prevent the French dealing with it and with this in view a railway had been built in its direction. An expedition was sent under General Sir Herbert Kitchener, afterwards Lord Kitchener, consisting of British and Egyptian troops in 1896. The Dervishes were defeated at the Battle of Omdurman in 1898 and Khartoum was captured. Order had been restored and the Sudan had been reconquered.

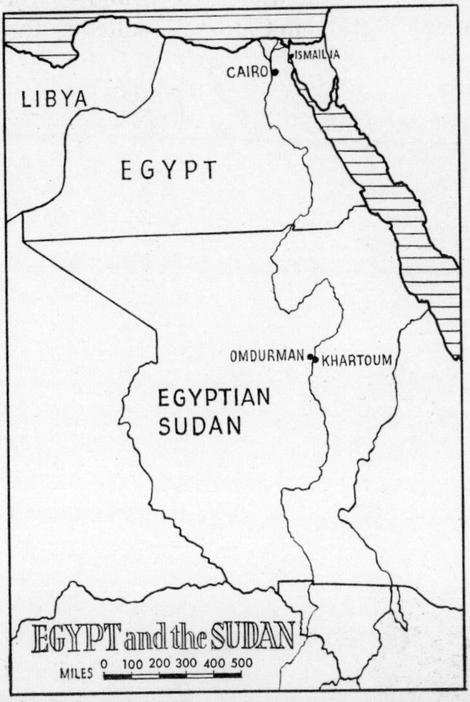

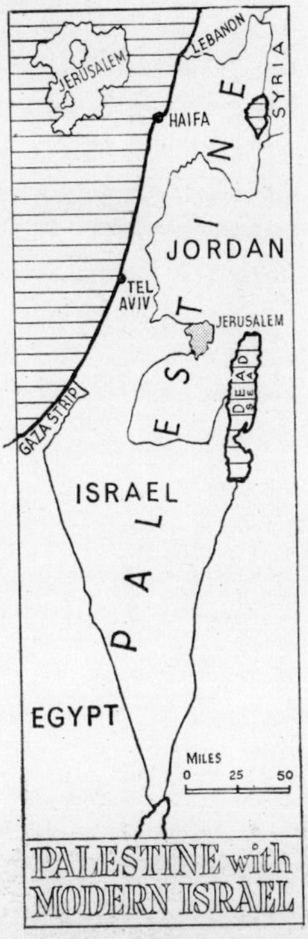

The same year a French expedition under Commandant Marchand occupied Fashoda on the Upper Nile. This 'Fashoda Incident' nearly brought about war between Britain and France as it was believed that France was trying to establish herself in the area. At length France withdrew the expedition and peace was saved.

The Sudan became an Anglo-Egyptian responsibility as a condominium and both British and Egyptian officials acted as administrators and both British and Egyptian garrisons were maintained there, though Britain had exclusive control.

Egypt Moves Towards Independence

When Turkey entered the First World War in November of 1914, as the territory of an enemy country, Egypt became a British Protectorate. An Egyptian Sultan was appointed and when the British Protectorate was ended in 1922, his successor became King Fuad I and Egypt became a monarchy. Egypt agreed that: (*a*) Britain should remain responsible for the defence of the Suez Canal; (*b*) since the responsibility should remain for the defence of Egypt, Britain might keep a garrison in the country; (*c*) Britain should also have the right to protect all foreign citizens in Egypt and (*d*) maintain a special interest in the Sudan. This latter was really a concern for the headwaters of the Nile. In all these matters there was to be free and friendly discussion and the *status quo* was to be maintained in the meantime.

In 1924, Sir Lee Stack, who was Sirdar and Governor-General of the Sudan, was murdered in Cairo. This resulted in a storm of indignation and protest in Britain and Lord Allenby, the British High Commissioner in Egypt, who was famous for his command of British

Lord Allenby.

troops in Palestine against the Turks in the First World War, presented an ultimatum to the Egyptian Government which resulted in the withdrawal of Egyptian troops and officials from the Sudan which was ruled virtually as a British colony until 1936. There followed a period of political crisis in Egypt, with many bitter struggles between political parties, for she was learning democracy the hard way. Lord Allenby resigned in 1925 and was succeeded by Lord Lloyd whose efforts led to a draft treaty between Britain and Egypt in 1927. The Nationalist members of the Egyptian Parliament refused to accept this and in 1928 King Fuad dismissed Parliament and ruled by Royal Decree until 1929 when new talks between Britain and Egypt led to the Treaty of 1936, after protracted negotiations. King Fuad died in 1936 and was succeeded by his son Farouk I. The Egyptian Government under Nahas Pasha accepted the terms of the Treaty freely and it came into force in August 1936. It provided for the full independence of Egypt; British troops and officers were withdrawn except from the Canal Zone, and the condominium of the Sudan was resumed. Egypt was admitted to the League of Nations in 1937.

Egypt became deeply involved in the Second World War when the Suez Canal was of great strategic importance. Italian troops invaded Egypt but were soon driven out by General Wavell's Commonwealth forces. Rommel's Afrika Korps also invaded Egypt, but the Eighth Army under General Montgomery won final victory after El Alamein in 1942. The Egyptians had always resented the presence of British troops and feeling between British and Egyptians was not improved by the war.

The Egyptian Government asked for the complete withdrawal of all British forces and for full control of the Sudan. The British Government was fully prepared to withdraw all troops but believed that the Sudanese people should decide their own future. The two Governments failed to reach agreement and the treaty of 1936 continued to operate.

In 1952 there was a military revolution, led ostensibly by General Neguib, which overthrew and deposed King Farouk, who left the country and went into exile in Italy. Soon after, the real leader of the rising, Colonel Abdul Gamel Nasser deposed General Neguib and became President of Egypt. Agreement was reached with President Nasser over the Sudan which became an independent country and decided to remain outside the Commonwealth.

British forces began leaving the Canal Zone in 1954 and the evacuation was complete by June 1956. Soon after this disputes over the financing of the Aswan Dam and Nasser's nationalisation of the

Aden: The army in charge.
This port is Britain's only major base between the Mediterranean and Malaysia.
(*Photo: Jeremy Ingham.*)

Suez Canal and seizure of its plant and assets led to the Suez Crisis. Israel's invasion of Egypt led to British and French forces seizing part of the Canal. After the intervention of the United Nations they were withdrawn.

Palestine

After British forces under General Lord Allenby had conquered Palestine from the Turks in 1917, it was made a trust territory under British administration by mandate of the League of Nations in 1920.

In 1917, Mr Balfour made his famous Declaration which stated that the British Government favoured the establishment of a Jewish National Home in Palestine. To the Zionists this meant a firm promise, but it was bitterly resented by the Arabs, mostly Moslems, who regarded the land as sacred by their religion. The Arabs claimed that they had been promised protection of their independence by Britain. There followed much strife and disorder.

By 1939, Jewish settlers had poured in at such a rate that they were nearly a third of the population and the British Government announced that it would allow no more Jewish immigration.

After the persecution of Jews during the Second World War, there were vast numbers waiting to come to Palestine. The British Government checked the flow and although many entered illegally, avoiding British naval patrols, this was resented by the Jewish people.

The British Government referred the problem to the United Nations and in May 1948 the new Jewish state of Israel came into being and British forces withdrew.

Jordan

Transjordan or Transjordania, as it was formerly known, was a part of the League of Nations mandated territory of Palestine.

In 1928 a new constitution was drawn up which allowed rule by an Emir or King, with a British Resident to advise. In 1946, Transjordan became fully independent and after the war with Israel in 1948 changed its name to Jordan since it had acquired territory west of the River Jordan.

Iraq

Mesopotamia, as it was then called, was a Turkish province which was conquered by British forces in the First World War. Britain was given a League of Nations mandate to rule the country in 1920. This provoked Arab resentment and some disorder followed. An Arab kingdom was set up in 1921 with the Emir Faisal as King. It still remained largely under British control until 1932 when the mandate was given up and Iraq became independent and a member of the League of Nations.

Aden: Modern architectural block. (*Photo: John Bulmer.*)

The moon rises over Aden. (*Photo: John Bulmer.*)

Aden and the Persian Gulf

Aden was first occupied by the British in 1839 as a part of British India. It was added to in 1882 while a large surrounding area became the Aden Protectorate in 1904.

It continued to be ruled by India until 1937 when it became a Crown colony under a governor with an Executive Council. In 1947 it received a Legislative Council which was enlarged and given a majority of elected members in 1959. Since 1958 there has been constant trouble with the state of the Yemen which claims Aden and the Protectorate as a part of its territories. This has resulted in considerable difficulties since the British, and British-officered Aden troops, have been in a great deal of fighting with Yemen forces along the borders. Egyptian forces have been in the Yemen in large numbers and the country is under Egyptian influence.

In 1959 the Western part of the Protectorate became the nucleus of the Federation of South Arabia and the Eastern part joined it in 1960. The small Arab states, ruled by sultans, amirs or sheikhs, were under a Supreme Council and a Federal Council from 1961 and a Federal Army was formed from the Aden Protectorate Levies originally organised in 1928.

Constitutional advances were made with the Colony of Aden which received Ministers in 1962 and in 1963 it joined the Federation. Further internal difficulties, undoubtedly fomented from the Yemen, led to Aden leaving the Federation, a state of emergency being declared in 1965. The British Government has since announced the intention of leaving the military base in Aden by 1968.

The Sultan of Muscat and Oman and the British Government signed a treaty of friendship in 1951 and there is a British Consul-General and British advisers with his army.

Bahrein has had treaty relations with Britain since 1880 and the Sheikh is advised by a British Political Agent.

Kuwait asked for British protection in 1897 and the Sheikh also has a British political agent. When Iraq claimed Kuwait in 1961, the Sheikh asked for British help and British forces were sent immediately. They were withdrawn when Arab League troops replaced them.

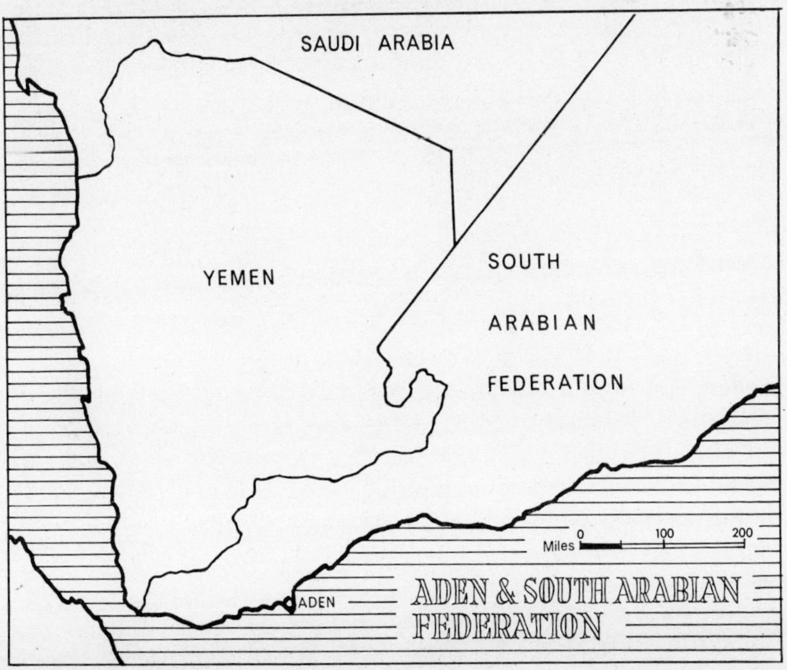

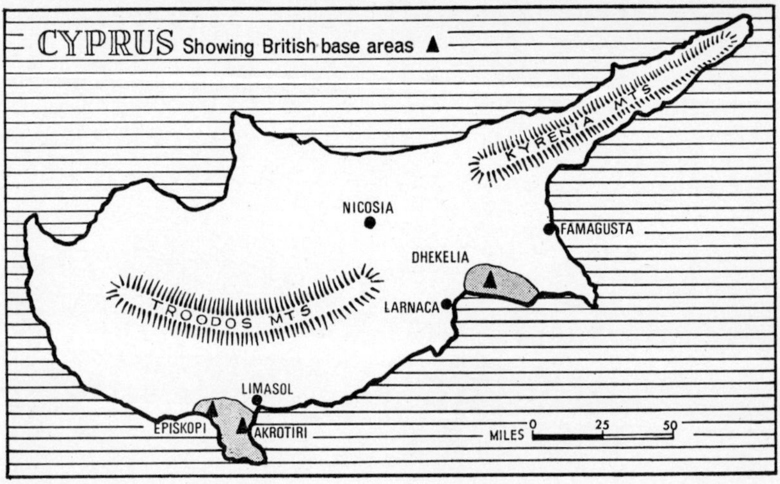

Cyprus

The island had been in Turkish possession since 1569 when it was conquered by Turkey. The Treaty of Berlin of 1878 placed Cyprus under British rule, although it was nominally under Turkish sovereignty and Britain paid an annual rent of £92,000 for it. When Turkey joined in the First World War on the side of Germany in 1914, it was annexed by Britain, who offered it to Greece in 1915, the offer being refused.

It was a Crown colony with a governor, an Executive Council and a partly-elected Legislative Council, and during this time benefited greatly from British rule. Railways, roads, irrigation schemes were provided and considerable afforestation was carried out.

Continuous immigration from Greece during British rule increased the population of Greek descent until it numbered almost four-fifths, while those of Turkish descent made up the remaining fifth. This meant that both Greece and Turkey were interested in the island although Greece had refused the offer of union in 1915. After the war there began a movement within Cyprus among the Greek Cypriots for union with Greece, known as Enosis. Since there was also clamour for self-government which the British Government seemed reluctant to grant, the discontent was channelled into the movement for Enosis.

This resulted in disorder and terrorism which built up until by 1954 a large number of British troops were involved and a state of emergency was declared in 1955. The organisation which carried out the terrorism and demanded Enosis was known as Eoka and was led by

Archbishop Makarios.

General Grivas.

Cyprus: Tragedy shows itself in the face of the womenfolk (*Photo: Donald McCullin.*)

General Grivas, a Greek officer. The leader of the Greek Cypriots, Archbishop Makarios, was found to be involved in the terrorism and was deported to the Seychelles Islands in the Indian Ocean by the British Government in 1956.

Eventually the British Government realised that Makarios was the only leader with whom they could negotiate. A settlement was reached at a conference in London in February 1959 which was accepted by all concerned and Makarios returned to Cyprus.

Under the Cyprus Act of 1960, the island became an independent republic with a Greek Cypriot President and a Turkish Cypriot Vice-President. Of the Council of Ministers, 7 were to be Greek and 3 Turkish and in the House of Representatives there were to be 35 Greek and 15 Turkish members. Britain was to retain two sovereign areas as defence bases. Archbishop Makarios was elected President and Dr Kutchuk, Vice-President, in December 1959, and Cyprus officially became a republic in 1960, Britain retaining the areas as military bases. In March 1961 it applied to be admitted to the Commonwealth and was accepted.

The Turks rejected the new constitutional proposals of Archbishop Makarios in December 1963. Disturbances which followed eventually broke out into serious violence and open fighting and, because of the interest of Greece and Turkey, Makarios asked for British troops to restore order. British troops took over, at first with Greek and Turkish forces, within a week. After the London Conference early in 1964, and Makarios' rejection of the suggestion for a NATO force, the United Nations sent a force, including British troops, in March 1964.

Malta

Britain captured the island of Malta from the French, who had taken possession the same year during the Revolutionary War in 1798. The Maltese people welcomed them as liberators and chose to become British. By the Treaty of Amiens, it was to be restored to the French and the British failure to do so was one of the causes of the Napoleonic War. After the defeat of Napoleon, Malta officially became a British possession by the Treaty of Vienna in 1815.

Malta then became an important base for the Royal Navy. A garrison was always maintained there and the governor was always the Commander-in-Chief.

In 1849 as a Crown colony, a Legislative Council was established and in 1887 it was given mainly elected members. It was granted responsible government in 1921 with a legislature of two chambers. The Senate was partly and the legislature Assembly wholly elected.

The Roman Catholic Church interfered in the politics of Malta and in 1930 instructed their members how to vote. The British Government considered this to be unconstitutional and the constitution was suspended by the governor. After the report of a Royal Commission the island was given a new constitution in 1936 which gave only a non-elected Executive Council, but in 1939 an elected Council was restored. However, this was not the restoration of responsible government and the Second World War broke out before any further changes were made.

During the war, Malta was under constant siege and continuous heavy bombardment from the air. During this period the people of Malta showed the most outstanding heroism, many were killed and injured and food and other supplies were short. In recognition of their behaviour King George VI awarded the island and its people the George Cross, and it has been known as Malta, G.C., ever since.

It was felt by the British Government that the people of Malta now deserved to be granted responsible government once more, and it was restored for internal affairs in 1947. It was given a Legislative Assembly and all men and women were entitled to vote.

In 1950 Mr Dom Mintoff, the Maltese Prime Minister asked that the island should become part of the United Kingdom. Britain had contributed a great deal of money towards the reconstruction of the island and there was a feeling that Maltese members should be sent to Westminster and that the island would progress better as a part of the United Kingdom than as an independent member of the Commonwealth. No agreement was reached, however. Concern had been caused in the island by the decision to close down the dockyard as the Royal Navy no longer required it. It was then taken over by the firm of Bailey's Ltd. for civilian use and this allayed the fear of unemployment. A new constitution which was to give Malta full self-government, except for defence and foreign affairs, presented in 1961 was not acceptable to the Maltese and a conference held in London in 1963 ended in deadlock. The British Government stated that independence was to be given by May 1964. There was still deadlock and after further talks a referendum was held which resulted in 54 per cent votes for independence which was finally granted as a state within the Commonwealth on 21 September 1964 after 164 years of British rule. Dr Borg Olivier became the first Prime Minister, and Britain retained certain defence facilities by agreement.

A crisis developed early in 1967, when the British government announced a partial closing of the defence bases and the Maltese government considered that the agreement had been violated.

SUMMARY

Egypt: Early British Interest

Early English mercantile activity in the Levant.—Communications with India paramount at end of eighteenth century.—Greek War of Independence (1821–29).—Mehemet Ali.—Syria question.—Hereditary Pasha of Egypt.—Opening of Suez Canal (1869).—Britain purchased shares (1875).—Ismail's bankruptcy.—The Dual Control (1879).—Arabi Pasha's rising (1882).—Rising crushed.—British control and reorganisation.—Mahdi's rising in Sudan (1883).—Murder of Gordon (1885).—Sudan under Dervishes for twelve years.—Reconquest of Sudan (1896–98).—Fashoda incident (1898).—Anglo-Egyptian Sudan.

Egypt Moves Towards Independence

Egypt as British Protectorate (1914).—Egypt independent under Fuad I (1922).—British responsible for Suez Canal, defence of Egypt and Sudan.—Murder of Sir Lee Stack (1924).—British rule in Sudan (1924–36).—Political troubles.—Treaty of 1936.—Egypt admitted to League of Nations (1937).—Second World War.—Disagreement over withdrawal of British troops and Egyptian control of Sudan.—Revolution of 1952 led by Neguib.—Neguib deposed by Nasser.—British forces left Egypt (1954–56).—Suez Crisis (1956).

Palestine

British conquest from Turks in First World War (1917).—Balfour Declaration (1917).—Jewish settlers in Palestine.—Restriction on immigration (1939).—British referred problem to United Nations.—British withdrew.—State of Israel founded (1948).

Jordan

Mandated to Britain by League of Nations after First World War (1920).—1928 Constitution.—Independent (1946).

Iraq

Conquered from Turks in First World War.—Mandated to Britain by League of Nations (1920).—Faisal as King (1921).—Mandate surrendered (1932).

Aden and the Persian Gulf

Aden occupied from India (1839).—Aden Protectorate (1904).—Crown colony (1937).—Trouble with the Yemen from 1958.—Federation of South Arabia (1960).—Muscat and Oman's treaty of friendship with Britain (1951).—Bahrein's treaty relations since 1880.—Kuwait under British protection since 1897.—Trouble with Iraq (1961).

Cyprus

Turkish possession since 1569.—Under British rule from 1878 by Treaty of Berlin.—Annexed when Turkey entered First World War (1914).—Predominance of Greeks in population.—Enosis.—Disorder and terrorism begin (1954).—Eoka.—General Grivas.—Makarios deported (1956).—Cyprus Act (1960).—Independent republic.—Readmitted to British Commonwealth (1961).—Further disorder.—British troops restore order (1964).—Referred to United Nations.—U.N. Force.

Malta

Captured from French (1798).—Officially British (1815).—Naval base.—Granted responsible government (1921).—Religious and constitutional difficulties.—

Constitution suspended (1930).—Royal Commission.—New constitution (1936). —Elected Council (1939).—Under siege in Second World War.—Malta G.C.—Responsible government restored (1947).—Request to join United Kingdom (1950).—Independence (1964).

QUESTIONS

Answer the following questions briefly:

1. (a) How did Mehemet Ali found the Egyptian royal family?
   (b) What was the Dual Control?
   (c) Who were the Dervishes?
   (d) What was the Fashoda incident?
   (e) Why was the Sudan called a condominium?
   (f) What effect did the Egyptian revolution of 1952 have?
   (g) What had Transjordan, Iraq and Palestine in common?
   (h) Why has there been recent disorder in Aden?
   (i) Why did Malta receive the George Cross?
   (j) Why did Malta ask to join the United Kingdom?
2. A declaration on British policy in Palestine was made by the British Foreign Secretary, Mr Arthur Balfour, on 2 November 1917. It said:

   > His Majesty's Government view with favour the establishment in Palestine of a national home for the Jewish people, and will use their best endeavours to facilitate the achievement of that object, it being understood that nothing shall be done which may prejudice the civil and religious rights of existing non-Jewish communities in Palestine, or the rights and political status enjoyed by the Jews in any other country.

   (a) What effect did this have on the Jewish people?
   (b) Outline the steps which eventually led to the establishment of Israel.
3. Describe the difficulties in Cyprus since the Second World War.
4. At 7 a.m. on 23 July 1952 General Neguib broadcast a proclamation from Cairo radio declaring that the object of the coup was to end Governmental instability and corruption in high places, and emphasising that the Army had no political aims and desired to work for the interests of Egypt within the Constitution. The text of this proclamation was as follows:

   > Egypt has undergone a critical time in her recent history. It has been a period of gross corruption and Governmental instability, and these factors had a great influence on the Army. People who received bribes contributed towards our defeat in the Palestine war. Traitors plotted against the Army after the Palestine war, but now we have purged ourselves, and our affairs within the Army have been placed in the hands of men in whose ability, character and patriotism we have faith. The whole of Egypt will welcome this news. No harm will be done to former military personnel who have been arrested. The entire Army is working for the interests of Egypt within the Constitution, and without any designs of its own.

   (a) What did General Neguib mean by 'a critical time in her recent history'?
   (b) What happened soon after this revolution?
   (c) What did General Neguib mean by 'in the hands of men in whose ability, character and patriotism we have faith'?

20 : The British Commonwealth Today

The Rest of the Commonwealth

THERE are a number of other colonies, protected states and dependencies which do not readily appear to be a part of a group or area and these are now dealt with here.

Gibraltar

An English fleet under Sir George Rooke and Sir Cloudesley Shovell captured Gibraltar in 1704 during the War of the Spanish Succession. By the Treaty of Utrecht in 1713 it was granted to Britain. A combined French and Spanish force tried desperately to recapture it during the American War of Independence and commanded by General Sir George Elliott, afterwards Lord Heathfield, the garrison withstood a siege which lasted from 1779 to 1793. Since that date it has been an important British naval base. The governor is also commander-in-chief and is always a high-ranking service officer. A Crown colony, it was given an Executive Council in 1922 and a Legislative Council, half elected, in 1949. A new constitution in 1950, amended in 1956, increased the size of the Legislative Council and the number of elected members. Spain has pressed for the return of Gibraltar in recent years and in 1965 General Franco imposed restrictions upon movement between the colony and Spain and made great difficulties for tourists. In 1965 a new constitution gave an Executive Council and an elected Legislative Council.

St Helena, with Ascension Island and Tristan da Cunha

St Helena was first occupied by Britain in 1659. It was captured by Holland in 1672 but recaptured in 1673 and has been British ever since. It was administered by the East India Company who used it as a station for their ships sailing around the Cape. The British Government took over the island between 1815 and 1821 when Napoleon I was in exile. He died there on 5 May 1821. It became a Crown colony in 1834. It is ruled by a governor with an Executive Council, advised by an Advisory Council. The Governor of St Helena is also responsible for the other islands in the South Atlantic, Ascension Island and the group of Tristan da Cunha. Ascension Island was occupied by

Gibraltar: General view showing half of the runway; the airfield was built during the Second World War. (*Photo: Armand Latourre.*)

Britain in 1815 in order to protect St Helena from attempts to rescue Napoleon, and was administered by the Admiralty until transferred to the Crown in 1922. It is governed by a Resident Magistrate responsible to the Governor of St Helena. Tristan da Cunha was annexed and garrisoned by Britain in 1816 for the same reason as Ascension. When the garrison was withdrawn the next year a Corporal of the Royal Artillery named William Glass, with his wife and two children, asked to be allowed to remain. He was joined by two ex-Royal Navy men, Alexander Cotton and John Mooney and three masons. In 1827 five coloured women from St Helena joined them and shipwrecked mariners and a few people from Cape Colony also settled on the island. From these, the present population of Tristan da Cunha is descended. For many years there was no formal government, the population governing democratically through a headman. In 1938 the group became a dependency of St Helena and now has an Administrator under the Governor of St Helena. In 1961 a volcano suddenly erupted and the population was brought to Britain where it remained for over two years. Nearly all elected to return to Tristan da Cunha, although some have come to Britain again since.

Falkland Islands

The Falkland Islands were discovered by John Davis in 1592 and visited by Sir John Hawkins two years later. France settled East Falkland in 1764. Spain bought the settlement in 1766. Britain annexed West Falkland in 1767, but it was captured by Spain in 1770, although after war had nearly broken out it was restored a year later. In 1774 the settlement was given up and for fifty years the islands were unoccupied. An Argentinian settlement begun in 1820 was destroyed by the Americans in 1831. Britain reoccupied the group in 1833 as a protection station for whaling and seal fisheries. The settlement was under naval control until 1843 when it became a Crown colony. It has a governor with an Executive Council, and a Legislative Council, some members of which are elected. The battle of the Falkland Islands between British and German naval forces was fought in nearby waters in 1914, early in the First World War. Among the dependencies of the Falklands are South Georgia and the South Sandwich Islands in Antarctica. The remainder of British Antarctica, the South Shetlands, the South Orkneys and Graham's Land, which were dependencies of the Falklands, became a separate colony in 1962, although the Governor of the Falklands is High Commissioner.

Mauritius

Holland annexed the island in 1598 and named it after their Stadtholder, Maurice of Nassau. It was used as a station by the Dutch East India Company until 1710 when it was abandoned. France annexed it as the Ile de France in 1715, but during the Napoleonic War in 1810 it was captured by a British expedition from Bombay. By the Treaty of Paris in 1814 it was ceded to Britain. The population partly British, but mostly of French descent, were joined by Indian labourers in the nineteenth century and by the end of the Second World War the Indians were in the majority. There are also Chinese. As a Crown colony, Mauritius has a governor with Executive and Legislative Councils. In 1948 the Legislative Council was given a majority of elected members and in 1958 the vote was given to all adults. It has been moving towards self-government and a conference was held in 1961 in London to discuss steps towards this and independence within the Commonwealth. Full internal self-government was granted in 1964 and after further discussions it was hoped that full independence would follow soon afterwards.

Seychelles Islands

Originally used as haunts of pirates, these islands in the Indian Ocean became French in 1756. They were captured by Britain during the Revolutionary War in 1794 and were occupied and ceded to Britain in 1814 by the Treaty of Paris. They were ruled from Mauritius until 1903 when they became a Crown colony. It has a governor and Executive Council, with a Legislative Council which is partly elected. Archbishop Makarios of Cyprus was exiled there in 1956. Amirante Island and the Aldabras are dependencies.

Maldive Islands

These islands, 400 miles south-west of Ceylon, came under British protection ruled from that island in 1887. They are ruled by a Sultan and in 1960 were given full internal self-government. Britain is responsible for external affairs and defence and has the rights to an R.A.F. base on the island of Gan for twenty years from 1960.

The Statute of Westminster, 1931

When Canada became a Dominion in 1867 it was a new conception in colonial history. Australia, New Zealand and South Africa followed and although by the Acts of the British Parliament which had brought these four Dominions into existence, Britain had authority to legislate for them or intervene in their affairs, in fact it had never done so. What is more, the services rendered to the Mother Country and the Empire by these nations during the First World War and the loyalty they had shown demanded recognition. After the war they had agreed to the Peace Treaty as separate nations and become members of the League of Nations. Although they were obviously independent nations, in theory they were still under the control of Britain. The Statute of Westminster, passed by the Mother of Parliaments, released them once and for all from British rule and made that independence a reality.

It declared that six of the states described as Dominions of the British Empire were to be absolutely independent. They were to be equal in status to Great Britain and to each other and were to continue to owe allegiance to the Crown. Britain renounced all authority over them and they, with Britain, were to form the British Commonwealth of Nations. These six members were Canada, Australia, New Zealand, South Africa, the Irish Free State and Newfoundland.

The Irish Free State, which had a long and unhappy history under British rule, was anxious to sever her connections with the Commonwealth and did so, declaring herself independent as the Republic of Eire in 1937. Newfoundland, after economic difficulties, had her constitution suspended in 1934 and became a province of the Dominion of Canada in 1949. Thus at the outbreak of the Second World War

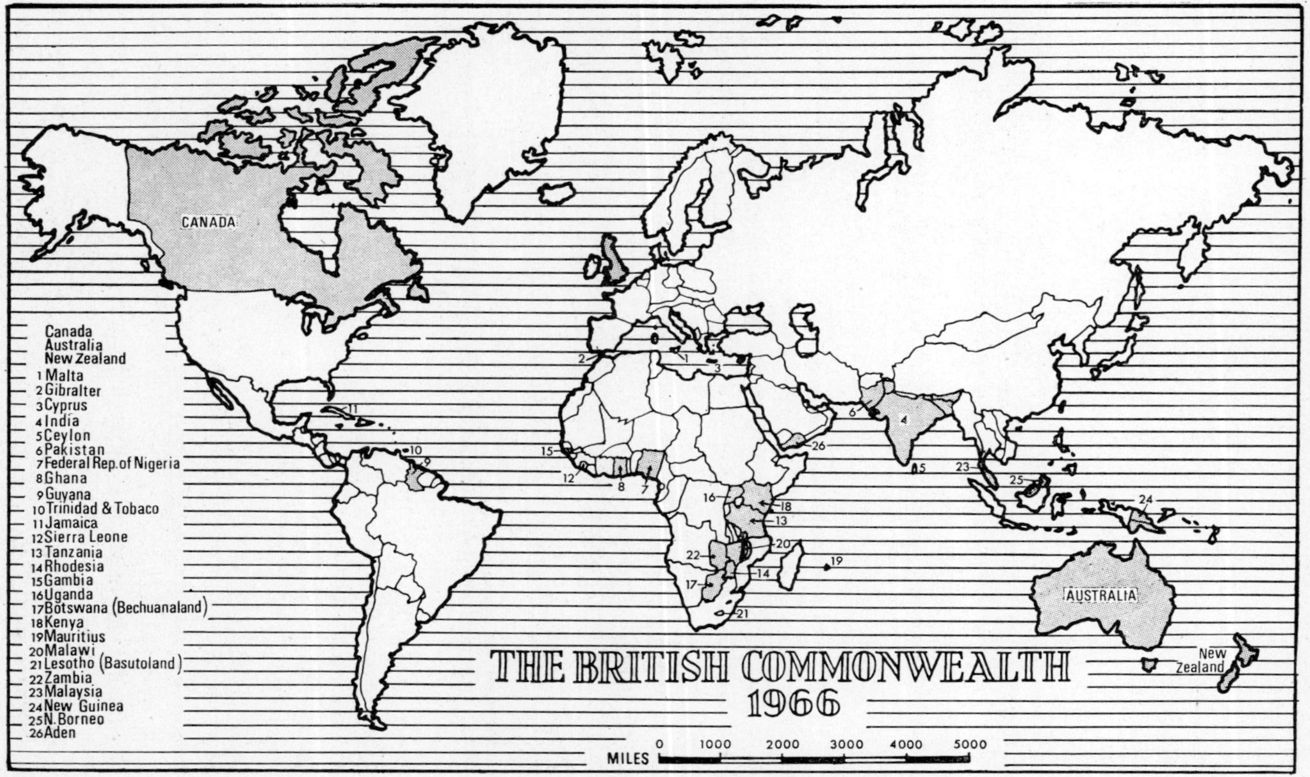
THE BRITISH COMMONWEALTH
1966
CANADA
AUSTRALIA
New Zealand
Canada
Australia
New Zealand
1 Malta
2 Gibralter
3 Cyprus
4 India
5 Ceylon
6 Pakistan
7 Federal Rep. of Nigeria
8 Ghana
9 Guyana
10 Trinidad & Tobaco
11 Jamaica
12 Sierra Leone
13 Tanzania
14 Rhodesia
15 Gambia
16 Uganda
17 Botswana (Bechuanaland)
18 Kenya
19 Mauritius
20 Malawi
21 Lesotho (Basutoland)
22 Zambia
23 Malaysia
24 New Guinea
25 N. Borneo
26 Aden
MILES
0
1000
2000
3000
4000
5000

the British Commonwealth of Nations consisted of Britain and four Dominions.

The British Commonwealth Today

Since the end of the Second World War one of the original four Dominions, South Africa, has left the Commonwealth, in 1961, while twenty-two former colonies have won independence and become full members.

These new members have not the ties of race and sentiment with the Mother Country which the old Dominions have, and the desire of some of them to become republics raised certain problems. India was the first Dominion to desire this and the difficulties were overcome by their renouncing their allegiance to the Crown, but by accepting the Queen as Head of the Commonwealth.

The Commonwealth is held together by slender ties. These include the acceptance of the Queen as its Head and common self-interest. At regular intervals Conferences of Commonwealth Prime Ministers are held in London, and many people believe that there should be a permanent Commonwealth Conference with representatives of all member states at Cabinet level. This might well make co-operation closer than it is. There are certain definite facts about the Commonwealth which emphasise its connection with Britain. English Common Law is the basis of almost all Commonwealth countries, and English is the common language. Indeed, India has found English is the only language fully understood because of the variety of dialects in the country.

The newly-independent states have found as the years passed that they wanted to follow the trade policy which suited them best. This applies to the old Dominions, too, although the newer countries, having less ties with Britain, have more tended to go their own way.

It has been fashionable in recent years to decry British Imperial history but it is undeniable that Britain achieved much with the countries which found themselves in her trust. Whether as Crown colonies with direct British rule, or by indirect rule through native rulers in protectorates such as in Malaya, Nigeria or Uganda, they learned the civilised way of government and moved gradually towards self-rule. Trade had been one of the great inspirations for colonial development and the Chartered Companies had played a considerable part in the exploration, settlement, development and administration of new territories. Although Britain benefited herself, the colonies and protectorates themselves have gained immensely and Britain has every reason to be proud of her colonial achievements, particularly as she has steadily handed over the government to the native peoples.

Yet the Commonwealth is now having to withstand great stresses and strains, notably with the crisis over Rhodesia's unilateral declaration of independence. It is to be seen in the future whether it can survive and continue as a great example of peaceful co-operation in mutual self-interest.

SUMMARY

Gibraltar

Captured from Spanish (1704).—Ceded to Britain by Treaty of Utrecht (1713).—Besieged (1779–1793).—Crown colony.—Executive Council (1922).—Legislative Council (1949).—Constitutional changes (1950 and 1956).—Trouble with Spain.—New Constitution 1965.

St Helena, with Ascension Island and Tristan da Cunha

St Helena occupied by Britain (1659).—Captured by Holland (1672).—Recaptured (1673); administered by East India Company; taken over by Government during Napoleon's exile (1815–21).—Crown colony (1834).—Governor, Executive Council and Advisory Council.—Responsible for Ascension and Tristan da Cunha.—Ascension occupied by Britain (1815).—Administered by Admiralty until 1922.—Resident Magistrate.—Tristan da Cunha annexed (1816).—Gradual settlement.—No formal government until 1938.—Under St Helena.—Administrator.

Falkland Islands

Discovered by Davis (1592).—French and Spanish settlements.—West Falkland annexed (1767).—Captured by Spain (1770).—Restored (1771).—Given up (1774).—Reoccupied by Britain (1833).—Under naval control.—Crown colony (1843).—Governor, with Executive Council and Legislative Council.—Dependencies in Antarctic.—Some became separate colony (1962) with Governor of Falklands as High Commissioner.

Mauritius

Annexed by Holland (1598).—Abandoned (1710).—Annexed by France (1715).—Captured by British (1810).—Ceded to Britain (1814), by Treaty of Paris.—Mixed population.—Crown colony with governor, Executive and Legislative Councils.—Majority of elected members in Legislative (1948).—Universal adult suffrage (1958).—London Conference (1961).—Full internal self-government (1964).—Hope for full independence within Commonwealth.

Seychelles

Haunt of pirates.—Annexed by France (1756).—Captured by Britain (1794 and 1810).—Ceded to Britain (1814).—Ruled from Mauritius until 1903.—Crown colony.—Governor, Executive Council and partly elected Legislative Council.

Maldive Islands

Under British protection (1887).—Ruled from Ceylon until 1900.—Internal self-government (1900).—Ruled by Sultan.—Treaty rights for R.A.F. base on Gan.

The Statute of Westminster, 1931

Six states declared to be independent.—Equal in status to Britain and each other.—Britain renounced authority.—British Commonwealth of Nations.—Withdrawal of Irish Free State as Eire (1937).—Newfoundland as province of Canada (1949).—South Africa (1961).

British Commonwealth Today

Changing nations of Commonwealth.—South Africa left (1961).—Twenty-two new states; some as republics.—Queen as Head of Commonwealth.—Commonwealth Conferences.—English as common language.—Different trade policies.—Britain's achievement.—Difficulties of Commonwealth.

QUESTIONS

Answer the following questions briefly:

1. (a) Name three colonies captured by Britain during wars and retained.
   (b) How did Tristan da Cunha become settled?
   (c) Why was Tristan da Cunha in the news in 1961?
   (d) Which of the territories mentioned in this chapter has a special treaty arrangement with Britain giving rights for an air base?
   (e) Which of the colonies mentioned in this chapter has been in the news in recent years in connection with the troubles in Cyprus?
   (f) Which colony is likely to receive independent Dominion status the soonest?
2. Why was the Statute of Westminster (1931) so important? Give its main points.
3. Sir Winston Churchill, in his *History of the English Speaking Peoples* (Educational Book Co.) says, 'Certainly the dawn of the twentieth century seemed bright and calm for those who lived within the unequalled boundary of the British Empire, or sought shelter within its folds.'
   (a) Apart from the two World Wars, what else has happened to break the calm within the British Empire during the twentieth century?
   (b) What has happened to 'the unequalled boundary of the British Empire'?
   (c) What does Sir Winston Churchill mean when he says, 'sought shelter within its folds'?
   (d) What are the main changes within the British Commonwealth since the Second World War?
   (e) What do you consider to be the main problems facing the Commonwealth today?

Biographical Notes

Adams, Samuel (1722–1803). American statesman. First came to prominence as a leader of the Sons of Liberty during the quarrel between the colonists and the British Government. He helped to organise the Boston Tea Party. He was one of the signatories of the Declaration of Independence.

Akbar, Jellaladin Mohammed (1542–1605). The greatest of the Mogul Emperors of India and the last to retain control of the whole of the continent. A great conqueror and a great administrator, he won for himself the title of 'Guardian of Mankind'.

Amherst, Jeffrey, Lord (1717–97). British soldier. He served at Dettingen and Fontenoy and in 1758 was appointed by Pitt to command British forces against the French in Canada. After his success, he was appointed first Governor-General of Canada and North America.

Arnold, Benedict (1741–1801). American soldier. He served with the colonial forces in the War of Independence, taking a prominent part in the battles of Crown Point, Ticonderoga, Quebec, Ridgefield and Saratoga and being wounded. He was eventually promoted Major-General but there were several cases of his being treated unfairly by the colonial government. He corresponded with General Clinton with a view to joining the British forces. A Major Andre met him to consider this but was captured with incriminating papers. Arnold was eventually made a Brigadier-General in the British army and thus is regarded as a traitor by the Americans.

Baden-Powell, Robert Stephenson Smyth, 1st Lord (1857–1941). British General and founder of the Boy Scouts movement. Served in Ashanti in 1895 and Matabeleland in 1896–97. Defended Mafeking 1899–1900. Lieutenant-General in 1908. Founded Boy Scouts movement in 1908.

Barton, Sir Edmund (1849–1920). Australian statesman. He joined with Sir Henry Parkes in the leadership of the movement in favour of federation. He became the first Prime Minister of Australia.

Bennett, Richard Bedford (1870–1947). Canadian statesman. He became leader of the Canadian Conservative Party in 1927 and Prime Minister of Canada in 1930.

Borden, Sir Robert Laird (1854–1937). Canadian statesman. He became leader of Canadian Conservative Party in 1901. Prime Minister of Canada in 1912.

Botha, Louis (1862–1919). South African General and politician. He opposed Kruger's policy against the Uitlanders and the declaration of war against the British. He commanded Boer forces with considerable success, however. He became the first Prime Minister of the Union of South Africa in 1910 and a firm friend of Britain.

Bradford, William (1590–1657). One of the leaders of the Pilgrim Fathers, who became Governor of New Plymouth colony. His wise rule was largely responsible for its success.

Bright, John (1811–89). British statesman and Liberal M.P. Noted for his advocacy of Free Trade and particularly his work with the Anti-Corn Law League.

Brooke, Sir James (1803–1868). British soldier and traveller. Was made Rajah of Sarawak by the Sultan of Borneo for his work against the Dyaks invading Borneo. The hereditary title remained in his family and they were known as the 'White Rajahs'.

Bruce, Stanley Melbourne, 1st Viscount (Born 1883). Australian statesman. Became leader of the Australian Liberal party and Prime Minister of Australia in 1923. He became High Commissioner in London in 1933.

Buller, Sir Redvers Henry (1839–1908). British General. He took part in the Red River expedition under Wolseley in Canada in 1870, the Ashanti campaign in 1873–74, the Kaffir War of 1878–79, and the Zulu War of 1879, in which he won the V.C. He was next on the Sudan campaign in 1884–85. He served in the Boer War of 1881, and was British commander in the first part of the Boer War of 1899–1902.

Burgoyne, John (1722–92). British General and dramatist. He commanded the British forces driving south from Canada in the American War of Independence which should have joined with Sir William Howe, and was defeated and captured at Saratoga in 1777. He wrote and published several plays.

Chamberlain, Joseph (1836–1914). British statesman. He entered Parliament in 1876 as a Liberal. He led the Liberal Unionists out of the Liberal party over the question of Irish Home Rule in 1886. He was Colonial Secretary in the Conservative Government of 1895–1903. He became an advocate of Tariff Reform or Protection.

Chancellor, Richard (d. 1556). In 1553 Chancellor made a voyage to the White Sea and thence overland to Moscow. The Czar showed him hospitality and made trading arrangements for English merchants. He was drowned returning from Moscow in 1556.

Clarkson, Thomas (1760–1846). English reformer. A founder of the Anti-Slavery Society, he collected much of the evidence for William Wilberforce and supported his efforts to end the slave trade and slavery.

Clive, Robert Clive, 1st Lord (1725–74). British soldier and administrator. He went to India in the service of the East India Company in 1744 and was commissioned as ensign in East India Company's army in 1747. Famous for his victories at Arcot (1751) and Plassey (1757). He was Governor of Bengal, and on his return to England in 1767 was accused of corruption. Although cleared he committed suicide in 1774.

Cobden, Richard (1804–65). British politician. Associated with John Bright in advocacy of Free Trade and in the Anti-Corn Law League. He became a Liberal M.P. in 1841.

Cook, James (1728–79). British sailor and explorer. He commanded a transport and navigated the River St Lawrence at the attack on Quebec in 1759. Famous for the voyage which led to the charting of the coasts of New Zealand and East Australia in 1768–70. He explored the New Hebrides and discovered New Caledonia and the Hawaiian Islands, where he was murdered in 1779.

Coote, Sir Eyre (1726–83). British soldier. He was a Major with Clive at Plassey in 1757 and distinguished himself in a 400-mile pursuit in 1760. In 1779 he was made a Lieutenant-General and Commander-in-Chief of India. His victory over Hyder Ali at Porto Novo against odds of five to one in 1781 is considered one of the greatest British feats in India.

Cornwallis, Charles, 1st Marquess (1738–1805). British General and administrator. He was the most successful British commander in the American War of Independence but was forced to surrender at Yorktown in 1781. In 1786 he went as Governor-General and Commander-in-Chief in India and defeated Tipu Sahib. He became Governor-General of India again in 1805 but died almost at once.

Cripps, Sir Stafford (1889–1952). British statesman. He became a Labour M.P. in 1931 and held office in the Labour Government. He led the mission to India in 1942, and was again a Minister in the Labour Government of 1945–50.

Curtin, John (1885–1945). Australian Trade Union leader and statesman. Became Labour Prime Minister of Australia in 1941 and was an able leader during the Second World War.

Curzon, George Nathaniel, 1st Marquess (1859–1925). British statesman. He became a Conservative M.P. in 1886 and was Viceroy of India from 1898–1905. He held several Cabinet offices between 1915 and 1924.

Dalhousie, James Andrew Brown Ramsey, 10th Earl of (1812–60). British administrator. He became Governor-General of India in 1847 and was responsible for many reforms notably in railways and other transport. He is remembered particularly for the 'Doctrine of Lapse' which was one of the contributory causes of the Indian Mutiny.

Davis, John (*c.* 1555–1605). British sailor and explorer. He served against the Spanish Armada. Between 1585–87 he made three voyages to find a North-West Passage and discovered Davis Strait. He discovered the Falkland Islands in 1592. He invented a quadrant used for many years by sailors.

Disraeli, Benjamin, later 1st Lord Beaconsfield (1804–81). British statesman. He became Conservative M.P. in 1837 and was Prime Minister of the Conservative Governments of 1868 and 1874–1880, the first Jew to hold that office; he had been baptised a Christian. He is regarded as the father of modern Conservatism and gained fame for his purchase of the Suez Canal shares in 1875 and his part in the

Congress of Berlin in 1878. Known by the nickname of 'Dizzy', he was a great favourite of Queen Victoria.

Drake, Sir Francis (*c.* 1545–96). British sailor and explorer. He sailed with his cousin John Hawkins in 1567 on a voyage and was nearly killed by the Spaniards. In 1572 he sacked the Spanish port of Nombre de Dios, crossed the Isthmus of Panama and captured a mule train of treasure. He was the first Englishman to sail round the world from 1577–80 and was second in command against the Spanish Armada.

Dupleix, Joseph François (1697–1763). French colonial administrator. He became Governor of Pondicherry and in charge of French settlements in India in 1741 and conceived the idea of driving out the British and making French power supreme through the native princes. Defeated by Clive, he was recalled in 1754.

D'Urban, Sir Benjamin (1777–1849). British General and colonial administrator. He served throughout the Peninsular War. He was Governor of Antigua and British Guiana before being appointed Governor of Cape Colony in 1834. He was admired by both British and Dutch for his firm and wise rule. The British Government rejected his advice after the Kaffir War in 1835 and this led to the Great Trek of the Boers and to his recall.

Durham, John George Lambton, 1st Earl of (1792–1840). British statesman. One of the promotors of the First Reform Act, he was known as 'Radical Jack' because of his advanced ideas. He was sent to Canada in 1837 as Governor-General after the Mackenzie and Papineau risings and was author of the famous Durham Report.

Fisher, Andrew (1862–1928). Australian statesman. He emigrated to Queensland at the age of 23 and became a Labour Member of the Federal Parliament in 1901. He became Leader of the Australian Labour Party in 1907 and was Prime Minister in 1908 and again 1910–13 and 1914–15. He was High Commissioner in London 1915–21.

Franklin, Benjamin (1706–90). American statesman and scientist. He invented the lightning conductor in 1747. He is well known as a man of letters. He was against the American colonies leaving the British Empire but once the War of Independence started supported the colonists loyally. He was one of the signatories of the Declaration of Independence which he helped to write and he went to France to seek that nation's help in the war in 1776.

Frobisher, Sir Martin (1532–94). English sailor. In 1576 set off to find the North-West Passage and made a second attempt in 1577. He was a subordinate commander against the Spanish Armada.

Gandhi, Mohandas Karamchand (1869–1948). Indian leader, who was partly educated in England. He gave up a £5,000 legal practice in Bombay to live on £1 a week in South Africa where he devoted his time to fighting laws which placed the Indians there at a disadvantage. He returned to India in 1914 and became the leader of the movement for Indian Independence. He was imprisoned by the British from 1922–24 for conspiracy. In 1930 he led a 200-mile march to fetch salt from the sea in order to defy the Government salt monopoly. He attended the London Conference on Indian Reform in 1931. On his return to India he renewed his civil disobedience campaign and was re-arrested. He continued in and out of jail until 1945, when he negotiated with the British for Independence. He was assassinated by an Hindu fanatic on 30 January 1948. He was known as Mahatma (Great Soul) Gandhi. His teaching of resistance by non-violent methods had a great effect in and outside India.

Gilbert, Sir Humphrey (*c.* 1539–83). British sailor and explorer. He sailed to St John's, Newfoundland, in 1583 and founded first British colony in America. He explored southwards and was lost on the return journey to Britain.

Gladstone, William Ewart (1809–98). British statesman. Entered Parliament as a Whig in 1833. After holding many ministerial appointments, he was Prime Minister of Liberal Governments from 1868–74, 1880–85 and in 1886.

Grey, Sir George (1812–98). British Colonial Governor and statesman. He was Governor of South Australia in 1841 and succeeded in restoring the colony. He was appointed Governor of New Zealand in 1845 and took over in the First Maori War, winning the confidence of the Maoris. In 1853 he was transferred to Cape Colony in South Africa as governor and suggested a plan for federation in 1859 which was very nearly successful. He returned to New Zealand as governor in 1861 and held office through the Second Maori War until 1868 when he returned to England. He again went to New Zealand in 1872 and was Prime Minister of New Zealand from 1877–79.

Hastings, Warren (1732–1818). First Governor-General of British India. He became Governor-General in 1773. When he returned to England in 1785 he was accused by his enemies of infamous conduct in India and after a trial lasting seven years was found not guilty and acquitted. The work he had done in India proved he was one of the greatest of Imperial administrators.

Hawkins, Sir John (1532–95). British sailor. Cousin of Sir Francis Drake. One of the early founders of the slave trade from West Africa. He carried on constant war against the Spaniards between 1562 and 1595 and was given a command as a rear-admiral against the Armada.

Henry, Patrick (1736–99). American politician. He was one of the leaders of the American colonists against the British Government's actions.

Hertzog, James Barry Munnik (1866–1942). South African politician. He fought against the British in the Boer War of 1899–1902 and remained anti-British afterwards, forming the Nationalist Party to fight for full independence for South Africa. He voted against Declaration of War against Germany in 1939.

Hofmeyr, Jan Hendrik (1845–1909). South African politician. Leader of the Afrikaaners in the Cape Parliament, he joined forces with Cecil Rhodes just before the Second Boer War to find a peaceful solution to the Transvaal problem.

Hughes, William Morris (1864–1952). Australian statesman. Born in Wales and went to Australia when he was 20. Became a trade union organiser and leader. Became leader of Australian Labour Party and Prime Minister of Australia in 1915.

Jameson, Sir Leander Starr (1853–1917). A friend of Cecil Rhodes, he was appointed administrator of Rhodesia in 1891. He organised the Jameson Raid in 1895 and was sentenced to 15 months' imprisonment. He was active in South African politics after the South African War of 1899–1902 as leader of the pro-British party.

Jinnah, Mohammed-Ali (1876–1948). Pakistani statesman. Became a barrister in 1897. President of the Moslem League which stood for a separate Moslem state. He became the first Governor-General of Pakistan in 1947.

Jones, John Paul (1747–92). American sailor. Born in Scotland he became a supporter of the American colonists after settling in Virginia. He was given a command in the American Navy in 1775 and became the most successful of their naval commanders in the War of Independence. In 1790 he became an Admiral in the Russian Navy.

King, William Lyon Mackenzie (1874–1950). Canadian statesman. His mother was the daughter of William Lyon Mackenzie, the leader of one of the risings in 1837. He became leader of the Canadian Liberal Party in 1920 and was Prime Minister of Canada from 1921–26 and after a break of a few months from 1926–30 and again from 1935–48.

Kitchener, Horatio Herbert, 1st Earl (1850–1916). British soldier. Sirdar of the Egyptian army from 1892, he was concerned in operations in the Sudan in 1896 and 1898. Served as Chief-of-Staff to Lord Roberts during the South African War of 1899–1902 and succeeded him as Commander-in-Chief. He was Minister of War at the outbreak of the First World War and was lost in the cruiser *Hampshire* on the way to Russia in 1916.

Kruger, Paul (1825–1904). South African politician. He went with his father on the Great Trek in 1836 into Transvaal, and his family's suffering developed in him a hatred of the British. He was President of the Transvaal between 1883–1900, his policy being largely responsible for the war of 1899–1902.

Lafayette, Marie Joseph Paul de Motier, Marquis de (1757–1834). French soldier and statesman. Supporter of American colonists in War of Independence. Served as volunteer and was made a General. Early leader in French Revolution, but fell from favour.

Laurier, Sir Wilfred (1841–1919). Canadian statesman. Prime Minister of Liberal Government in Canada from 1896–1918.

Lawrence, Sir Henry Montgomery (1806–57). British soldier and administrator. Defended Lucknow during Mutiny and was killed in the siege. With his brother, Lord Lawrence, did much to settle and develop the Punjab.

Lawrence, John Laird Mair, 1st Lord (1811–79). British administrator. Was Lieutenant-Governor of the Punjab during the Indian Mutiny and helped in the capture of Delhi. Governor-General of India 1864–69. Previously did much to settle and develop the Punjab together with his brother Sir Henry.

Lawrence, Stringer (1697–1775). British soldier. Served at Gibraltar, in Flanders and at Culloden. Went to India to command East India Company's troops in 1748. Clive served under him and they became life-long friends.

Livingstone, David (1813–73). Scottish missionary and explorer. Won regard of the natives in Africa as a missionary. As an explorer, discovered Lakes Ngami, Shirwa, Nyasa and Bangweulu and also the Victoria Falls. He was the first white man to traverse the length of Lake Tanganyika.

Lugard, Frederick Dealtry, 1st Lord (1858–1945). British administrator. Served as a soldier in Afghan War (1879–80), Sudan (1884–85) and in Burma (1886–87). He led an expedition against slave traders on Lake Nyasa in 1888 and was severely wounded. He was sent to Uganda by the Imperial British East Africa Company in 1890 and subdued the area with one British officer and a small force of Sudanese soldiers. High Commissioner of Nigeria 1900. Governor of Hong Kong 1907–12. Governor of Northern and Southern Nigeria 1912–19.

Lyons, Joseph Aloysius (1879–1939). Australian statesman. Became leader of United Australian party in 1931 and Prime Minister of Australia from 1931–39.

MacArthur, Douglas (1880–1964). American soldier. He commanded American forces in the Philippines from 1941 and in 1942 was Supreme Allied Commander in the Pacific, a post he held until final victory. He was then Supreme Commander in Japan. He commanded U.N. Forces at the beginning of the Korean War.

MacDonald, Sir John Alexander (1815–91). Canadian statesman. He went to Canada as a child of five. He became leader of the Canadian Conservative Party and was Prime Minister of Canada in 1857. He was one of the authors of the British North America Act of 1867 which led to Dominion status and was Prime Minister of the Dominion Government from 1867–74 and 1878–91.

Mackenzie, Sir Alexander (1755–1820). British explorer. He entered the service of the North West Fur Company of Canada in 1779 and in 1789 led an expedition to explore the north-west. He penetrated to the Arctic Ocean and discovered the territory and river which bears his name. He led another expedition to the Pacific Coast in 1793.

Mackenzie, William Lyon (1795–1861). Canadian politician. He led one of the risings of 1837, highlighting the grievances which led to the Durham Report. He fled to the U.S.A. after the rising was crushed, but returned in 1849 and was active in Canadian politics.

Menzies, Sir Robert Gordon (b. 1894). Australian statesman. Prime Minister of Australia 1939–41 and 1949–66. Became Lord Warden of the Cinque Ports in 1966.

Milner, Alfred, 1st Viscount (1854–1925). British administrator and statesman. He served as Under-Secretary for Finance in Egypt 1889–92. He became Governor of the Cape of Good Hope in 1897 and was responsible for the negotiations with Kruger before the Second Boer War. He took part in the peace negotiations and was Governor of Transvaal and Orange River Colonies until 1905.

Montcalm, Louis Joseph, Marquis de (1712–59). French soldier. He was appointed to command the French forces in Canada in 1756 and led them in several actions. He was forced to retire to Quebec and was there killed in the action with Wolfe's troops.

Mountbatten, Louis, 1st Earl (b. 1900). British sailor, military leader and administrator. He entered the Navy in 1913. Captain 1937. Vice-Admiral 1942. Chief of Combined Operations 1942. Supreme Commander South-East Asia 1943–46. Viceroy of India 1947. Admiral of the Fleet 1953. Chief of Defence Staff 1959–1965.

Nehru, Jawalarlal (1890–1965). Indian politician. Educated at Harrow and Cambridge. He was one of the leaders of the India Congress Party and an associate of Mahatma Gandhi. Prime Minister of India 1947–65.

North, Frederick, Lord (1732–92). British statesman. Prime Minister 1770–82 during the quarrel with the American colonies and the War of Independence. He was leader of the party dominated by King George III.

Oglethorpe, James Edward (1696–1785). British soldier and philanthropist. He served under Prince Eugène. He did much to alleviate suffering of debtor prisoners and formed an association for the establishment of a colony for them in America. He founded Georgia in 1733 and was governor for thirteen years.

Papineau, Louis Joseph (1786–1871). Canadian politician. He was leader of the French Canadians in the rising in 1837 which led to the Durham Report.

Parkes, Sir Henry (1815–96). Australian statesman. He emigrated to Australia in 1839 and became Prime Minister of N.S.W. in 1872. He was the leader of the federation movement which was eventually to lead to the foundation of the Commonwealth of Australia.

Penn, William (1644–1718). English Quaker. Founder of Pennsylvania. He helped to found a Quaker colony in West New Jersey in 1676. He secured a grant of territory to be known as Pennsylvania in 1681 and founded the colony in 1682.

Pitt, William, 1st Earl of Chatham (1708–78). British statesman. He joined the Ministry of Newcastle in 1757. He was the architect of the British victory in the Seven Years War. He vigorously opposed the policy against the American colonists, but ill-health prevented his maintaining it.

Pitt, William (1759–1806). British statesman. Younger son of William Pitt, Earl of Chatham. He became Prime Minister in 1783 at the age of 24 and led the country during the Revolutionary War with France and until 1806.

Pretorious, Andries (1799–1853). A descendant of an early Dutch settler in South Africa, he was one of the leaders of the Great Trek in 1836. He became a military leader of the Boers, first against the Zulus and then against the British in Natal. He crossed into Transvaal and once more led the Boers against the British. He concluded the Sand River Convention in 1852 by which the British recognised the independence of the Transvaal. Pretoria was named after him.

Raffles, Sir Thomas Stamford (1781–1826). British administrator. He entered the service of the East India Company in 1795. He was responsible for the extension of British influence in the Far East and founded a settlement at Singapore in 1819.

Raleigh, Sir Walter (*c.* 1552–1618). English soldier, sailor and writer. He was a favourite of Queen Elizabeth. He was associated with Sir Humphrey Gilbert's voyages and in 1584 he sent an expedition to what is now known as North Carolina but which he called Virginia. He founded a colony there which was unsuccessful. In 1595 he went on a voyage of exploration to the coast of South America.

Revere, Paul (1735–1818). American patriot. He was a Second-Lieutenant in the artillery at Crown Point in 1756. He was one of the leaders of the Boston Tea Party in 1774 and he made a famous midnight ride from Charlestown to Lexington on April 18–19th in 1775 to give warning of the approach of British troops from Boston.

Rhodes, Cecil John (1853–1902). British statesman. He went to Natal as a young man because of ill-health. He became interested in the diamond industry and made a vast fortune. He had a vision of a British Africa with a railway from the Cape to Cairo. In 1889 he secured a charter and formed the British South Africa Company to develop Rhodesia. He became Prime Minister of Cape Colony in 1890, but resigned after the Jameson Raid.

Riel, Louis (1844–85). Canadian rebel. He was a half-breed who led the Red Rising of 1870. He escaped capture and on return to Canada became an M.P. He led another rising in 1885 and this time was captured and hanged for treason.

Roberts, Frederick Sleigh, 1st Earl (1832–1914). British soldier. He won the V.C. in the Indian Mutiny. In 1880 he led the famous march from Kabul to Kandahar and became Commander-in-Chief in India in

1885. He went to South Africa in 1899 as commander of the British forces in the Second Boer War. His only son was killed winning the V.C. at the Battle of Colenso in 1899.

St Laurent, Louis Stephen (b. 1882). Canadian statesman. Prime Minister of Canada 1948–57.

Simon, Sir John, later Viscount (1873–1954). British statesman. Liberal M.P. from 1906–18 and 1922–40. He held several Government offices and in 1927 went to India as Chairman of the Royal Commission. He was created a viscount in 1940.

Smith, Adam (1723–90). British economist. In 1776 his book the *Wealth of Nations* was published which began a new trend of thought in political economy. He particularly advocated Free Trade and the Whigs and later the Liberals adopted this as a policy.

Smith, Sir Harry George Wakelyn, Bart. (1787–1860). British soldier. He served through the Peninsular War, and the war with the United States in 1814 and at Waterloo. He went to South Africa in 1828 and commanded a division in the Kaffir War of 1834–36. His advice and that of Sir Benjamin D'Urban was rejected by the Government and the Great Trek resulted. He went to India in 1837 and took part in the Sikh War of 1845–46. He returned to South Africa in 1847 as Governor of Cape Colony and defeated the Boers in the Orange River Sovereignty in 1848. The towns of Harrismith and Ladysmith were named after Sir Harry Smith and his wife.

Smith, John (1580–1631). British soldier and colonist. He led the settlers to Virginia in 1607. He was captured by Indians and released by the intercession of a chief's daughter, Princess Pocahontas. He became President of Virginia in 1608.

Smuts, Jan Christiaan (1870–1950). South African soldier and statesman. He was born of Boer parents and went to Cambridge University. He fought with brilliant success against the British in the Second South African War. He was a Minister in the first South African Government of 1910. In the First World War he commanded South African Forces in E. Africa. He became Prime Minister of South Africa on Botha's death in 1919. He was a firm friend of Britain and a leading Commonwealth statesman in the Second World War.

Steuben von, Baron Frederick William Augustus Henry Ferdinand (1730–94). German soldier. Born in Prussia he fought for Frederick the Great in the Seven Years War. He went to America in 1777 to help the colonists in the War of Independence and in 1778 trained Washington's Army at Valley Forge.

Wakefield, Edward Gibbon (1796–1862). British colonial statesman. He became interested in colonial subjects in 1828 and is chiefly known for his *Letter from Sydney*, actually written in England in 1829 in which he advocated his ideas on systematic colonisation. He was active in the projects for the settlement of South Australia in 1836 and New Zealand in 1839.

Washington, George (1732–99). American soldier and statesman. In 1755 he joined the staff of General Braddock and took part in operations against the French. When the War of Independence broke out he was appointed commander-in-chief of the American colonists. It was his personality and leadership which held the army together in spite of difficulties. Rather against his wish, he was prevailed upon to become the first President of the U.S.A. in 1789 and was largely responsible for the constitution.

Wellesley, Richard Colley, 1st Marquess Wellesley (1760–1842). British colonial administrator. He became Governor-General of India in 1797 and held the office until 1805. He was in India during a great part of the French Wars and he consolidated and extended British control.

Wellington, Arthur Wellesley, 1st Duke of Wellington (1769–1852). British soldier and statesman. He was the younger brother of Marquess Wellesley. He entered the army as an ensign in 1787. He was sent to India in 1796 and fought some brilliant actions there while his brother was Governor-General. He left India in 1805 and in 1808 was sent to command in the Peninsular War. He won fame for his conduct of the campaign, and was created Duke of Wellington in 1814. He led his victorious army over the Pyrenees into France in 1814. He commanded the Allied forces and defeated Napoleon at Waterloo in 1815. He entered politics and became Prime Minister in 1828 until 1830.

Wilberforce, William (1759–1833). English philanthropist. In 1788 he threw his whole energy into the cause of ending the slave trade and freeing the slaves. After a long, exhausting and bitter struggle he succeeded in getting the Act of 1807 passed by Parliament which ended the slave trade. He continued the fight until slavery was ended in 1833.

Willoughby, Sir Hugh (*c.* 1500–54). English explorer. In 1553 he was sent to find a North-East Passage to India and Cathay. After his little fleet was dispersed by a storm off Norway he and his crew died of scurvy after reaching Lapland.

Wolfe, James (1727–59). British soldier. Commissioned into the army in 1741, he fought in Flanders and Prussia in 1742–45 and at Culloden against the Jacobites in 1745. He distinguished himself at Louisburg in 1758 and was then given the command of the force which was to attack Quebec. He was killed on the Heights of Abraham.

Wolseley, Garnet Joseph, 1st Viscount (1833–1913). British soldier. He joined the army in 1852 and was in command of the Red River expedition in Canada in 1870, and in the Ashanti Campaign 1873–74. In 1882 he was appointed to command in Egypt.

Glossary

Administration. Name given to a system of government. Often refers to the officials appointed by an American President, although it is used by other countries.

Afrikaaner. A Dutch South African, formerly known as Boer.

Allegiance. Duty or loyalty of a subject to King, Queen or Government of a country.

Anarchy. Complete absence of any Government. Anarchist—supporter of movement which seeks to end all government.

Assembly. Name given to committee or Parliament of a country or group of countries.

Bantu. Language spoken by many Africans. Also used by South African Government for all coloured inhabitants.

Battalion. A formation of infantry, usually consisting of between 700 and 1,000 men.

Boer. Dutch South African—literally farmer.

Brigade. A military formation, usually of three battalions.

Bull. An edict or order issued by the Pope.

Charter. Written grant of rights by authority.

Chartists. Those who fought for the Peoples' Charter in the nineteenth century. They demanded votes for all adult men, secret ballot, equal voting districts, abolition of property qualification for M.P.s., payment for M.P.s., annual Parliaments.

Colony. Settlement in a new country which remained subject to the state from which the settlers have emigrated. Crown colony: British colony subject to direct rule by British Government.

Commando. The formation of troops used by the Boers in the South African War. A highly mobile body of men. The name was borrowed by British Army in Second World War.

Commission. An authority to a person or body of persons such as that given to an officer in the Navy, Army or Air Force. A committee or body set up for a special purpose.

Concentration camp. A camp used for prisoners, civilian and military by British in South African War.

Condominium. A state controlled jointly by at least two other states.

Confederation. A union of sovereign nations or states for common action.

Congress. A meeting or conference. The U.S. Parliament.

Conquistadores. Name given to the Spanish conquerors of the Spanish Americas, particularly in the sixteenth century.

Constitution. A document that lays down the way in which a country shall be governed. The duties and powers of the Government are clearly stated.

Contravention. The breaking of a rule or agreement.

Convention. 1. A practice which has become accepted.
2. An American meeting to select a presidential candidate, or a meeting generally.
3. An agreement.

Dervishes. Mohammedan religious fanatics.

Division. Military formation usually of three brigades and supporting troops.

Dominion. Colony which has become independent and self-governing and whose head of state is the King or Queen of Great Britain.

Dyarchy. Dual form of government, as in India after India Act of 1919.

Dynasty. Line of hereditary rulers.

Emigrant. One who leaves his country to settle in another.

Ensign. 1. A flag.
2. The lowest commissioned officer in the infantry, now usually known as second-lieutenant.

Exports. Goods sent out of a country to other countries.

Factory. Originally a foreign trading station at which goods were stored.

Federation. The grouping together of a number of states under one Government. Each state controls its own affairs while the Federal Government governs the affairs of the whole group (such as foreign affairs and defence) e.g. U.S.A., U.S.S.R.

Franchise. The right to vote in an election, especially for M.P.

Free Trade. Trade between nations free from customs or taxation barriers. The opposite policy to protection.

Frontiersman. One who lived on the old frontier, i.e. the limit to which settlement in a colony had reached.

Governor-General. Representative of the King or Queen of Great Britain in a Dominion, or a large colony.

Habitants. French colonists.

Hanseatic League. A commercial league of towns in North Germany, particularly important in the Middle Ages and sixteenth century.

Huguenots. French Protestants.

Humanitarians. Those concerned with the condition of other human beings and active in the cause of their betterment.

Immigrants. Those who come into a country from outside with the purpose of settling.

Impeached. To be accused of treason, i.e. disloyalty to the Crown.

Imperialism. The idea of the extension of an empire, i.e. a country's possessions overseas and the policy resulting from this.

Impi. A unit or regiment of Zulu warriors.

Imports. The foreign goods brought into a country.

Indentured. Bound to a master by signed agreement. The worker was unable to leave his employer.

Inquisition. Roman Catholic tribunal for the suppression of heresy (disbelief in Roman Catholicism), particularly in sixteenth century.

Irregular. Term used for a soldier who was not in a regular army or recognised reserve force.

Jesuits. Members of the Society of Jesus founded by Ignatius Loyola in 1533 as a militant movement against the Reformation.

Khedive. Ruler of Egypt.

Kraal. South African village within a fence or a corral for cattle.

Laager. Boer encampment, especially a circle of wagons.

Legislature. The law-making body of a state, usually an elected parliament.

Maharajah. Indian Prince.

Mahdi. A leader whose coming is looked for by the Mohammedans.

Mandate. Command or authority to act for another person or group. Used in connection with the right of the League of Nations and United Nations to administer a Trust Territory.

Mausoleum. Tomb or monument.

Mercantilism. A belief that money and wealth were virtually identical and thus a policy encouraging maximum exports and minimum imports.

Migration. Movement of peoples.

Militia. Force of soldiers called out from among ordinary citizens in case of need.

Mogul. Originally a Mongolian conqueror of India. Later the Great Mogul was the Mogul King.

Nabob. Indian Prince or nobleman.

Navigation Acts. Acts passed in 1651 by Oliver Cromwell to damage Dutch trade which limited the carriage of goods to or from the colonies to British ships.

Nawab. Indian Prince or nobleman.

Nizam. Indian Prince or nobleman.

Pasha. Turkish officer of high rank.

Pass Laws. Laws of the South African Government which direct that all coloured people in South Africa must carry passes. If found without a pass or in an area other than that for which the pass is valid they are subject to severe penalties, including arbitrary arrest and imprisonment.

Petition. A request for some action made to a King or Queen or any authority.

Philanthropist. One who sets out to do good to his fellow men particularly by giving money to charitable causes.

Plebiscite. A vote in which the people of a country are asked to say yes or no in answer to a particular question.

Preference. In international trade, a favoured position granted to nation or country by which its goods pay a lower tariff than others.

Protection. A system of tariffs to protect the home market.

Protectorate. A state which has accepted the protection of a larger nation without being annexed.

Province. A large division of a country. A division of Canada.

Puritan. An extreme Protestant. Member of the Protestant party which sought a more complete Reformation, i.e. purifying the Church.

Radical. In politics, one who seeks change and reform.

Rajah. Indian prince.

Reconnoitre. To make a preliminary survey of an area or position. Particularly used in military operations.

Referendum. The direct vote of the people on a matter of importance. Similar to a plebiscite.

Renaissance. The rebirth of learning. The revival of interest in art and literature in the fifteenth and sixteenth centuries.

Responsible Government. Government in which a state is responsible for its own affairs without necessarily being independent.

Representative government. Government in which elected representatives of the people take part.

Republic. A Government without a King or Queen; usually with a President as head of state.

Resident. British political representative or agent in a semi-dependent state such as a protectorate.

Residuum. The remainder; what is left. Particularly used in describing powers left by a constitution after some are specifically detailed.

Revenue. The money raised by a Government by taxation.

Secession. The act of withdrawal from a federation or similar body.

Seigneurs. French ruling class in Canada at time of British conquest.

Sepoy. An Indian infantry soldier, especially in British-Indian army.

Sirdar. British commander-in-chief of Egyptian army.

Stadtholder. Governor and ruler of United Provinces (Holland).

Status Quo. The state of affairs as it was up to a certain date.

Suffrage. The right to vote at elections.

Tariff. A customs duty—that is a tax which has to be paid on certain goods imported into a country.

Tenure. The conditions under which a piece of land is held.

Treaty. An agreement or contract formally signed between states.

Ultimatum. The last document which contains certain terms which the receiver can either accept or reject. If it is rejected certain action mentioned in the ultimatum (e.g. a declaration of war) is automatically carried out.

Viceroy. The person who represents the King or Queen.

Index